Who'd Have Thought It

A Community Healing Project

Also By Colin Bloy and Suzanne Thomas

I'm Just Going Down To The Pub To Do A Few Miracles

Other articles and booklets by Colin Bloy
to be found on website
https://www.fountaininternationalmagazine.com
Free quarterly Magazine and monthly Newsletter

Who'd Have Thought It

A Community Healing Project

Colin Bloy
&
Suzanne Thomas

Fountain International Magazine
c/o 35 Padacre Road
Torquay
Devon
TQ2 8PX
England

Also available:
Reprint of Colin Bloy's book "I'm Just Going Down To The Pub To Do A Few Miracles" in paperback.

On the free/donation Fountain International website –
https://www.fountaininternationalmagazine.com
Quarterly Magazine
Monthly Newsletter
Plus other Fountain International info

ISBN: 978-0-244-53414-1

Dedicated to
All past, present and future Fountaineers

Contents

Acknowledgments

My grateful thanks go to Jan Stewart for her corrections. Vivienne Shanley and Jan Bayliss for the book cover.

I would also like to mention, Ba Miller, Christopher Miller, Paul Broadhurst for their support, and of course Colin Bloy and Hamish Miller for making their presence felt whilst writing.

Introduction

Who would have thought it, indeed! Out of very small beginnings, came Fountain International, a world-wide, free community healing project, open to all, and based on the simple notion that communities, like people, suffer from dis-ease, and may be healed. The concept, which is at the heart of Fountain International activities, came about after many years of research by Colin Bloy and friends. Colin remained a leading light and exponent of Fountain until his death on 12th May 2004, (and some would say he still has his finger on the pulse). I continue to promote the idea through the website www.fountaininternationalmagazine.com and the e-magazine.

In this book, I am going to take you on a spiritual journey of discovery, and the process that led to Fountain and beyond. But first, I would like to give you hope that, in these dark days of global changes **you are not powerless, and there is something you can do.** By using the "concept", (which I will explain later), whether alone, or in a group for your community, you are of great value, no matter what you, or anyone else thinks.

Within these pages there are two sets of spiritual journeys, Colin's and mine, although the majority will be Colin's as the main instigator and visionary of Fountain. But before we get started, I would just like to say that both Colin and I are very "down to earth" people, and not given to flights of fancy. Although when you read on, you may think differently, real life is some-times stranger than fiction.

Both of us started down the path in an innocuous way. After recently failing to become an MP, Colin had gone over to a parliamentary friend's house for afternoon tea, and to talk politics. But as he was sitting down, a couple of bent coat hangers were thrust into his hands, and he found himself being given a lesson in dowsing. He had only gone along with it because he trusted the other's judgement and sanity. If you had talked to him about dowsing before that day, he would have told you, that you were mad. It took him a few false starts, before he became one, with the rods. The friend had previously seen a utility man dowse for a gas pipe which needed fixing, and found it in extra quick time. This inspired, the friend to teach himself to dowse, for his water pipes etc. As these things do, one thing lead to another, sending Colin on a journey, that could rival the Da Vinci Code, and often made him doubt his sanity and the morals of what he was doing. But unlike the Da Vinci Code, this is not a book of fiction, but a true account into his research of energy lines etc, and what occurred out of those findings!

For me, the hook which lead to Fountain wasn't dowsing, but all things healing and spiritual. Fountain International, (at this point just known as Fountain,) had in 1986 organised a conference at Exeter University, the speakers were of general interest to me, but the real pull was my childhood favourite Michael Bentine, (of the Goons, Potty Time, TV and radio fame,) which peeked my interest. Michael did not attend the conference due to illness, (and I never did get to meet him). But I was enthralled by the other speakers and their subjects. At that point in my life I had reached a plateau. I had been a healer for some years and was looking for something new. Now I had found it. Indeed, a whole new world opened up, and it was difficult to contain my excitement and enthusiasm.

My background has little in common with Colin's. He was the CEO of the family run business of Bloy Inks, traveling the world on business. Colin would often say that he was related to Spanish royalty. How true this was, is unproven, but Colin did not have an ego complex, so he was probably right.

I on the other hand came from much lower stock. Born in Solihull, England, my father was a television engineer, and my mother a housewife. In the mid 60's we moved down to Devon from Birmingham as a family. Looking back on it, energetic magnetics seem to have been in play, drawing us down to where we needed to be. Spiritually, this put me in the right place, and right time to begin my journey, and meet many wonderful people along the way, including some from previous lives. Sometimes I wonder what would have happened if we had stayed in Birmingham. Would I be spiritually where I am today, (but by a slightly different route), or I be in a totally different place

When I first met Colin, I suppose that he was in his late fifties/early sixties and I was in my late twenties. Colin was fluent in Spanish, and spent extended time in Spain, where he used his skill of healing people. At one point, he did a healing meditation on a National Radio station in Spain, with great success, (more of this later.)

During his research, Colin became great friends with Michael Bentine. They had a similar background in that during WWII both had been used by the Intelligence Services for their language skills and both had an interest in the same things. Michael would often go with Colin on his dowsing trips, and site workings. Michael was a very spiritual man, writing autobiographical books which included esoteric matters. He also wrote "fiction". One of his books was called, "Lord of the Levels" in which Colin Bloy and other known people appeared.

Colin was a kind and generous man, who never spoke a bad word about anyone. One of the main ways he would like to relax, was to have friends around and cook for them, although I'm told he wasn't too good with the washing up. Like myself, he was an inquisitive man, enjoyed research, and knowledge on areas of interest. Colin was the second great healer in my life. The first was Barney Camfield, who taught me to heal. Colin did healing very differently to Barney, though that's not to say that one was better than another.

3

Colin for example, would send distant healing via the telephone. If the person to receive the healing was not there, he would leave it on the answerphone. I can personally confirm that this approach was effective, (it is all about intention). He was also known to be able to do "Psychic Surgery." Colin was very charismatic, and a raconteur which is why so many flocked to his cause or were interested in what he was doing. But for all this Colin Bloy was not a man of ego and was humble in the way that he went about life, and a true gentleman.

Colin and I had in common, and abiding interest in earth energies. Also, such subjects as the Knights Templar, Cathars, Arthurian legend, the Essenes, sacred geometry etc, etc. Our backgrounds may have been miles apart, but our spirituality and interests ran along parallel lines.

However, for me, and I am sure of Colin, the most important part of our journeys, (and this book) relates to the Fountain Concept, and how anyone, whatever circumstances, colour, religion, or political beliefs, can use it as a tool to help heal their community, and ultimately the world/earth if they desire.

If you feel that spiritual mumbo jumbo is not for you, that's fine, and not a problem. **But please consider Part 3 on what Fountain International is, the concept, and how to use it.**

Don't just let the world happen to you, make a stand, and work towards a better world.

If you are still with me, and not vanished into Part 3, or put the book back on the shelf. My hope is, that you will find the book empowering, and insightful. Take from it what you will. There are many things in heaven and on earth that we don't understand.

So, when did I have the first inkling of this book? It was back in January 2000, a fellow healer Roger Keenan, was energetically augmenting my intuitive faculties for me to see my spiritual future, and like any person on a spiritual journey it is good practice to jot down your findings and experiences. What follows is my writings on the event.

January 2000

The images came easily and strongly, as I lay on a therapy table.

The first picture was that of a whirlpool, with people dotted around the edge. As the whirlpool turned, the people became closer together. There was no feeling of fear, or horror in the impression. My mind whirled in the process of trying to think what the purpose was of this whirlpool. Or more importantly what happened at the bottom and would it hurt? It felt that in order for the people to move together, that they would need to be physically moving closer. When we did get to the bottom of the funnel, we joined up and light went out in a sort of network effect.

The next image was that of walking through a wood. I seemed then to be looking up at this gate, with a rose on it. Then the rose appeared on a ring, which unseen hands were giving me. (In June 2000, I looked up the symbolism of the gate, rose and ring. The ring denotes the symbolism of eternity, continuity, divinity of life. It also represents power, dignity, strength, protection, delegated power, (I did an "Oh shit", at that one,) completion of cyclic time. The ring is equated with the personality, and to bestow a ring is to transfer power, to plight a troth, to join the personalities. It is also a binding symbol. The rose relates to the heart and love. The gate shares the symbolism of the threshold as an entrance. It's a passage from the profane to the sacred, entering a new world. As a boundary symbol, it is the line of meeting of the natural and supernatural; this is ritually

5

defined in the ceremony of "beating the bounds," redefining the realm of space in the same way in which the New Year ceremonies define time. Entering a dark forest is another threshold symbol of entering the perilous unknown. Vestal goddesses of virginity are the goddesses of the threshold, as are Lares. Guardians of the threshold, who must be overcome, before the sacred realm can be entered are; dragons, serpents, monsters, dogs, etc. In psychic and spiritual realms guardians prevent man from going too far, too fast and meeting or seeing more than he is able to handle in occult, (hidden), or esoteric knowledge. The gate is also the protective sheltering aspect of the Great Mother. In Christianity, the Virgin Mary is the Gate of Heaven.

The final scene was that of a scene of rolling green hills, with a cottage nestled in a dale. Again, streams of light are coming out of the cottage, as a network, mainly in the form of talking, writing and telepathy. Had a feeling that some-one was either going to give me an idea of a book or would ask me to co-write one. The place had a feeling of great calm and balance, I felt very comfortable here. To me this is not a place in the outside world, but somewhere to which I could work from on the inner planes. Another wow escaped my lips.

I've always had trouble in knuckling down to a daily meditation, so I think "higher management" saw their chance, and threw down everything that they had, just in case they couldn't get my attention again. Sorry boys, I will try harder with the routine stuff.

With this book, I hope to bring a little light, and inspire you. Wishing you well on your journey in life. All you need to do is take the first step.

Suzanne Thomas – July 2017

Part 1

Colin Bloy's Early
Research - In His Own Words

A Pattern in Time

I learnt to dowse in Kent in 1968. One day a good friend, Harold Wicks, stuck into my hands two halves of a wire coat hanger, both shaped to form a right angle, of which the short ends were held loosely in either hand. After a few false starts the wire rods in my hands, which were pointing straight ahead, moved and turned towards each other. "That's my water main," he said. They crossed again. "That's my drain." The first time I dowsed a ley line I did not know what I had found, for I did not know that ley lines existed. By the end of the day I turned to my friend and said, "Now look what you've done". Harold did say that he felt like Mary Shelley, of Frankenstein fame, but he said it with a smile.

(During this time period, all energy lines were commonly called "ley lines", after a term coined by Alfred Watkins, energy lines that crossed the ley of the land. I would equate energy lines to the nervous system of the human body, with major, average and minor energy lines.

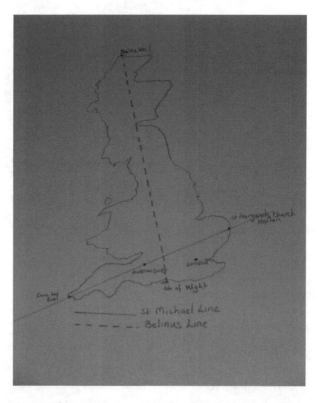

Although the term ley line is still relevant to large energy lines that cover massive distances, crossing the ley of the land. For example, in England, the St Michael Line that passes through St Michaels Mount in Cornwall, crosses the country, and then out through Bury St Edmunds in Suffolk, which is investigated in the book "The Sun and the Serpent" by Paul Broadhurst and Hamish Miller. Or the Belinus Line that runs through the Isle of Wight travelling up through England, and out through Scotland, investigated in the book "The Spine of Albion," by Gary Biltcliffe and Caroline Hoare. - Suzanne).

I believe anyone can dowse. Although what happens to cause the dowsing reaction, I am not able to say. There are those that claim that when the body passes through a force field, such as that created by underground running water, the muscles react involuntarily to cause whatever is held in the hand or hands to move. Many countryside dowsers use the forked hazel twig and, it is said that some of the violent reactions can cause the dowser distress, for example when the hazel twig strongly flips and hits them in the chest. I think that the type of dowsing tool used is just what suits the dowser, and in my case, it was a wire coat hanger. Which is provided with ever increasing profligacy by dry cleaners and laundries. *(The wire coat hanger is straightened, broken in two equal halves. Then picking up one of the halves, bend a quarter of it to a ninety-degree angle, making it look like an L shape, and repeat with the other wire. Well Done. You have just made a pair of dowsing rods of your very own. Take one in each hand, holding the shorter part of the rods, hold them loosely towards the crook of the rod, but with just enough pressure to prevent them from moving of their own accord in the wind - Suzanne).* When a dowsing zone is entered, the long end is held pointing away from the body, will of their own accord cross inwards, and stay in that position until the dowsing zone is left. In this way, a dowsing line may be followed at walking pace without difficulty.

Suffice it to say here…It works… a conclusion whose accuracy is unequivocally demonstrated by the fact that many employees of those eminently practical and prosaic organisations, such as the Gas Board, habitually employ the rods to locate unmapped gas mains. For me, dowsing for gas or water-mains soon palls, unless you have a professional interest in it, and I did not.

Harold, who introduced me to dowsing moved to Suffolk, acquiring another rural property. The garden and surrounding fields were full of fossils. We thought that we would try to locate them by dowsing and we did on occasions, but as there were so many, the laws of chance were on our side. During this exercise, I found two straight lines: one, on excavation, revealed a land-drain and the other, on excavation, nothing. I was detecting more and more of those enigmatic lines which clearly had nothing to do with the Gas or Water Boards but, equally clearly, existed. And they were not only straight but curves, spirals and circles. What on earth, or rather what in earth were they? And there the matter rested until, three or four years later, and I came across two books about ley lines.

I suppose it was inevitable that I should eventually stumble upon the works of two men, Watkins and Underwood, who could offer a dramatic clue to the mystery, a clue which first led me to the South Downs church of Alfriston, and then half way round the Western hemisphere. The discovery of Watkins' book "The Old Straight Track," first published in 1924, and Underwood's "Patterns of the Past", was inevitable, because after being greeted with first mocking hostility, and then obscurity, both books have emerged on the current wave of interest in the "occult". Anyone with any interest in mysterious lines in or below the earth's crust would eventually encounter the work of these men.

Alfred Watkins was a Hereford solicitor who, at the age of 65, was sufficiently unconventional to have a revelation. This took place, as

10

John Michell recounts in his note to the recent Abacus paper-backed edition of "The Old Straight Track", when Watkins became aware of a network of lines, standing out like "glowing wires" all over the surface of the country, intersecting at the sites of churches, old stones and other spots of traditional sanctity. And so, in a single flash, he had perceived the existence of the ley system, and in his book, he proceeded to describe it.

Using his profound knowledge of the countryside around Hereford, he was able to show, by both map and fieldwork that a great number of objects or sites of objects of prehistoric antiquity, churches, so called "camps", castles, standing stones, clumps of trees, tell-tale place names, etc., all formed straight alignments across miles of countryside, these he called "leys". He interpreted them as "old straight tracks", masterpieces of accurate surveying by men (traditionally held to be stone-axe wielding painted savages), designed to mark the ways by which the population of those days moved around the countryside. The fact that early churches appeared on these leys is accounted for by the instruction of Pope Gregory V in the sixth century, that Britain would be Christianised more easily if the new churches were to be built on sites of pagan religious significance. In the development of his thesis, Watkins goes on to show that through these alignments there survived the ancient beliefs and religions of Britain.

King Cole, celebrated in the nursery rhyme as a "jolly old soul", and his daughter Helen, of Romano-British date, gave rise to place names such as Coldharbour, Cole's Farm, Colchester and many others. "Coel" would appear to be of Celtic origin. It meant omen or belief, hence Coel-bren, a piece of wood used in choosing or balloting: Coelcerth, omen of danger, beacon, bonfire; Coelfain, the stories of omen. Helen was none other than the mother of Constantine the Great, the Christianiser of the Roman Empire, (also Elen, goddess of trackways and communication!) It is said that Helen found the "true cross" in Jerusalem when her son won the city back. Through the book, we shall try to show that the "true cross" was not a wooden cross that she found, but a cross of ley-lines. Helen appears as Sam Helen, the causeway which transverses Wales. In the same way, Old King Cole became the king of the "Old Straight Track".

The Greek god, Hermes, is also associated with the ley-system, taking it back much further in time. He was known for guiding wayfarers on unknown paths in this world and the next. Later he became associated with, or progenitor of, the Roman god, Mercury, whose symbol was an upright stone. But going back to Egyptian times, it is generally agreed, he was the Egyptian year god, Thoth. As Hermes, he is held to be the inspiration behind the development of hermitages and hermits, whose real function in life was "to help the traveller on his way", in both a physical and spiritual sense. As Thoth in another early representation, he was the moon god and, later by association, became god of reckoning and learning in general. He was held to be the inventor of writing, the founder of the social order, the creator of languages, scribe, interpreter and advisor of the gods. In the myth of Osiris, Thoth protected Isis during her pregnancy and healed the injury inflicted by Seth on her son, Horus. Thoth weighed the hearts of the dead and reported his findings to the chief of the gods, Osiris. He makes his appearance in the ley-system in names such as Tothill, Tooting, Totteridge, etc. Mounds with the Tot-derivation abound in Britain. There is one in Hassocks, Sussex, unmarked on the Ordnance Survey Map. At the same time, Thoth-Hermes was the father of the hermetic sciences, alchemy and astrology and the supposed author, under the name of Hermes-Tresmegistus, of the Kabbala.

Meticulously assembling his evidence, Watkins showed that the ley system he discovered through his flash of inspiration had its origins in the mists before recorded history – and that they existed before the construction of Stonehenge, itself incorporated on various leys. The leys were a thing of wonder, mystery, and were indeed so old that Watkins suggests that "civilisation destroyed it" – along with the coming of metal. All this is a splendid contribution, along with the work of Professors Thom and Hawkins, to a better and indeed awe-inspiring appreciation of the realities of the straight track society and megalithic man. Yet it leaves us with a puzzle. As Watkins himself says, if these lines were intended for travel, why did they pass over the peaks of mountains and through ponds and lakes? He discovered evidence of foundations laid through water – and over precipices. Having admitted this as an objection to the theory of tracks, he dismisses it effectively saying that it is not for the 20th century man to judge the travelling habits of his early ancestors, as he may have had his own very good reasons for not circumnavigating natural obstacles. But at the same time, he gives us tantalising hints that his vision of "glowing wires" was perhaps more meaningful than the superficiality of his straight track theory as a means of navigation. He describes it as a fairy chain across the country, and says "I feel that ley-man, astronomer-priest, druid, bard, wizard, witch, and hermit, we are all more or less linked by one thread of ancient knowledge and power".

Watkins' work provided the pragmatic, measurable basis for the infant art. It is not yet, or indeed ever likely to become a "science" in the current meaning of the word, because it is partly subjective – but none the less real for that. Watkins' son believes that his father was aware of the mysterious dimensions behind his discovery, but in his published work Watkins limited himself to what could be demonstrated through maps and conventional surveying techniques. Indeed, so restrained is his work that one is hard put to understand why he created such venomous hostility among professional practitioners of archaeology. It was another man, Guy Underwood, who was to take an allied concept, a very significant stage further.

Underwood was born in 1883 and, after his schooling in Dulwich College, started out as a solicitor. This palled and he subsequently involved himself in such matters as researching genealogical trees, constructing electrical apparatus, water divining and archaeology. In 1969, five years after his death, what appears to be his one and only work, "The Pattern of the Past", was published. Notwithstanding its content, it is a book of charm and warmth. In the first chapter, he explains how Reginald Allender Smith of the British Museum first suggested there might be some connection between the location of ancient monuments and the presence of underground water. Smith, Keeper of the British and Roman Antiquities Department of the British Museum and Director of the Society of Antiquities, was also a water diviner, although he kept quiet about it. In 1935 Underwood read a paper to the British Society of Dowsers, in which he said that at the centre of every prehistoric temple there would be found a spot, from which a number of underground streams would form a radiating pattern. He called these spots "blind springs", and said that they existed at Stonehenge, Avebury, Stanton Drew, and all similar sites, as well as at every prehistoric barrow.

Underwood did not claim originality for his theory, he points out that two French archaeologists, Louis Merle and Charles Diot, published papers on the subject in 1933 and 1935. They said that all prehistoric burial places and similar stone structures in France were surrounded by underground streams, and that the famous stone avenue at Carnac was aligned upon underground streams running parallel with each other. Reginald Smith points out that "the constant presence of underground water at the exact centres of these circles and earthworks is a significant feature easily verified by others. If this is allowed to be intentional, then the selection of sites by the Druids

14

and their predecessors no longer appears arbitrary but dictated largely by geological traditions."

In the main body of the work Guy Underwood tells us of his findings by water divining at prehistoric sites and medieval churches exhibited similar dowsing phenomena. He saw them as located by geomancers who determined the siting of sacred sites according to the geodetic formulae of particular places. He explains how he became a dowser by chance, after sceptically observing water diviners at work. He designed his own dowsing rod and refined the art almost to a point of a spring-loaded pen recording on the drum of a barograph. (I was not initially as sensitive as this.) It is not condescending to point out that rod dowsing in general had been the province of "country folk" until Guy Underwood refined it into a delicate art. His touch indicated much more than the professional reluctance or incoherence of the country dowser has ever revealed. Underwood was no fantasist. He himself points out that *"Sir Oliver Lodge has stressed the difficulties and dangers of research into new subjects, as being far more formidable than those encountered when extending knowledge in some existent field, for there is usually one obvious line of work, and also of course, instruments which will assist the worker. When water divining constitutes the prime method of research the hazards are greater. The sole media whereby the investigator may detect or measure any phenomenon by his own perceptions, can mislead him. Auto suggestion is his enemy, and preconceived ideas may blind him to important facts when these seem impossible or produce some chance and unrepresentative results. And while he is labouring to translate the intelligible, he may miss the plain facts or else subconsciously set them aside in fear that their emergence will compel him to scrap somebody of previous work. He must also bear in mind that no manifestation can be accepted as valid until it has been repeated many times with identical results and has been observed on several occasions by chance at a time when it is unsought."* (So true, as I was to find by bitter experience.)

Underwood made archaeological dowsing his life's work and, indeed, it was the first-time dowsing was used for archaeological purposes. He discovered and recognised new archaeological sites, established by his dowsing techniques. He took dowsing and rationalised it into something approaching an exact science. I do not propose to recount his theories exactly. Effectively at present, he was a more-subtle dowser than I, but I was now experienced enough to put his theories to a field test.

The first dowsing expedition was in January 1975. A site I suspected to be of antiquity, but which was held to be a chalk pit of recent date, was the object for attention of a team consisting of myself, my brother David, a friend and his wife, and a covey of assorted bewildered children. David came equipped with wire, pendulum and coffee, and my friend and I came with wires and brandy. (My brother had also developed the skill to dowse, and on an earlier visit to him at his home, in a jocular vein, I offered to write a word on his lawn spiritually whilst he was out of sight. When he came back to dowse for the word, he got about halfway through then he looked up at me watching from an upstairs window and said, "I'd be obliged if you wouldn't write words like that on my lawn." But he laughed as he said it.) A January day on the South Downs requires prudence. Our purpose was to dowse the site and see if we could obtain results like Underwood's, thereby showing the site to be of antiquity. The venue was on the western side of Wolstenbury Hill, a strange plateau about the size of a football field, half hollowed out of the hillside, and half dependent on chalk that had been excavated and pushed outwards and downwards, the whole area was covered in grass. Some yards from the foot was a long barrow, and access was by a series of parallel converging and diverging hollow ways from the valley through which the London to Brighton road passes. I had been intrigued by the site for some time, as it stands stark against the hill, and is plainly visible from the road. What on earth was this football field doing sticking out from the top of a Sussex Down, on the peak of which was a so-called hill fort? I had made a preliminary reconnaissance with my son, Nicholas, and the impression from ground level was confirmed – "a football field" projecting from the hillside and clearly part of a system of earthworks. I had written to the Sussex Archaeology Society to see if they recognised it as a site of antiquity, and after some preliminary sparring, in which they gave the view that it must be a relatively modern chalk or marl-pit, they apparently wrote me off as tiresome, and the correspondence ceased.

To dowse it, we met at 10am on a Sunday morning, and our motley crew wound its way up the hillside, looking like an object of curiosity to ramblers observing the group of people holding pendulums and half coat hangers. In the excavations at the bottom we dowsed Underwood's spirals without difficulty. The earthworks winding up the hillside revealed the triple line which Underwood called an "aquastat". We followed the round the side of the plateau, even more stark against the hill as we got nearer on to the plateau itself. On the forward part there was nothing, but in the backward part excavated out of the hill various spirals were dowsed, and around the area of the excavations, smaller spirals. Within the hill fort area, we dowsed a variety of curved lines and an apparently straight line pointing to Clayton Windmills about a mile away.

On the return journey David announced he had found a straight line going down the middle, carrying on through the artificial slope, and then down the natural hill. We tried to take a sighting but the heat haze on this warm winter's day made it impossible, although the view was commanding. At the time, although we had destroyed several 1inch Ordnance Survey Maps drawing straight lines all over the place, ley lines were not foremost in our thoughts. Our main purpose then was the testing of Underwood's findings, which did not involve straight lines. We left satisfied that we had some evidence to show that modern chalk-pits are not made at the top of a hill, and that chalk miners do not level off their site immaculately when they have finished. The long barrow revealed the spiral phenomena that Underwood indicates. Later I pondered on the straight line, how far it went, and wondered. Remembering a particular tree on the lower lip of the hill that appeared to be in line as a marker, the next time I passed along the road, I looked in the other direction, and saw a church, not visible from the top, Newtimber Church. It was one of those moments when one feels oneself to be on the brink of something. The following day I decided, as I drove to the office, to take one rod with me and attempt to dowse the potential line from a moving car. It worked!

Car dowsing was an extremely important discovery, on two counts. Firstly, by further dowsing on foot at Newtimber Church, I was able to establish that the line really did enter the church at the east end and, secondly, that car dowsing was a fact. This was later to enable me to start rapidly building up the ley map of the South Downs, rather than spend a lifetime wandering around on foot looking for starter points. I later established that the same reactions were obtainable from aircraft, whether on a De Havilland Dart, flying at 400mph to Manchester at 10,000 feet, or a Boeing 727 at 26,000 feet flying at 650mph to Frankfurt. The latter experience showed that the ley system not only existed on the other side of the English Channel, but in the English Channel itself! I now felt that I have achieved a breakthrough, and set about building up enough data to confirm my initial findings I further discovered that if you established yourself on a line and followed it, the rod (for really only one is necessary), stayed crossed and only opened if you moved off it. Another helpful thing was that you could dowse a ley line on the run, and as it has been my desire (if not my recent wont), to go running in order to achieve some semblance of physical fitness, I was able to combine business with pleasure and dowse at a sprint, if necessary.

Having established car dowsing as a fact for my own satisfaction, a whole new possibility opened itself up. Happily, I drove from my home in Brighton to my office in Crawley 25 miles away, and back every day, and there are many minor diversions one can take without overtly extending the time taken. I was able to rapidly record dowsing responses over wide areas, noticed from the car. But for entirely different reasons, my car was examined by a policeman who, on noticing the rods enquired whether they might be lock picking instruments. A practical demonstration of their function served, if not to convince him of dowsing, at least to persuade him that their purpose was innocent. It became clear, however, that helpful as the car experience was, actual leg work was essential in following up the vast number of clues which the car dowsing provided. I may say that it takes a little boldness to run the gauntlet of incredulous shoppers when you pass amongst them holding a rod with an intense look on your face, or to brave the suspicions of a vicar, (or worse, his wife,) who descends upon you whilst dowsing in the churchyard, enquiring as to what you might be doing. However, the English have traditionally the good manners to ignore the activities of the eccentric, and this story is marked more by the number who politely chose to ignore or assist this curious happening, than by those who subjected me to ridicule. It is also a tribute to the innate courtesy of the many when approached for permission to dowse their property or churchyard, did not dismiss me out of hand, but listened, assisted, tolerated and encouraged, even though the subject was one at which the sceptic could easily jeer.

Following up on Underwood, yet with growing conviction that there was something more to discover, I dowsed Newtimber Church. It was revealing. I dowsed my first triple line, which ran more or less the length of the east-west axis of the church. This was later to be recognised as a virtually universal feature of pre-Reformation churches and fonts. The triple line went in a flattened circle upon which the main line of the church ran. Further single lines revealed themselves as follows, on the south side a blocked -up window marked one, on the same side a blocked- up door another. What was interesting was that this line left the churchyard by a stile. A single line appeared at each end of the east-west axis along the triple which later left the axis to form a circle. On the northern side, a niche in the wall seemed to be the indicator of another line, making five in all.

All this seemed to be making fascinating sense. Some weekends later we drove to Alfriston, a delightful Downs land village, whose medieval church was cruciform and beautifully kept, is known as "The Cathedral of the Downs". I noticed on the north wall a Gothic arched doorway, blocked up, but its white pillars clearly visible against the black Sussex flints that faced the church. These blocked up doorways are known as Witches or Devils' Doors. They were blocked up by tradition to deny the practitioners of Wicca (the witches' ancient religion) access to the church through the doorway that had always been for them. The Church as it were, acknowledging its debt to earlier religions. A line came through this doorway. I followed as it passed through the churchyard wall and thence into the water meadow, going along the Cuckmere River to the road bridge, passing it just to the west and then crossing over the river itself. It continued north to Milton Court Farm. I took the car and at the northern end of the farm from the road, I saw the long barrow, encircled by water and almost shimmering in a grove of fallen and curiously twisted trees. (This is known as Burlough Castle – no interment found). This is another moment where the breath suddenly becomes short and the body tingles.

I sought out the farmer's wife and begged permission to go on her land. I picked up the line smartly and followed it across the field to where an earthen bridge crossed the water surrounding the barrow. The line continued under a fallen tree, still alive but arched over the line. It disappeared into a myriad of spirals covering the barrow. It was a strange feeling on the barrow, for it was a truly magic place, a monument put there for his purpose by man of many millennia ago. Looking back over the water meadow to Alfriston Church in the grey, misty, early spring afternoon, I realised that I had found and walked my first straight line, and it had led to another significant site, which I did not know about when I started. It was not marked on the one-inch Ordnance Survey Map. I was now convinced that the energy lines existed, and that they linked Christian and Pre-Christian sites, the purpose or cause of which was a matter for the most extraordinary speculation and investigation. I felt that NOW I had found my first ley line.

Over the next few months I dowsed some sites, modern as well as prehistoric, Christian as well as pagan, constructed as well as "natural", accepting only repeatable phenomena, building up slowly a corpus of information that would serve as guidelines. I lived and worked in Sussex and therefore Sussex provided the main, locale for these early hesitant explorations. Almost any other part of the country would, I suspect, provide similar discoveries. I was also fortunate in that Sussex is particularly rich in sites which are recognised by academics as being of enormous antiquity, and many sites as yet unrecognised. Each of the dozens I visited provided yet another clue, another stepping-stone to a still yet unknown destination.

The Emerging Pattern

Throughout my first hesitant months I was vividly aware of the opposing hazards of self-delusion and prejudice that beset anyone engaged upon such a voyage of discovery. The problems were succinctly expressed by Underwood in that remark of his that I have already quoted: "Auto suggestion is the (dowser's) enemy, and preconceived ideas may blind him to important facts when these seem impossible or produce some chance and unrepresentative results." Underwood was speaking of his own experience and though I too encountered the hazards, I was more fortunate than Underwood for I had his own work as a datum point against which to check mine. And at this point it seems appropriate to discuss in rather greater detail the ideas in his seminal work, "Patterns of the Past."

Underwood refers to his lines generally as geodetic or telluric; that is to say forces which originate in, or represent peaks of electromagnetic, gravitational or odic fields. These lines are never single, but triple, double, two triples, three triples and so on. They divide into three main categories:

The Water Line width varies considerably. When small, it consists of three slight lines. When large, each line will be seen to be a triple in its own right. When 6ft wide, nine triples may be perceived, even up to 27 triples.

The Track Line consists of two parallel triples, width 22 – 24 inches. It is of little significance in the layout of sacred sites, but all old roads are aligned on them and almost all animals follow them.

The Aquasat consists of two pairs of triples.

Geodetic lines normally, says Underwood, take winding courses and may be zig zag, looped or folded into hair pin bends. They usually maintain one general direction for considerable distances. Multiple lines had special religious significance, and their presence is frequently indicated on sacred sites by notches or groves in the stones of the site.

Sites such as Stonehenge or the Bradbury Circle at Bradford on Avon, which he discovered by dowsing, have loops and spirals formed by these primary lines. He then refers to "blind springs" and "primary spirals". "Blind springs" are centres upon which primary lines converge and from which they emerge. Their effect is to cause the converging lines to take a spiral course. These spirals are called "primary spirals". They enclose the spring and after numerous coils terminate upon it. The blind spring was the esoteric "centre" of the Old Religion as well as being the actual centre of its monument. It was holy ground. These spirals may expand their radius by about 3 feet from January to June, contracting from June to January, but primary lines remain stationary so far as their main axis is concerned. Parallel lines do, however, expand and contract between 8am and 8pm GMT. They are shortest at night and attain their maximum at 3.15pm. This is something, incidentally, that I have never positively checked. Neither have I received any indication that this is so in respect of ley lines.

In his book, Underwood produces a wealth of dowsing evidence to show that our so-called "primitive" forbears arranged their habits, society and agriculture according to geodetic considerations, and he says that geodetic phenomena were accepted as divine manifestations of the Life Spirit. Because these phenomena were complicated and invisible it was natural that priests in charge of arrangements should evolve some system, whereby they could be recognisable to the initiated, while still remaining incomprehensible to outsiders. They did this by means of mounds, banks, ditches, stones, dolmens, stone circles, walls, terraces, roads, pits and ponds in varying arrangements. (I believe that this relationship is correct, but I hope to show later on that these were not only markers for the initiate but rather causes and stimuli of the phenomena.)

Underwood further asserts that dowsing reveals that the greater proportion of minor topographical features are man-made and that some of the major features, such as the shape of hill tops and the courses of rivers, have been considerably altered by man. It is difficult to accept that the great coombes sometimes found in association with important prehistoric structures in hilly country are entirely natural – try looking at the Deans and Dunes around Brighton. I hope to show later that certain tremendously important topographical phenomena in Sussex cannot be natural. At any rate, none of prehistoric man's work exists without geodetic dowsable phenomena. Underwood tells of his dowsing experience at Stonehenge, (which he found bewildering in its complexity), the Acropolis, Avebury, Carnac. Even the individual stones at Stonehenge have their own internal geodetic subtleties. The Slaughter Stone has notches on it indicating the passage of multiple water lines. Hill figures such as the White Horse of Uffington are geodetically orientated.

In his chapter, "Freemasonry and Medieval Architecture", he jumps a millennium or two, and points out that English pre-Reformation churches exhibit the same dowsing phenomena as prehistoric monuments. We saw earlier in the book how Pope Gregory V gave specific instructions that the pagan British were to be Christianised by building churches on their traditional religious sites. What is remarkable, however, is not that geodetic phenomena should be present in pre-Reformation cathedrals and churches, but that these buildings were constructed so as to take account of them. He points out that many ecclesiastical buildings are not even straight or based on a rectangle. Southwark Cathedral has a bend in the nave, choir and retro-choir out of line. Pisa is most odd. Many churches are otherwise inexplicably sited. Some are half a mile from the village that they serve. Some are built on unsuitable ground. Winchester is built on a swamp. Some were totally disproportionate to their community's needs. He says, *"The results of my visits to a great many medieval buildings, established without doubt that an almost identical system was used for their location and layout as had been followed in respect of prehistoric temples and other early monuments...the escapable inference was that the secret preserved so closely by the Freemasons was their knowledge of the geodetic system and the observance of certain rules in connection with it."*

He goes on to explain, just as I found, that this is a subject on which there is no recorded history, or that is, recorded in a way intelligible to contemporary man, who is only just becoming adept at storing data in non-visual ways. He also says that this esoteric knowledge was hidden from all by men unlikely to risk the fate that would be incurred by a public statement. Indeed, it has become obvious that the Knights Templar, protectors of the operative Masons in their day, and heirs to the pagan, gnostic, occult tradition (for all their external Christian trappings), were destroyed by an unholy alliance between the French monarchy and the papacy, not only for their temporal wealth but also for their preservation of arcane pre-Christian secrets.

However, the manipulation and understanding of the Earth Force is perceptible, according to Underwood, and I certainly subscribe to this view, to analysis by the established exact sciences, although it involves a multiplicity of disciplines and specialisations that may be difficult to harness in a concerted effort. Nothing that he says, or that I shall seek to say at this stage, should cause us to relegate dowsing to the realms of the occult. This is a term often used by established science to dismiss and thereby avoid "difficult" subjects, or by those who seek to impress us by mystery and prevent serious investigation which might undermine their subjective credulity. Rather I seek, just as Underwood, to indicate that dowsing is a means (albeit empirical) of providing data that may open doors for new targets in atomic science, in wave physics, in philosophy, sociology and archaeology. Indeed, it could result in a new evaluation of man and his relation to the cosmos, that could involve all the –ics, -isms and –ologies at the end of the day. I seek to show that dowsing is not just a country "art". It is a means of showing, by the use of certain tools that we are influenced by changes in the force field around us, subtle as they may be. Furthermore, these force fields are not just fields that influence man but may be influenced by man and harnessed to his purpose for good or ill.

Guy Underwood refers to Alfred Watkins and "The Old Straight Track" only in passing and makes no attempt to link his work with that of Watkins. However, he correctly recorded the dowsing phenomena associated with the works of this earlier civilisation. I say this in the full belief that Guy Underwood was a more-subtle dowser than myself, but his interpretations of the phenomena as causal in the siting of ancient monuments I do not necessarily believe to be exclusively true. As I began to extend my research to include the great monuments of Europe, in particular the cathedrals, I became more and more convinced that this theory was too simplistic. Charpentier, in his book "Le Mystere de la Cathedrale de Chartres", is clear that the present position of the Cathedral and its earlier ancient druidic site is due to a particular telluric power point that occurs there. He is not arguing from anything other than a theoretical or mystical consideration of the telluric currents. Not being a dowser nor having access to dowsing information, he was not aware of the particular lines of Chartres which relate specifically to architectural features, doors, towers, etc, of the construction. The question is, do these lines exist because of the design of the Cathedral or does the design of the Cathedral arise from the lines?

I do know of a site in the South Downs of Britain, which exhibits all the dowsing characteristics of a small church, that is to say, a triple line circle, such as one would find passing through a font. Or, is in the middle of a football field, and I can find no record of any church having been there. My experience of water dowsing is minimal, but it may well be that this is an indication of one of Guy Underwood's blind springs, and that the siting of churches and stone circles was indeed determined by such a factor. The siting of the font on these circles, (which range from 2 yards to 300 yards in diameter), gives some sort of credence to the fact that the placing of the fonts over blind springs was in order to get the "charging" benefit of the blind spring below; a continuance of the pagan mysteries of the Earth Goddess. Chartres Cathedral, for instance, has a huge six bar circle which is flattened on one side and running the length of the nave via the west door, as are others of such magnitude. Lesser churches are not bothered by such niceties and only the font relates to the circle.

I am prepared to accept that these sites were indeed determined by such considerations as Underwood, a unique pioneer, indicated. However, as we noted elsewhere, Underwood did not dowse between sites and so missed the ley line effect. He did state, however that various lines did enter and leave by doors, but did not observe that they were straight, dismissing them as underground water courses. An interesting point occurs at this time. He may be right (and so might I be) in saying that the ley lines exist but are not based on underground water courses. It all comes back to the dowsing phenomenon; the dowser's mind is enormously selective. If it were not so, dowsing a London street would be impossible as the sewers, electric cables, gas pipes, water pipes and telephone lines would produce a mishmash of reactions as to make the whole exercise impossible. Yet a GPO engineer can use the rods quite satisfactorily to locate his underground services and so can the gas man. Neither involves himself in the other's affairs. In the same way, it is curious that in setting out to check Underwood's result I had ley lines in mind. He always had water in mind. What we have both found coincides in part but diverges in important aspects. In the cathedrals we have both dowsed, I have found some of the things that he found and other things that he did not. Our dowsing maps of Stonehenge are not identical. I cannot find his spiral in the centre, for instance, perhaps that is a water spiral. However, I find the following pattern at both Woodhenge and Stonehenge. In the case of Stonehenge, the extant stones are within the central circle, in the case of Woodhenge the pattern is within the layout of posts. We both find the six lines emerging from the Heel Stone with six notches, but Underwood's run off in a meandering direction. Mine go straight to Woodhenge.

What I began to suspect was that we may well be dealing with a phenomenon that exists on various levels. Underwood was in fact dealing with an exoteric phenomenon; the application by the megalith builders of underground water and blind springs in choosing their sites. What I stumbled on by chance is the esoteric aspect, the transformations of the energy of blind springs, etc, by the use of purpose built structures, and its injection into different fields of force, along with energies from other sources (celestial from the earth temples of Wolstenbury, Malling, etc, and the so-called hill forts,) which create the ley lines. These are superimposed upon and feeding on the naturally occurring telluric phenomena. To the extent, I had reason to suspect that upon the ley system is imposing or developing a macro system of broader fields of force on which the planetary conjunctions exert themselves. But that is a story for another time. Teilhard de Chardin's "noosphere" would be involved here, I feel. Therefore, Underwood's results and mine would not coincide in all aspects because we did not look for the same thing. I always had ley lines in mind when I checked his findings.

But the basic problem was, do the lines determine the structure or do the structures determine the lines? Clearly, an architect of a medieval church or cathedral was unlikely to be a violent atheist or he would not have been selected for, or inclined to build, religious monuments, and so the effect might be the same, as he would be spiritually open to such unconscious considerations. I did not feel, either, that a ley conscious architect would necessarily have a precise plan of the ley system that would result from his design. When he had selected, or been given his site, I had no doubt many exoteric and esoteric factors were involved in his plan and I had equally no doubt that I was only dimly aware of a few. And the lines on churches and cathedrals do not always associate with deliberate architectural features. In some way that I could not fathom the basic form and style of architecture was relevant. The abandonment of the Roman for the Gothic arch is highly significant. As well as permitting much higher roofs the thrust pattern thus produced would be entirely different and would create a new factor in whatever is transmitted from that site.

It is relevant here to note that we have been able to show that it is possible to create ley lines today. This is done by arranging the charged or "sacred" stones in particular patterns, but they are always consistent, or so it would appear. Such lines always lock into the nearest feature of the ley system in their path. The megalith builders created their sites and therefore a ley system. Woodhenge connects to Stonehenge and 49 bar line goes south east from Stonehenge to a point which I do not yet know. It is argued that medieval church builders built on old sacred sites and therefore built within the ley system and did not interfere with it. Consequently, ley hunters seeking projected lines on maps linking these sites will come up with fairly spectacular results. Yet I cannot always dowse predicted lines. From this I concluded that the building of the medieval churches did affect the living ley line system and altered it for two reasons: 1) they were not necessarily always on ancient sites and 2) they produce a different ley configuration from conventional megalithic or druidic monuments. This interruption of the system (and a cathedral would do this massively) would impose different channels on the leys, rather as a series of magnets and iron filings in a particular configuration would produce a particular pattern in iron filings, and the introduction of a new and powerful bar magnet would immediately change the pattern as a new equilibrium of forces were established. Thus, a new church might divert an earlier line onto or from a feature not foreseen by the architect of the latter. At the same time, lines from doors, etc., are not necessarily perpendicular to those doors. It appears that they may have been originally, but later sacred features of the landscape may have made greater demands and pulled them away.

In his conclusion, Underwood explains his initial reluctance, later overcome by certainty, to believe that he was onto something. He states that what he has experienced through dowsing is the Earth Force, a force recognised by science but not understood. Our forebears had certainly come to terms with it. He says, *"I became absorbed by the discovery of the extreme importance of the serpent symbol in prehistoric religions and the subsequent emergence of the serpent as a god believed to control fertility, and always associated with water and usually with the moon. As the serpent is one of the land-living vertebrates which naturally and frequently reproduces all geodetic spiral patterns, it seems reasonable to assume that both the serpent and spiral symbols are representative of the geodetic spiral"*. Dragon is a word of Greek origin – drakon – and it originally meant any large serpent, and the dragon of mythology remained, for all its embellishment, essentially a snake. In Egyptian lore the god Apepe, was the great serpent of the world of darkness. The Greeks and Romans generally accepted the serpent as an evil power although sometimes the drakontes were held to be beneficent dwellers inside the earth. For the Christian Church, the dragon-serpent was symbolic of sin and paganism. The great dragon killing Saints were George and Michael. Many early paintings show one or other delivering whole townships from dragons and converting them to Christianity. It seems likely that the religion of the megalith builders was one of serpent worship. Indeed, one of their greatest monuments, that of Avebury, not far from Stonehenge, was originally conceived in the form of a serpent. As it has been partially destroyed, we assume this, owing to the felicitous activities of a man well ahead of his time, Dr W Stukely, Minister and Freemason. He perceived the temple of the serpent at Avebury and in his book, "Avebury in 1763", reproduced a drawing of what he saw. Unhappily, its destruction by pillagers of stone for building has established archaeologists reluctant to accept that the present-day Avebury circle is in fact part of a greater serpentine whole. It must be noted, however, that Stukley was a man steeped in the Old Tradition and was seeking to find some elusive unifying pattern behind the prehistoric features of Britain. For him there was no doubt that this was the serpent passing through the circle, the twin symbols of alchemical fusion. Underwood says that his own observation of the dowsing lines at Avebury confirms Stukely's statement.

Alfred Watkins, in "The Old Straight Track", first drew attention to the fact that some of his leys could be associated with St Michael because of the occurrence of his name at various points, mainly the terminal points, for example, St Michael's Mount in Cornwall. In the 1980's, the late Hamish Miller and Paul Broadhurst, (both Fountain International members,) took on the Herculean task of testing the theory, and were the first people to follow and dowse the line, later to be known as the St Michael Line along the whole length of its path across Britain. So, starting at Carn Les Boel , then St Michael's Mount, the line went through such places as the Cheesewring, St Michael's Church at Brentor, St Michael's Church Trull, going across Glastonbury Tor and Burrow Mump, both with ruined churches dedicated to St Michael, Stoke St Michael Church, straight through Avebury, Ogbourne St George, St Michael's Church Clifton Hampden, Royston, Bury St Edmunds, where there is another great medieval abbey, St Margaret's Church Hopton, and finally leaving Britain on the east coast between Lowestoft and Great Yarmouth, many months and a few broken cars later. This line is remarkable for the number of hills and churches dedicated to St Michael that fall on its route, Hamish and Paul's journey along this continuous line can be found in their book "The Sun and the Serpent". This task established that an energy line, such as the St Michael line, does exist in a dowsable form across the country.

Ley lines can also be known as dragon lines, and dragon legends may be found in abundance throughout Britain and, as John Michell observes in "View over Atlantis", where such legends and dedications occur the places "appear always to coincide with sites of ancient sanctity". Indeed, in Sussex itself, the dragon legends persist. St Leonard slew a dragon in St Leonard's forest near Horsham. The "nuckar" has emerged from his deep pond in Sussex folklore from time to time. On one of his escapades he fell prey to the cunning of one Jim Puttock. It appears, according to Jaqueline Simpson in "The Folklore of Sussex" that "dunnamany years ago," a Nuckar was swimming in the Arun River, snapping up cows and men, and even "sticking his ugley face up agin the winders in shipyard when people was having their tea." So, said a Sussex hedger recorded in 1929. Clearly something had to be done about this anti-social behaviour and the Mayor of Arundel offered a large reward to anyone who would put an end to the "nuckar" or "knucker". The dragon came to a bad end, due to a dubious "pudden" that was fed to him by the aforesaid Puttock who, upon onset of the anticipated collywobbles, cut off his head with an axe. Puttock is a modern version of one Jim Puck who earlier was the hero of a similar adventure. Jim Puck was alleged to be buried under an ancient tombstone in Lyminster churchyard, his tombstone showing a battered full-length cross superimposed over a herring bone pattern which, according to local tradition, represents the hero's sword laid across the dragon's ribs. Even in the 1930's somebody still decorated the stone with fresh snapdragons.

The word "Nuckar" is thought to derive from "nicor" in Scandinavian languages meaning a water monster, and the Anglo-Saxon epic, "Beowulf" describes "nicoras" as serpents of both sea and freshwater pools. Several hundred "knucker holes" exist in Sussex, and Jacqueline Simpson quotes Miss Helena Hall, in whose "Dictionary of Sussex Dialect" the knucker holes are defined as follows: *"Springs which rise in the flatlands of the South Downs. They keep at one level, are often 20ft across, and are reputed to be bottomless. The water is cold in summer, but never freezes, in frost it gives off vapour, being warmer than the air. Knucker holes are found at Lyminster, Lancing, Shoreham, Worthing and many other flats".*

Dragon legends abound across the length and breadth of the land, whether in Loch Ness or Loch Neagh, in Sussex, or in Berwick, where the Lambton Worm was finally dispatched, and where the deeds of St George, St Michael, St Patrick and St Catherine are remembered. And, of course, Apollo slew the python dragon at Delphi and thus created the most sacred shrines of Ancient Greece. What does it all mean? It means the cult of the serpent, dragon or nicor was a feature of the pre-Christian religions of these islands. It means that the folklore or racial consciousness has recorded the vanquishing of Paganism by Christianity in the slaying of the dragon by St George. As with all folk memories, we would do well not to dismiss them as a symbolic reference to something of greater reality. The dragon lines of Britain were real before Christ and are real to this day. The dragon myth is, I believe, an attempt by unlettered man to embody the truth about the serpent meanderings of that telluric force we now call the ley system, and by knowledgeable man to express in a harmless symbol the dangerous truth.

Certainly, the dragon wreathed his mighty coils around that part of Sussex where my metal rod inexorably led me, to the Templar Church near Hilaire Belloc's windmill at Shipley, and the discovery in the water meadows beside it. For the thought started to develop in my mind, as I had by this point dowsed Stonehenge, that perhaps there was a minor system in the South Downs which developed into the major system based on the 6-bar line on the Slaughter Stone. If that were so, then Wolstenbury tumulus was a key local interchange and the Coldharbour Wood embankment was a junction. Where, therefore was an interchange, where the triple became the 6-bar line? I followed the triple system through various Sussex churches going north towards Horsham. When I conferred with David, he had always been interested in Shipley Church to the south of Horsham, as it was said to have been the southern headquarters of the Templars and, as we have shown, the Templars seemed to have had more than one hand in the whole affair. He nagged me until I went there.

The Warriors of God

Discoveries in the Templar Church at Shipley

Sometime in the early 12th century, probably between the years 1125 and 1130, Philip de Harcourt, Dean of Lincoln, gave the Knights Templar "the land of Heschapelis and the church of the said village". The Templars immediately began to rebuild, erecting the solid, rather sombre building that now stands beside the bank of the Adur, one of the oldest and architecturally most important church in Sussex. I first saw St Mary's, Shipley, on a June day in 1975. It was an idyllic scene, a "Country Life" cover picture of rural England if ever there was one. Swans glided majestically between the water lilies on the clear meandering river, and small boys fished. A little distance away the white mass of the windmill that had been Hilaire Belloc's home reared itself above the vivid green of early summer trees. (Joseph Hilaire Pierre Rene Belloc was and Anglo-French writer historian. He was one of the most prolific writers in England during the early 20th century. Belloc was known as a writer, orator, poet, sailor, satirist, man of letters, soldier and political activist). Beyond, the little village drowsed in the afternoon sun. It was a charming scene of which I was only partially aware at the time, for almost immediately I found what I was looking for and hastened to follow it up.

The triple line, which off and on I had been following through Sussex for weeks, arrived at one of the corners of the altar end of the church at an angle of 45 degrees. At the north-east corner, a 6-line emerged, and I had found the changeover point. The new sextuple went towards Dragon's Green where the "George and Dragon" pub stood. Along the side of Dragon's Lane and partially on it, the sextuple line ran in a northerly direction. The road turns to the left, but the sextuple continues, marked by a line of well-established oak trees that successive farmers have allowed to remain standing across the field, until it joins a low earthwork in a hedgerow. Here there is a strange trackway about 8 feet wide between an impenetrable wood and the hedgerow. The low earthwork dowses like those at Coldharbour Wood. Some 20 yards along the earthwork the sextuple line, running parallel to and on its right hand (south – north) side along the earthwork, split in two, one branch running across the field to the north east, the other easterly through the impenetrable wood.

I drove along some of the nearby lanes, one ran past a house marked on the map as Knight's Farm. Most Templar churches had farms of their own. There are many Mr Knights, but it was worth a try, for a sextuple line crossed the road at 90 degrees and went toward the house. This was strange because its other direction was to Shipley Church and I had only found one sextuple there which I had traced in another direction. The following day I visited the church again, with the same results, but this time I went outside to the graveyard and into the meadow to the south. The churchyard was clearly elevated some 4 feet above the meadow and, at a point where it extended some 10 feet a right angle in a southerly direction before carrying on, I found a westerly sextuple line that equated to the one at Knight's Farm.

Going to the churchyard, I found the vicar, and engaged him in conversation. He had only taken over the parish at the beginning of the year and was still in the process of informing himself as to its antecedents. When he was questioning the verger, who had informed him that grave digging had revealed signs of a building in the corner where I had encountered the second sextuple. He believed this to be the Templars' Preceptory, referred to earlier. He also told me that the 15 feet wide River Adur which passed the church used to be navigable and the knights had embarked there for the Crusades. Indeed, it was alleged that the ironstone bollard in the entrance to the church had been found at the water's edge and bore what might be marks of mooring chains. It dowsed! But then it was ironstone, at least that was what I supposed at the time to be the reason.

I enquired about Knight's Farm and he said it was believed to have Templar associations. The lady who lived there would be pleased to talk to me. A Mrs Gretel Little, the owner, welcomed me in, gave me a life-saving beer on a hot summers day, and showed me around the house. She explained that it was alleged to be a Templar's hospice, it was clear that much of the house, albeit restored, showed little sign of antiquity. The sextuple line ran through her drawing room, once a kitchen, and partly outside the house. It stopped some 10 feet the other side. Two days later I came back and met Mrs Little's partner in her horticultural business, Bob Phillips. He was a parish councillor with a deep love for and intimate knowledge of that beautiful stretch of countryside, and I was fortunate indeed to have a so knowledgeable a guide. Bob showed me many things of dowsing interest in the area – old wells, strange woods and so on. Accepting what I had to tell him, he took me to see Abraham's Well, for which recently he had obtained modest funds from the parish to renovate with his own hands. It was a mysterious and slightly disturbing, if singularly beautiful spot, the well – or rather spring – was about the size and shape of a large cauldron, perhaps 2 feet across and only 2 feet deep. But no matter how hot the outside temperature was, the water was always bitterly, numbingly cold. Bob Phillips told me that the well changed its water every two and a half minutes and that Hilaire Belloc used to insist on churns of water from Abraham's Well being sent to him by train whenever he was staying in London. The 6-bar line went through it.

On my next visit a few days later, Gretel Little welcomed me in her accustomed style. "Do you do ghosts with your thingummyjig?" "Well, I don't know," I said. "Possibly. Why?" "Well I have visitors who say that one of the bedrooms is haunted." I asked her permission to dowse the bedrooms, she agreed but she said that she should not tell me which it was. I dowsed them but the only reaction was the straight 6-bar line which passed through her living room and the bedroom above. She told me that was the room where a particular visitor said a nice young man was always there. I proceeded to follow the 6-bar line back and I went to the field opposite, where next to the sextuple line I found two circles. My first reaction was an idle speculation that the 6-bar line circle was the same diameter as those I found in the interim at Chartres Cathedral which I had visited a few days before. It was 33 ½ of my paces, and so were the Shipley circles.

Gretel took me later to a little bridge of obvious antiquity over the River Adur on her property. It was a splendid little bridge built without mortar, and its stresses were distributed, and its fabric supported by its massive stones which formed a Roman arch. The river authority had been at work, dredging and "preserving". They had pulled out of the river some very large stones which had fallen from the coping, they were about 100 kilos each. She told me how they had also found heavy stones laid under the bridge below the water. The stones dowsed or gave a reaction. The bridge itself which could support a modern tank was on a line junction, an exact cross, but the bridge was with a circle into which the lines did not penetrate. The centre of the circle also dowsed. I took a fragment home. It dowsed. Later, on another visit with Bob Phillips, we explored the lines on the bridge. They were different from other lines I had encountered, single lines about 10 feet wide. Normally they are 3 feet or less. The northern line ran to a grove within a hollow, with configurations like the classic clover leaf pattern of the "earth temples". Within the complex a star shaped line system met the main line where is disappeared. We did not know what to make of it.

We returned to Abraham's Well to examine it at greater length. Bob had brought his three children and I put my spare rods in their hands. As we crossed a sextuple line, they began to say, "Daddy the rods move!" The well was beside the road, and on the other side, some few yards into the wood, I could see a low earthwork. We went in. It curved in a gentle arc some 25 yards either side of the six as it crossed the road. It dowsed just like Coldharbour Wood! Its curve took it back across the road to a hollow, like the chalk pits, on the side of the well and, leaving the earthwork on the other side, the single 6 bar line split into three sixes in a north-west quadrant. Bob stopped in his tracks and said, "I can feel them too, as well as the children". We paused to consider, Bob this time concentrating very hard. The sympathy he had initially shown me hardened into certainty that at least I wasn't a wandering mad man and whatever it was, he and his children knew it was there too. He then said, "There's a meadow I know nearby I want to show you. I've always felt odd there since I was a boy. It is an area where things don't grow." We made our way over there with the children, and the children were idly dowsing in the meadow, when suddenly one said that he had found a circle. I went over to check, not really believing the child, but sure enough I dowsed a circle where he had found it. (In some ways children take to dowsing easily because they have less preconceptions or hang ups). Soon the children found more and more which I verified. Many of the circles were 33 ½ paces in diameter perpendicular to Knight's Farm, and Shipley Church. What was interesting was that a complete dowse of the meadow in question revealed, in an area about 100 yards square, a group of 49 circles, each about 18 paces across. There are similar circles and dimensions around the apse of the cathedral of Chartes, and all cathedrals have such circles, albeit in different dimensions.

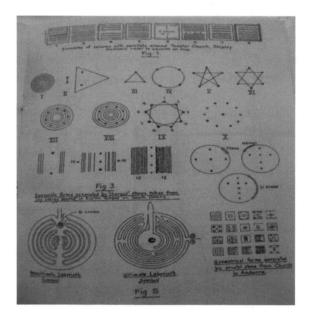

We continued to the "odd" place that Bob mentioned and found spirals, not one or two, but a complete system of interweaving spirals over a large area, in the format of 7 X 8. I began to feel there was something very important here in Shipley.

I returned to Shipley a few days later, then again and again. Working my way first through the water meadows immediately surrounding the church and then through the fields beyond. In the water meadow to the south of the church I came across similar dowsable circular forms 7 X 7, which enveloped Church Farm South. Each of the three farms was in, or next to, similar phenomena. As I moved into another area around the windmill owned by Belloc, I found dowsable squares. Again, in groups of 49. Inside each were different combinations of parallel lines, within the combinations the numbers, 1, 3 and 7 were important.

It was slow work, for I was no longer dowsing on open down land but on farmland, and where there are arable crops it is possible to work only during the relatively short period between reaping and sowing. But fortunately, Shipley lay more or less on the route between my office and home, and so it was possible to stop over at odd moments and add a little more to the map that I was building.

It was becoming more apparent that I was not simply dowsing ley lines, or even Underwood's aquasats, but something much more complex and deliberate. Eventually with assistance, I was to uncover more than 600 symbols centred round Shipley Church, symbols, not patterns which might have been produced by chance movements of underground water, symbols which, though possibly employing that blind natural force, had communication as their object. This was what my rod was revealing, and in due course I found different classes of symbol. One of the most elaborate of these was something which resembled a line in music, a representation of Ram's horn spirals, based on factors of seven. And the circles were in groups of 49, as were the squares with the linear symbols inside.

Map of Shipley Church symbols

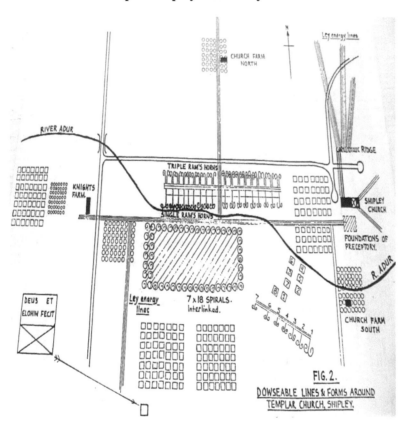

FIG. 2.
DOWSEABLE LINES & FORMS AROUND
TEMPLAR CHURCH, SHIPLEY.

Another phenomenon I tried to chart, (but eventually gave up as impractical, although not impossible,) was a link-up group of 126 (or 7 x 18) spirals I referred to earlier. I had noted that they were linked, but when I started to sort out the linkage I found myself involved in a most intricate pattern. The spiral at one corner might be linked to another 100 yards away, and also linked to the next one 15 yards away and so on. I recognised a symmetrical interweaving pattern, such as one might find on a Persian carpet or interweaving forms of Celtic art, but I didn't have time to pursue this. It would take a team of three or four dowsers, and a day or so. If it is shown to be important, it will be done. What I particularly noted was that the huge display of symbols, at least a mile long and wide, always followed the natural features of the landscape. They scrupulously observed the serpentine banks of the river. All of which was not an unpleasant way to spend a summer or two, particularly when one knew one could always repair to Gretel Little's for refreshment or a chat with Bob Phillips, (who by now had become a first-class dowser), at the end of the evening. If nothing else, one had made good friends on this strange quest.

(Four years later I rechecked findings in the area, and they had remained the same.)

By July 1975, I had found enough to convince me beyond argument that I was not looking at merely another function of the ley system. But what had I found? Before one could even begin to answer that question, it was necessary to have some corroborative investigation. Bob Phillips had worked side by side with me and confirmed my findings. But had I been unconsciously influencing him? What was needed was a dowser of experience who could confirm or deny the findings by basing them on his own experience.

I made enquires of Guy Underwood's publishers as to whether there were any unpublished papers, and they directed me to his Estate's solicitors where I was courteously received. Upon announcing the nature of my enquiry, they said that all his papers were on loan to a Mr Robert Cowley. They gave me his telephone number and permitted me to use their telephone. We talked for half an hour before I realised that I was abusing the hospitality of the solicitors. I think that we both realised we had a lifetime in which we were going to talk. "Come down next weekend to Wolstenbury," I said, and he agreed. Harold and his wife came too. We all struck up the firmest of friendships from then on. My meeting with him was only one of many such meetings that illuminate this story. Bob was a senior member of R.I.L.K.O. (The Research into Lost Knowledge – website www.rilko.net). This admirable and unpretentious society, which publishes works of the most fundamental importance, was founded under the auspices of Mrs Janette Jackson to rehabilitate the reputation of Frederick Bligh Bond, the man who excavated Glastonbury Abbey under the direction, it later transpired, of automatic writing from a medieval monk. His great discoveries were then hurriedly suppressed by the ecclesiastical establishment. How extraordinary that such evidence of survival of the human spirit after death should cause embarrassment to the very institution which has preached it for two millennia.

I kept Bob informed of my findings, and he did visit Shipley himself, and generally agreed with my findings. One day, he phoned me and said, "Look, Bill Lewis is in London for the weekend. He will come down and look at what you have found." I was delighted for I knew Bill Lewis by reputation as one of the best dowsers in Britain. As it happened, the previous week, I was in Watkins bookshop in Charing Cross Road and fell into conversation with a complete stranger, a young man called Stephen. We got talking and I said, "Why not come to Shipley and see what is going on? He did, and he came with another young man called Dylan, an advanced yogi, who was also a dowser. Thus, quite by chance, a remarkable gathering of people quite suddenly took place. It was with a great sense of anticipation that I drove to Shipley from Brighton. This was for two reasons, firstly, my findings might be rejected by a better dowser than I, and all the work I had put in be rendered useless, secondly that it might receive confirmation, in which case I would receive another form of emotional shock. For, notwithstanding my intellectual appreciation of the dowsing results, there was still one part of my mind which kept telling me it was all idle fancy, an attempt by the subconscious to provide relief from the wholly materialistic culture of which I was a product.

We met at 11am that Sunday morning. I don't know what the vicar thought when he saw this strange group of people coming together outside the church. Bill Lewis was introduced, and he looked at me with a twinkle in his eye. "So, you think that you can dowse, do you? We shall see." He was a man in his sixties from Welsh Wales, and as I got to know him during the day, a gentle and knowledgeable man, if ever there was one. Dylan, the yogi, and I went off in one direction, whilst Bob and Bill went in another. Dylan cut himself a hazel fork of the traditional dowser and I held my rod. We marched together across the sextuple line from the church. As the hazel worked and jumped in his hands, so my rod moved back and forth through its quadrants. We were both marking the same phenomenon. I explained to him about the symbols and we moved into the area where they were. He dowsed them, and then something quite extraordinary happened. "I can see them," he said. As in all strange events, at the moment strange things happen, you take them in your stride. It is only later that the full impact hits you. "Oh yes?" I said. "What's over there then?" And he proceeded to explain to me that he could actually see, the square symbols. I had painstakingly dowsed and drawn a map of them, which he had not seen, so I asked him to tell me what he could see. Then he demonstrated to me that he could identify, by his own particular vision, what was present. He agreed with my map! Then I asked him to describe them. They are like huge cubic polythene bags, blown up."

Now in our dowsing of the South Downs that at points where these energy paths entered the so-called earth temples, there were holes in the chalk, and over a two-year period they generally got bigger. We also noticed that, where the energy lines ran through flint walls in particular, holes appeared in the walls. It was beyond chance. What was interesting, was that the stones appeared to have been taken away, and it was some time before Jill Wicks supplied the answer. "They are being removed for magical purposes." David Conway, tax inspector turned magician recommends that when you make your magic circle, of which the four points are earth, air, fire and water, for the earth point a sample of stone or earth from a place where the old foot paths cross was very efficacious. We figured that they were therefore charged in some way, which made us take away some ourselves. Setting them out in various forms provoked various dowsable forms.

They represent the various geometrical forms of the Pythagorean Tetracts. We also noted that, if you set them out in the form of a cross, a set of dowsable lines appear.

"Let's make an experiment," I said. I had brought with me the charged stones we had collected from various sites where lines started divide into two branches. We set them up in the carpark of the church in the form of a rood cross, which we knew produced a projection of lines. "What's happening now?" I asked him. "It's as if a current of air is blowing through the squares, the cubic forms are being blown aside, they are bending in the breeze", he replied. "It's linked to the ironstone in the church porch". I asked him to move into a position in which he could feel the strongest impressions, but from which he could not see me, and I would disassemble the stones, to see if he would know when it was done. I did so, and when I had put the stones back into their bucket, he came around the side of the church almost immediately, claiming that it was like a punch to the kidneys when I removed the cross.

As it was lunch time, we went to the "George and Dragon" inn, whilst Bill Lewis and Bob Cowley had gone off inside of the church itself. Bob took notes of Bill's findings. Lewis felt that the church was based on a series of converging underground springs, forming a "square of Pegasus". The ironstone in the porch was part of a larger and much earlier stone temple site and was important in today's system. Much later, I found out that the constellation of Pegasus was a key symbol of the Templars, whose church this was.

Bill and I got to know each other better over a beer and a sandwich, after which we went to the area of the spirals. Bill certainly found them, although he kept associating them with underground water. As a test, I got out the charged stones and set them up in a way that would interfere with the patterns when Bill was not looking. I walked away leaving him to it, but when I returned the stones, that I had placed in the grass in such a way that they would not be visible were back in the bucket. He waved an admonishing finger at me and grinned. What was interesting was that he agreed with what I had found, but his interpretation was more on Underwood's lines.

By now Bill had realised that Dylan could see what was going on psychically and asked him if he could see auras. Dylan agreed that he could, but today was the first day that he could see such things! Mischievously Bill said that he was going to steal my aura, he took me by the right hand and with his left hand swung the pendulum to the right. I felt a distinct tingling. When asked to confirm if my aura had gone Dylan nodded, and added that Bill's was now twice as big. Indignant I asked for my aura back. Obliging he swung the pendulum the other way, and again I felt the tingling sensation. Dylan reported that my aura was now back. Now up until that time, although the rods had always worked, I could never get a pendulum to move, but from that day the pendulum came alive in my hands and I was generally a better dowser. I often wondered if I didn't get something from Bill as a result of this action but was later grateful as the use of a pendulum became important in my research.

We moved up onto Abraham's Well. Dylan found the six bar lines there. Bill said it was the convergence of two radio-active stress lines whose origins were thousands of miles away.

Bob Phillips told us that the present name of Abraham's Well, had only been in place for the last 80 years. Previously it had been a dedicated shrine in the name of some saint or other some 750 years ago. Circa 1900 B.C. it had been the centre of a temple, at which time the spring, previously a blind spring, had been opened up so that the waters emerged. Bill proceeded, using a wire spring, which he thrashed in the air with one hand, to give an analysis of the water and asked Bob Cowley to call out the periodic table, and spelled out the sort of analysis one is accustomed to read on the label of mineral water bottles. Calcium was the predominant trace element, with potassium and magnesium second and third. He expressed percentages of others to six places of decimals. When traces of Strontium 90 were found, Bill remarked that it was a wonder that all the sheep weren't psychic. Later I came across a belief in occult circles, that the release of Strontium 90 into the environment was raising man's perception. (Perhaps, this is why Belloc had barrels of water from this spring sent to London when he was there.)

At the end of the day we went over to Gretel Little's house for a farewell beer together. Whilst there, I asked Bill to take a look at my photograph of Wolstenbury with the hemispherical bubble, (now normally called an orb). He dowsed it with his spring apparatus and concluded that it was a manifestation of ley energy, Theta radiation. Many people take photographs like this, but thrown them away, as they think that the light has somehow ruined the photograph. Interesting, but it merely removed the problem one stage further.

Today, what had we found at Shipley? What was the explanation of this huge complex of inter-related symbols? The conversation went back and forth, the speculation circling around the subject until I said, with some diffidence. "Are we looking at the equivalent of a school child's blackboard? Could it be, say, a permanent display setting out geometric truths for the benefit of the Templar neophytes and, in the Preceptory, those who come after them. People like us for instance. It is perhaps a code, or a form of simple test. Only when the neophyte has perceived them and explained them, is he fit to move on." I lacked confidence because the theory was startling to say the least. But I had good grounds for advancing it. Over the last 18 months or so that I had been visiting Shipley, I had naturally been building up some background information on the Templars. It was sketchy, hesitant material. At this point in time there is no history of the Templars or, rather, to be exact, the history of the Templars has only been written by their enemies. They were wiped out totally in 1305, and their traditions subjected to vicious, hostile propaganda which sought to show them as degenerate perverts who also dabbled in the black arts. But "truth is the daughter of time," and over the succeeding centuries independent researchers have been throwing light on aspects of Templar tradition and motivations. All this I tried to explain that evening with my fellow explorers. Sceptical at first, they became more and more interested.

I began to think of a link between their quiet Sussex churchyard and that violent story wrapped in the mists of time of the Albigensian Heresy. In a month's time, I was going to Andorra to spend the summer in the family chalet high up in the Pyrenees. I had bought a map of Andorra and gave it to Bill Lewis to be dowsed by him, to which he agreed. He promised to write to me with the results for I had told him I had discovered a legend that the Grail of the Cathars was buried in a cave in Andorra. The reason why thoughts form in one's mind and why one does certain things is not always easy to explain in a logical way. I had read certain books about the Cathars or Albigensians by French authors over the past year, as they were appearing in a series about "occult" matters in Spain. I acquired them

48

as they were published, for I was also interested in the surrounding history of Andorra. My interest quickened when I noted, in Gerard de Sedes' "El Tesoro Cataro", his reference to the work of Fernand Niel who had indicated that the castles and chateaux of the Cathars had been built on geomantic lines, that is to say, in keeping with the ancient canon of measurement and orientation I had read about in John Michell's "View Over Atlantis". Maybe the Cathars had been in on the secret as well, whatever the secret was. The connection between geomantic buildings and ley lines was also a point made by Michell, and by Paul Screeton in his "Quicksilver Heritage". Furthermore, the Cathars were clearly associated with a strange group of men called the Cagots, a guild kept in ridged apartheid in that area, who built the churches and who unequivocally traced back their origins back to the Master Hiram, builder of King Solomon's temple. Here one was right back in again to that Masonic stream with which the Templars are inevitably associated. I shared Underwood's view that all this was a "Masonic" phenomenon.

During this period, I had also read Trevor Ravenscroft's, "The Spear of Destiny". This also dealt with the feminine grail symbol, the chalice stone, and I was now therefore familiar with Wolfram von Eschenbach's "Parzifal" and the alternative Grail cycle in which the Grail Knights or Templars, had received the Grail and guarded it in the castle of Montsalvat, quite specifically in the Pyrenees. Wolfram had said it was a stone fallen from Lucifer's Crown. Montsalvat, said some, was the same as Montsegur, last redoubt of the Cathars who were synonymous with the Templars in knowledge and objective. Both were exterminated for heresy. In a little book called "The Templars" by Pierre Morizot, given to me by Bob Cowley, the connection between the Templars and the Cathars was spelled out, both were grail adepts and guardians. Could it be, I wondered, that the grail symbol cloaks the esoteric truths of ley lines and geomancy? And the thought began to form in my mind that the quest was perhaps a sort of search for the Holy Grail. Even when I found the reference to its being buried in a cave in Andorra, it was still with a light-hearted gesture that I gave the map to Bill Lewis.

Discovery in the Pyrenees

Three weeks after that bewildering and rewarding day in the water meadows at Shipley, I was 5,000 feet up in the Pyrenees, struggling to make sense of an extraordinary series of phenomena which my rod had revealed in the mountain village of Arinsal. The discovery of the line from Wolstenbury tumulus led me eventually to Shipley. There, the necessity to make some sense out of what was appearing around the church led me to investigate the known surviving aspects of Templar history. This in turn demonstrated unequivocally that there was some relationship between the Order of Knights Templar and the massacred sect known as the Cathars. The last refuge of the Cathars was high upon the towering mountain of Montsegur.

The events that brought me to Andorra were perfectly commonplace. I used to spend part of each year in Spain, combining business with domestic arrangements. In 1975, my wife suggested that we go to Andorra for a weekend. In that weekend, we both fell in love with that mountainous area, a survival of the Middle Ages, and bought a holiday chalet, in the most remote and delightful valley of Xixerella, The fact that I was able to spend a reasonable time each year in the Iberian peninsula was to have a profound significance at a later stage of my explorations.

Shortly before that summer of 1975 I had come across a book called "Le Defi Cathare" by Paul Guillot, in which Guillot draws the reader's attention to a legend which tells of how four Cathars left Montsegur, on the 12th March 1244, by an underground passage with the "treasure of the Cathars". No-one knows where they went. According to tradition the Cathars were in possession of the Holy Grail and this is what they were alleged by some to have taken with them. Guillot discusses various possibilities and legends, including one which stated that they went from France to Andorra, a land nurturing a sturdy independent folk, more or less outside the jurisdiction of the Inquisition, and in particular to a cave in the valley of Arinsal. They later merged into the local population, successfully claiming them for "Protestantism".

My first expedition was naturally to Arinsal but, not having been to Andorra since my discovery of the lines, I made a preliminary survey. At the frontier with Spain, I ran into groups of circles like those at Shipley, and further determined that a line about 30 metres wide was running up the valley. It went all the way to Les Escaldes, where a branch about 10 metres wide went up via La Messana to Arinsal. When I made my detailed survey of Arinsal, I followed the thick line to a point above the village, where it ended more or less where the tarmacked road becomes a dirt track, and a pattern of squares and circles developed into a mini version of Shipley. My interest quickened. They were spread over a substantial area and, on taking the newly installed chairlift to the top of the mountain, I found them on the way up, and at the top, thus proving that dowsing in a chairlift is also possible. On descending to the road again, I looked for a possible source of the lines. There was a small Romanesque church at the side and away from the village. Building materials surrounded it and the area appeared to be under reconstruction and excavation. Human bones were stacked in random heaps around the place. I dowsed outside the church, and a V-shaped triple emerged from the circular apse. The door was a round wooden one and padlocked. I wandered around it again, dowsing idly. The rod picked up some extra single lines, and I was startled as they had not been there the first time. My niece Caroline was with me, (and I had

51

established earlier that she could use a rod), so I asked her to see what she could find around the church. After a while she came back and said that there were hundreds of lines. Once again, I made the mistake that 12 yr olds cannot dowse as well as adults. "You've got it wrong, let me have another go." She was right, there were hundreds of lines. I went to the area of the circles and re-dowsed. The circles were now squares with four triple parallels inside. Even more puzzled, I thought that was enough for one day!

Coming back the following day, further tests showed that the multiple phenomenon could be produced on request. On filling out some of the lines it was evident that they joined up with what could have been the remains of a stone circle, most of whose stones were buried or partly visible.

I returned to the church, this time alone. The triple V-shape was there, but nothing else. Then an idea struck me, telepathically I asked the church to show me the lines, and it did! A thrill went through me and I was amazed. This was the point of no return, the discovery that the so-called "ley-system" was living and could be actively used. I glanced at the church, knowing that I needed to gain access to further the mapping. There was no one around to ask, so I went to the nearby café for a coffee, and to enquire about obtaining a key for the church. The waitress said that the church was owned privately by a Senor Amadeo Rossell, who was reconstructing it, (local villagers went to church elsewhere). Senor Rossell was a man of mature years, and the owner of Andorgas, the propane and butane distribution company. He was happy to talk about the church and explained how he thought that he had bought some apparently virgin ground, presumably to build a house. When he came to look at the land, he discovered the ruins of a 12th or 13th century church on it, which appeared to have been destroyed at some time in an avalanche. The building had been flattened, leaving about 4 feet of walls above the foundations, but the original stones were there. Bravely he had decided to reconstruct the church as it had been. It was an expensive project, but he wanted to leave something in Andora by which his grandchildren would remember him. He was not skilled in the area of reconstructing a 12th century church, so Senor Rossell gained advice from M.Pierre Cantury, a noted Andorran archaeologist. (A bell rang in my head as soon as he said Cantury's name. In Guillot's book, he acknowledges Cantury as the source of his information about the Cathars in Andorra, and the cave in Arinsal. Unfortunately, at that moment Cantury was away on holiday). Senor Rossell explained that he did not have the key to the church, and that it was with two students who were working in the church at Pal. He gave me permission to get it from them.

Pal is in the next valley, so I drove over and went into the church at Pal and saw the two students on ladders carefully chipping away plaster, to reveal the medieval paintings behind. I announced my business, and they immediately gave me the key to the church at Arinsal. These archaeology students had rebuilt the church at Arsinal stone by stone, (apart from one stone). I explained that I wanted to dowse in the church, and they looked at me wide eyed, so I gave them a demonstration and dowsed inside the church at Pal. Under the floorboards that they had yet to take up I found a zone but then my eye was caught by the side chapel, with an altar cut from the living rock. A single line emerged, and the pendulum, which I could now use, gave a positive reaction. The students were very curious, but I was a bit pressed for time, and said I would answer all their questions later.

Back inside the church at Arinsal, with a group of people, I located the source of the energy at the base of the altar, which was obviously new, and I looked around at the rough stone floor of the 12th century church. My experiment the other day showed that the energy system responded to command, so taking it one step further, with myself and the people who were with me, we all sent out a thought of love. Suddenly I noticed a zone of activity had spread halfway down the tiny church, where nothing had been before. This again showed that the energy system responded to thought, which was interesting. As I left, I noticed that the dowsing phenomena outside the church had also changed. It was now based on concentric rings in groups of seven around the church, and extended to my chalet, fading after two hours.

As so often happens with my journey, one thing leads to another and next day I went to the church with my trusty tape recorder/cassette player tucked up my arm. Now I knew what would happen when a certain type of thought, in this case love, interacted with the energy in the church. So, what would happen when certain pieces of music were played? Firstly, I played the "Hallelujah Chorus" from Handel's "Messiah". The power went out of the church, albeit huge squares centred on the church, phenomena were present over a large area, and I was able to check them as far away as Les Escaldes, some 11 kilometres away.

On the following day, I tried a different piece of music, this time from "Jesus Christ Superstar," the song "Ho-sanna, Hey-sanna", which has a verse, when Jesus is talking to Calaphas on Palm Sunday:

Why waste your breath moaning at the crowd?

Nothing can be done to stop the shouting.

If every tongue were still, the noise would still continue.

The rocks and stones themselves would start to sing.

I played the opening bars of the overture and switched to the song. The source of the power in the church, if that's what is was, appeared from the base of the altar, and expanded rapidly and bolted like a rabbit out of the door. It obliterated all other phenomena, and was dowsable at La Massana, 5 kilometres away, some sixty minutes later, in concentric rings of seven.

Another experiment using an act of spiritual love produced a wall of energy, that came at me from the crude altar and went past at an increasing speed, leaving a dowsing vacuum inside the church. Outside there were squares, in groups of 49, about two yards across each square. Within the square was a symbol.

Groups of 49 such squares were all over Andorra, at least up to 12 km away. They decayed after several hours. Gregorian Plain Chant from a cassette recorder produced similar results.

I arranged to meet the students, Eudaldo and Toni at Arinsal church. Eudaldo and Toni were by now expressing the keenest interest in what was going on. I agreed to instruct them in the art of the rod which they readily took to and agreed with my findings. They even activated the church that they were working on in Pal and noticed that the living stone altar was doing the same thing as the church in

Arinsal. Later on, I was to establish that I could discern whether they were working in the church or not, simply by dowsing in our front garden some miles away, finding sides of huge squares being emitted due to their presence in the church, and to there being in a state of awareness. The interesting thing was that I had dowsed my garden every day for a fortnight before I met them without noticing anything untoward. Now just by there being there, the altar was emitting. One thing was clear, however. They believed that what I had told them was true. Sometimes I had to go up to the church and remonstrate with them as the emissions were affecting my experiments. It would shut down on request at the source itself and later I was able to shut it down at distance by a mental request of some concentration.

During our visit to Arinsal Church, Toni and Eudaldo drew my attention to a stone they had found at the side of the altar in the ruins. It was a pentagon in form, not of equal sides, but as follows; tapering upwards and cut off at the top before it came to a point. They couldn't work out where the stone should go in the church but thought that it was interesting. The stone was a sedimentary type, white as if aerated, and there was a quarry of this type of stone in Andorra. I took it outside and dowsed it. Each facet emitted a line, and with the student's permission I took it home. But in doing so, I had the strangest feeling of hostility, so I left the stone in the car overnight.

The next morning, I placed the stone on the window-ledge and dowsed it. Nothing. Then remembering our switch on and switch off experience in Arinsal Church, I conducted similar experiments with the stone. It worked in the same way. "Give me some squares?" I said, and it did with four triple lines inside. "Something else?" and it produced single line circles. "Next please". It was like talking to a colleague operating a slide projector, and so it went into a square. At lunch time I put it away until the next day, when I would put it to work again. It opened up with the same series of symbols, just like those I had found at the Templar Church at Shipley, except those at Shipley were always static. This stone was putting up different lineal symbols on request. It moved to squares, circles, rectangles, E shapes, and circles within squares within circles in strange and apparently meaningless combinations. I recorded 300 of them and began to lose patience. What does it mean? I thought, after a long question and answer session with the stone. How many frames must I go through? The answer came back 1,000, at which point I broke off to try and make sense of it all.

I told my son, Nicholas about the results. "Ask him his name, Dad". The stone replied by spelling out its name. PIOTAM. Nick was excited, "Let me ask Piotam some questions. I'll write them down without telling you, and you find the answers." (We used a yes/no system of answering.) A thirteen-year-old doesn't boggle like forty-year-old. Some of the questions were serious, others cheeky. Nick's final question was, "is the source of this intelligence on this planet?" No." In our galaxy?" Yes. "Where?" The thought of what is a double E went through my mind.

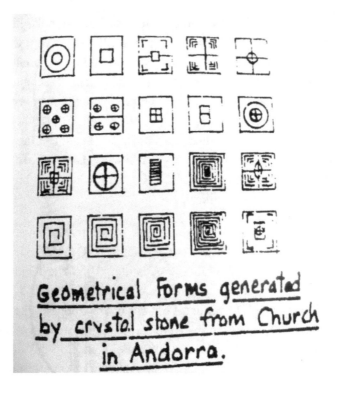

Geometrical forms generated by crystal stone from Church in Andorra.

So ended one of the most remarkable communications of my life, it was the precursor of many, much more remarkable. I persisted at various odd moments in trying to establish more facts from Piotam, as he was now affectionately known in the family, sitting him in his place of honour on the mantelpiece. I established again that he was not the Cathar Grail, that was still in an Arinsal cave, (which encouraged us to make the expedition recorded later). We decided to visit Montsegur in France, the last redoubt of the Cathars. Piotam indicated that he had been to Montsegur and would like to accompany us on the journey, which he did.

It was when Pierre Cantury returned from holiday that some light was thrown on the original purpose of the stone. Toni and Eudaldo had noticed at a church at Encamp, that there was a small square building at the side of the church, which had a Piotam type stone on the roof, surmounted by a metal cross. I checked it out, and it performed. During this investigation, it was established that the small house or chapel was on the cardinal compass points and took some measurements. But these were useless, as I later learned that the building was reconstructed. I was more than fascinated, because in previous conversations with Piotam, I had questioned him closely as to what part of the church he had come from, and had been firmly told that his position was on the roof, projecting upwards, towards the skies, and that was where he wished to return to eventually. At this point I was able to meet Pierre Cantury, the director of social services in Andorra, whose responsibilities include archaeology. He is a man of considerable reputation in the area, and the students had already primed him about my visit, and he was not disposed to mock. Little by little, I went through the story with him. When asked about the little "chapel" at Encamp he was immediately forthcoming. "It is a magic house," he said, and went onto explain that there had been others like it in the area, now destroyed. A magic house was an adjunct to the church where the priest would conduct magical rites, which would not meet with the bishop's approval if carried out in the church. These included summoning and dispelling storms. Made of the same stone as Piotam, there had been an altar inside the "Magic house". He himself had seen an old lady of the town conjure up a storm by going to the square and using a stone axe head, and a Christian cross, chanting to the four points of the compass. Many Andorran village households still kept these axe heads as talismans.

Later, Cantury called me to his office to examine the reliquary that had been found under the altar at Arinsal during the excavations preceding the restoration. It was carefully constructed, again in the same stone as Piotam, and after taking the lid off, another smaller container revealed itself, but was found empty. It performed as Piotam. I later noticed its curious resemblance to the altar he had drawn for me. In my travels, I found another chapel near Encamp with a Piotam high up in the campanile and formed the hypothesis that the church builders of Andorra were aware of the powers of the Piotams', and built them into their works deliberately. I also found evidence that the Piotam phenomenon was not first associated with Christian churches, because I noticed near the church at Arinsal what appeared to be a standing stone, which performed the Piotam routine. This stone is connected via other stones to the church and to another larger, clearly cubic stone some half a mile away. This in turn, is connected to the terraces. Following, we discovered others which indicated the Piotam system to be extensive and to involve Christian and Pre-Christian sites. We also discovered that Piotam was on call even out of a ram's horn spiral in the mountains. When Piotam 1 had been removed from Arinsal the wide line in the valley appeared smaller. When I restored Piotams 1 and 2 to Arinsal, the Arinsal line exceeded its earlier width.

It was mid-August when I decided to look for the cave at Arinsal, and one courteous inhabitant led us part of the way. "It's up there on the right," he said, pointing to a gully running precipitously up the mountain, "although I've never been in it." Nicholas and I started the ascent. It was not easy, for much of it was on loose stones. I entered the cave on hands and knees, but after a few yards I was able to crouch. Nick followed me in. At one stage we could stand upright, but after twenty yards or so the roof descended to a gap of 18 inches. Nick crawled forward at poked his head under. He could see a chamber on the other side. When I dowsed with my pendulum, it gave a reaction indicating the existence of a "power" source nearby. I realised at this point that we were ill-equipped to go further.

Protective helmets were essential, more than one torch, candles etc. So, we called it a day.

Happily, it was soon to be my birthday, so I was able to prevail upon the family to give me helmets, haversacks, water bottles etc., as birthday presents. On my birthday, with a much better equipped expedition, I set out with a friend, who was a practising speleogist. and founder of the British Cave Rescue Service, Paul. We went in under the 18-inch gap, and on the other side we found ourselves in a small chamber, perhaps 12 feet long and 6 feet wide. A further smaller tunnel led off to another smaller chamber in which we could stand up, but it was only 3 feet in diameter, and that was the end of the system. An investigation revealed stalagmitic activity. The cave must also from time to time have been filled with water, because every upper surface was coated in a clay like material. The floor was an unknown depth, and a mixture of stone and clay-like earth. By dowsing we found a spot where we needed to dig, but unfortunately, we didn't think that we would need digging tools, so we had to call it a day, (to return two days later with trowels.)

In my earlier discussions with Piotam, it was emphatic that we would find the Cathar Grail in this cave, and that we would find it this day, my birthday. That very morning, I had received a letter from Bill Lewis stating that the Cathar Grail, according to a map dowse, was in Arinsal, although I had not given him that name. Our expectations were high. In the cramped circumstances of the cave I used the rod and found a straight line. Other lines developed and a simple calculation based on these indicated the spot in the cave which was the source, as the different lines met there. I remembered Piotam's statement that I would find the Grail on my birthday, and I felt perhaps we had really discovered the position of something, even if we had not seen it.

In the interval before our next visit, I questioned Piotam. I was told we had located it, and that there were scrolls in the cave as well as objects of copper, gold and silver. Becoming more fascinating, we set off again on Monday 25th August 1975, taking food, stimulants and proper excavating tools. Piotam said I would find it within the hour, and at 12.15pm we started to dig. At 1pm we had set aside in a bag various objects of small size, including some chips of material that glinted in the candlelight, but nothing of obvious interest. I persisted in the area indicated by the rod and, amongst some stones of indeterminate and insignificant shape, began to isolate one which was different. It contained a cross like shape protruding from a flat base and, on loosening it from its position, I put it in the bag for further examination. We went on digging and at 1.15pm Paul said that our hour was up. I took out the pendulum and obtained a nil reaction, likewise with the rod. "Ask if we should go on digging," said Paul, and the answer came back as no. I then asked had we found it, and the answer was yes, it must be in the bag I thought, and I think that it is that strange stone. After our exertions, we decided that it was time for lunch, and went outside the cave and perched ourselves on the ledge. There was no room to walk around, and I took the strange stone, still coated in clay-like mud, and placed it in the recess on the mountain. I invited it to produce squares and it did. Paul was able to dowse them too. It performed like Piotam. "Who are you", I asked. "Piotam it replied. "Are you the Grail?" "Yes," it said. We ran a few more tests. It performed. When I got it home, I gave it a wash as it was encrusted with clay. The strange shape was confirmed; an equal armed cross, (a Cathar cross,) on a base all made of a crystalline material and translucent.

That night a huge wind blew up, and I had to get up in the night, to close the shutters and check the house. When I got up the next day, the telephone lines were down and snow was on the mountains, something the Andorrans could not recall having seen before in

August. I was extremely depressed, nervous, and could not stir myself to contemplate the object, but after lunch I got it out, feeling rather dubious. The fragments that had broken off during the excavation had glinted in the candlelight, and we had seen the equal-armed cross shape of this odd stone in the daylight at the mouth of the cave. It proved to be completely composed of a crystalline material which glinted at the edges. We had brought out a bagful of assorted fragments which I also subsequently washed. Many of them were of the same material and looked as if they were fragments of a broken plate. One piece was like a geode broken in two, with the crystals clearly standing out like a fragment in a jeweller's window. So, there it was. I set the strange stone out on a window ledge and considered. It was no artefact that I could identify. Man does not make crystals they are formed by nature. The strange shape was undeniable, although it was embedded in a clay-like earth. What was strange was that the Cathar symbol was the equal armed cross. Only a fragment resembled a geode. The rest appeared to have been formed within a mould. It made no sense to my tutored geology. Putting all that to one side, the fact remained that the object performed.

For 24 hours, I could not come to terms with the experience, and put the object away. Finding a Grail was a totally new experience for me. My approach to the whole affair, had been fairly jocular and lighthearted. But to have found, at a designated spot, a crystalline object, with the form of an equal armed cross, was an unlikely coincidence, if nothing else. That night a huge gale blew up. In the morning the lower mountains were covered in snow. The locals said it was unheard of, for snow at this time of year.

The next day I washed the object and washed it well. Then together with my son and daughter, we started to dowse it. The result of hours of questioning seemed to be that the crystalline object which I termed the "grail stone," was a sort of master control of the various Piotam stones, one of which I had acquired previously. That is, in talking to Piotam, we were also talking to the Grail, who was Piotam. In response to further questioning we learned that Piotam was a person who lived in our galaxy, but not in our Solar System, in the constellation of the bears, for Trionis, (symbol ooo), in Latin means Great and Little Bear. Linking to the Arthurian Grail Legend. Another coincidence? This constellation and its association with Arthur, Charlemagne and many other zodiacal myths would be the subject of a book called "The Ancient Wisdom" by Geoffrey Ashe. Some-time earlier on a visit to Montsegur, (supposedly the home of the Grail Stone I had unearthed), on dowsing the meadow where 300 Perfecti were burned alive in 1244, we had dowsed message which read: DEUM ORRIFLAMIFEREM RERUM TRIONIUM DIFFICILEM FIDELEM DEUM DOIT ROMA. As time went on it became apparent that the double E symbol was the symbol for Elohim, who emerged as a separate intelligence from Piotam, as he now stated his name to be. At any rate in the early communication, Piotam kept referring to the Elohim as being the people who understood the symbols. I had always understood Elohim to be plural, viz. Genesis Elohim, the sons of God who gave children to the daughters of men. However, Paul established that Elohim was singular, and in the book of the Kabbala, I discovered that Elohim was one of the names of God. This seemed to account for a somewhat confusing exchange with Piotam, and we came to the conclusion that Piotam was a separate intelligence, and that Elohim was another, who claimed to be of God. Sometimes I felt we were holding conversations with our subconscious selves. However, I was always sure that at times something was going on independent of myself, as I had too many surprises. When Toni and Eudaldo started their dialogues with a Piotam stone, they became convinced, and one was bound to accept that something most extraordinary was going on. Nevertheless, I continually voiced my fears about self- delusion.

I was idly re-reading a book called "Les Templiers Sont Parmi Nous," by Gerard de Sede, when I came across a reference to Pope Sylvester II, a strange 12th century Pope. The Knights Templar, in their secret statutes, observed that it was only during his reign that the real Church of Christ on earth existed. Apart from making some striking technological inventions, a new type of clock and a steam organ, he was supposed to have a copper head which answered questions and foretold the future. The author pointed out that it only answered "Yes" or "No" and functioned like a binary computer. Could it be that we were dealing with some strange phenomenon? If this were the case, we should have to be very careful with our questions. For instance, the word "important" could mean a hundred different things. Important to whom, and relative to what? It was a wholly contingent word, and we would have to use only absolute questions, even though it made discussions tedious, and involved many supplementary questions to get at the truth, or the real opinion of the intelligence. Furthermore, I suspected that communication was telepathic rather than verbal. We should have to discipline ourselves to frame absolute questions and rid our minds of the jumble of mental static that goes with most intellectual activities. The result of this was to make sessions shorter and quite tiring. It did, however, appear to be the right approach and cleared up many misconceptions. The idea that what we had found in the cave was unimportant turned out to mean that the object itself was unimportant, whereas the intelligence behind it was not.

One day in 1976, I wrote to Michael Bentine, after seeing a television programme in which he indicated his interest in strange energies and stone. He telephoned me immediately he received the letter, and we talked for an hour. Between us we had a lot in common – even the same tutor, John Leslie. Within a couple of days, he came to visit me. I explained my research so far, then gave him a fragment of the quartz like material which had detached from the strange stone.

Michael phoned a few days later, "Look, I was fascinated by your story and took the fragment to Joe Benjamin, the well-known psychometrist, but I am sorry to tell you that he couldn't make anything sensible of it, it's very disappointing". I felt very downcast, but asked him what Benjamin had said?

"Well, first of all he mentioned a connection with RICO, or RICHO or ARICO. He was holding the fragment in a packet and didn't know what It was. Then he said Bligh". "Ah you mean Colin Bloy", I said. "No, not Bloy, Bligh. Bligh Bond. I'm sorry, it's all nonsense."

"Do you know what RILKO is?" I asked. "Never heard of it," he replied. "And Bligh Bond means nothing to you? "Never heard of him", came the reply. I told him what they meant, and he shouted out loud. Finally, I told Michael that Bligh Bond's last book was on the Holy Grail. What Joe Benjamin said may be of supreme importance, or the most absurd coincidence. Michael and I have worked together ever since.

The Circle in Andorra

We spent the August of 1976 in the family chalet at Xixerella, Andorra. The last symbol given, the Grail symbol, was still in the garden. An idea formed in my mind that, if I were to do anything with the garden, it ought to be based on the symbol. So, I decided to build a circle of stones sunken into the garden which would double as a barbeque area. Against a background of cynical family tolerance, the work was completed. I say completed, because I had originally intended to cement the floor, and pick out the Grail symbol in the mosaic. However, I had noticed shortly after we arrived that the line had become a triple and, after completion of the circle, over a period of a week, it started to multiply until it was a 49-bar line. In dowsing the area, I noticed that behind the house the Tri-onis symbol was permanently there.

I questioned Elohim from time to time, and he certainly approved of the work. I asked about the purpose of the symbol, and the essential Yes/No routine revealed that it was a magic circle which could only be used for white magic as it was the Grail symbol. I enquired as to why the feeder line was multiplying, and was told it was charging up the circle, as a defence against misuse. Accordingly, on Sunday 5th September at 11pm Andorran time, (9pm GMT) I stood in the centre of the symbol where the seven circles were, and said to myself, "In the name of Tetragrammaton, Elohim, Jesus and the great seven, may the power in this circle be used to neutralise the activities of practitioners of evil everywhere, so be it." I dowsed the circle and the symbol had disappeared, to be replaced by the F symbol, the circular part being formed by my masonry. The Gothic arch leading into the sitting room remained. I asked Elohim if I had done well. "Yes," he said, "but the Grail symbol would never return to that spot, the F symbol of love would however remain."

Afterwards I went inside and poured myself a whisky and wrote down what had happened. I am sorry if there appears to be an air of cynical levity about it all. In a sense, I believe it is my protection. None of this is a purely emotional experience, or a spiritual one, in the sense that I perceive things in a welter of emotional turmoil. All of it is perceived through the rod, and is therefore entirely prosthetic, to the extent that, if a neighbour caught me at it and engaged me in conversation, I would break off without a second thought and talk to him about this and that, and carry on later. Nevertheless, I remain entirely convinced that this was a meaningful and real experience.

Perhaps this is material man's way back to his spiritual origins, having set aside the priest.

The question is whether or not I am dowsing my own subconscious, and I am the first to consider this possibility. There is no doubt in my mind and, I hope, in the readers' that the lines as such, have an objective reality. What is more doubtful is whether the related phenomena do. What concerns me somewhat is the extent to which my own subconscious can project lines and symbols whose reality depends solely on me, and not something external. What is at stake is of much more profound importance. Do these experiences have a reality which depends on intelligences and forces operating in other dimensions? Circumstantially the evidence I have is "Yes", but then only I know that I knew nothing of the significance of Elohim, the Tri-onis symbols, Arturus the constellation, the Great Bear, Arthur and the Round Table, etc, before they were written out for me. The cynic will quite rightly say, "Ah yes, but they were all in your subconscious anyway." My reply would be that I have searched my mind as far as one is able, and I can honestly say that I knew nothing of these things.

The fact that another may follow my own dowsing experiences as they take place is not conclusive of external intelligences at work, or indeed that my activities have some effect on events. Following the arguments I have put forward elsewhere, namely that the dowsing experience is a question of "tuning in" can equally well be dowsing my subconscious. Yet even if that were the case, it would not necessarily invalidate the experience. Positivist science is a dead end. How many more sub-atomic particles can we discover and how far can the theory of anti-matter go? It is feasible to posit that ultimate reality may well be reducible only in terms of a relativist approach. As a non-scientist, I can only dimly grope towards these things, but I recognise that I need to show the Elohim experience to be an objective one and not a dowsing of my subconscious, fascinating as that may be.

The evidence for ley power being used for magical purposes I hope I have established. The Druids and their spokesmen seem to be powerful corroborators of that. Apart from field evidence, the use of symbols for magical purposes has been genuinely established, but the operations of Elohim and his mission less so, unless of course you believe in the Bible or Rudolf Steiner, or even Aleister Crowley. *(Symbols are used in Reiki for the practice of healing – Suzanne.)* But if you don't, I have a problem and I don't know how to overcome it. Certainly, I seek to tell the truth, as I see it.

Shortly afterwards, I received a phone call from Antoni, one of the students, whilst in Madrid. Telling me that he had just visited Campo de la Cryptana in La Mancha, the very place where Don Quixote had set out on his quest, and around one of the famous windmills, geometrical forms similar to those generated by the stone, were picked out in brick. I went there immediately, and this is what I found.

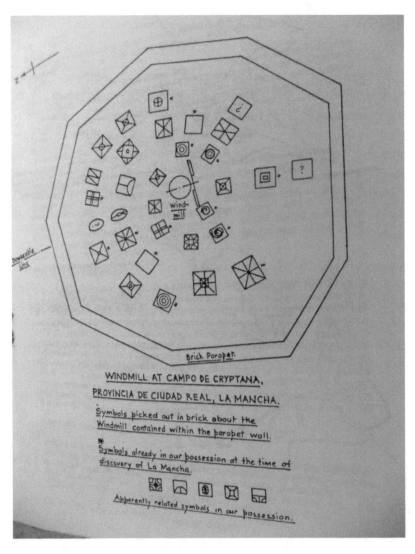

WINDMILL AT CAMPO DE CRYPTANA,
PROVINCIA DE CIUDAD REAL, LA MANCHA.

Symbols picked out in brick about the
Windmill contained within the parapet wall.

* Symbols already in our possession at the time of
discovery of La Mancha.

Apparently related symbols in our possession.

The windmill belongs to this day to the Order of Monteso, the military order into which many Spanish Templars went after their persecution and disbandment.

I have obviously cut corners in the narrative to date. We had established that ley energies existed and got involved with some huge displays of geometrical forms around the Templar Preceptory at Shipley, we had looked for the Cathar Grail and found something odd to say the least. There appeared to be intelligences involved, one of whom, or they, identified themselves as ELOHIM, a name which meant nothing to me, the number 7 seemed to be important in it all, the constellation of the Little Bear, number, form and so on. Just what did it all mean?

It was important that if number and form were important, then the Gnostic doctrines, Masonic teachings, Pythagorean teachings, Kabbala and the like, would have something to tell us in explaining it all. Most of the next two years was spent in literary and historical research to seek out a frame of reference for it all. We liked the illustration in Bligh Bond's book "Gematria," showing a cube with the stars super imposed on the seven-visible point plus the eighth from which they depend. I discovered in the Kabbala, the path of the Sephiroth BINAH, its god name Jehovah Elohim, its symbol the chalice, and the Vesica Piscis, it is also the first manifestation of form, says Gareth Knight, can be defined as the interlocking of free moving forces into patterns which then operate as a unity. I felt this to be a good working hypothesis as to what the geometrical forms were all about.

Elsewhere Gareth Knight says "Forces of stellar magic can be contacted through Binah and the constellations of the Great and Little Bear, which have particular significance for this Universe as our Solar Logos is said to have undergone previous evolution on those stars we associate with these constellations. The Great Bear also has reference to the Round Table and the Little Bear to the Holy Grail."

So, that might be what TRIONIS was all about! Perhaps GOD is a Kabbalist.

One thing we quickly did notice, and the maze of symbols were a clue to it was of course that such symbols were on various cathedral floors, and a tour around many of Europe's cathedrals revealed this, and also showed other forms on the floors as well. The double square form may be found in Pisa, Florence and Sienna cathedrals, but it took us a long time to work out why this form kept occurring in situations that one might evaluate as "good" empirical basis. Apart from being a planographic representation of the Masonic and Melchizedek double cube altar and involving the proportion 2:1. It was some-time later, in the course of an investigation into the Great Pyramids of Egypt.

But I am getting ahead of myself, if we go back to 1976.

Bahrain and Cairo

In November 1976, I visited Bahrain where the Company had shares in an aluminium atomising company. I had been a frequent visitor there in earlier years, but had not had the opportunity to visit for some time. I always supposed the ley system was world-wide, but this was to be the first time I had looked for it outside Western Europe. The route was overland all the way – Munich, Zagreb, Istanbul, Syria, Kuwait and down the gulf to Bahrain. The ley system could be felt all the way, even across the Gulf. Bahrain Airport is on the nearby island of Muharraq, connected to the mainland by a causeway. Driving in the taxi along the outskirts of Muharraq Town, I soon picked up lines crossing the main road, and on the causeway, a wide line was evidently following part of the way, before it changed direction and the line went off at an angle to the road and continued to the mainland. I found similar indications in Manama Town.

It was a day or so before I had time to do some serious dowsing, but I soon contacted and paid my respects to the Earth Spirit whose name was OLO. He told me that everything in Bahrain was in order, which was confirmed by Elohim, whose presence could be felt. It was not long before I could dowse my first mosque. It was not one of the first-class ones, being a little dowdy and elderly. The mosque only boasted one minaret, but it's base was octagonal. In walking around the mosque, I found a triple line of two points forming a right angle at the base of the minaret, nothing else. I followed one of them and after a while it arrived at the gate of the Juma Mosque, the largest in Bahrain. The line did not go to the minaret but straight through and out the other side, through a sort of half tower projecting from the wall. Where it went on from there, I did not have the time to establish, but I did note another triple line, apparently unconnected, left the minaret in another direction. I followed it and it ended in the Bahrain Law Courts built in 1937. "Work that one out," I said to myself.

Later just before I left, some colleagues and I spent a quick ninety minutes touring certain sites in the island. Bahrain has several important mythological traditions attached to it, and an esoteric history that is not to be dismissed. The land of Dilmun was looked on as a terrestrial paradise by our forebears in that region. Singular amongst its ancient monuments is the huge necropolis near the village of Ali, where more than 100,000 people are buried, or so it is said. They stretch out as far as the eye can see. I had once taken part in an excavation of one of the tombs, which I regret. It did however give some idea of what was in those burial mounds. Carefully cut stones form a double burial chamber one above the other with a beehive roof. These are then covered with desert scree to form a tumulus. Everything is orientated to the East or with the key stone to the West. Archaeologists have said that such a necropolis could not have been sustained by the population of Bahrain alone, and that it may well have had a huge catchment area for wealthy people, perhaps across Arabia. The stone in which the tombs are so carefully made is not indigenous to Bahrain. Clearly it is no ordinary cemetery. Specialists have dated it at about 5,000 B.C. Most of the tumuli have been opened at some time in their history by ancient and modern vandals, I was regrettably one of them.

In any event, that Necropolis was emitting a 49-bar line due north, but it did not go very far, for within 100 yards or so, it hit a shallow tumulus at which it went more or less due east. I could not follow it further than this. I believe the necropolis to be tremendously important in the system. The only other 49-bar line I know, (that is to say in its natural quiescent state,) is the Pyramid of Cheops. The necropolis has now been scheduled as an ancient monument. Next to the necropolis in the village of Ali are some very large tumulus tombs, otherwise called the Tombs of the Kings. They are also in the system.

Another landmark in Bahrain is the Old Mosque which is thought to be circa 700A.D. Its twin minarets remain, now restored. On the way to visit it we passed a tumulus at a bend in the road, festooned with green prayer flags, and I recalled that these sites around the island, (although not recognised officially,) were used as places of prayer by Bahrainis and were said to be the tombs of holy men. We stopped the car, and I dowsed it. It was on a triple. One axis went to another similar site with its green flags and the other to the Old Mosque. The watchman let us in. The line was to one minaret. Inside was a double square symbol, and the line continues again from the other minaret. We picked it up again around the Ruler's Palace, it did not go through it, but skirted round the back through two fairly modern mosques, (perhaps 200 years old).

On that same day, I caught a delayed Egypt Air flight to Cairo. Cairo Airport was chaotic, and I made various attempts to book myself a room by telex, but nobody answered. In a way, it was just as well, or I would probably have ended up in the centre of Cairo instead of the Mina House Hotel, underneath the pyramid itself. It was a delightful place and not expensive, at least not by Gulf standards. As it was now 1am, I went to sleep and when I awoke there was the Great Pyramid of Cheops silhouetted in the still misty early morning. It was huge. A great deal has been written about the pyramids by terribly respectable Egyptologists, mathematicians, occultists, romantics, lyric-writers and so on, and has been on the travel list of everyone from Herodotus, Alexander, Napoleon to Aleister Crowley, (to name but a few famous and infamous tourists,) and every aspiring tourist that ever was. I walked out of the hotel with the rod at the ready. A silent "Whoof", if I can explain it that way, made itself apparent. The rod dragged itself to the right in the hotel drive. I went to investigate, and there I found a negative symbol. I enquired of the local earth spirit and a double E symbol came up, except that it had a bar down the middle of this (a square with 4 squares within).

I was accosted by a multitude of potential guides and settled for one young Egyptian in an exceptionally clean robe, who said the best thing was to take a horse and buggy, as the complete tour was rather long. As we rode up the hill the sheer size of the pyramid became apparent. Dowsing in a buggy presents no difficulty, but we were a long way around the Pyramid of Cheops before I picked up a line. I dismounted, and with my guide watching with a mixture of curiosity and pity. Between the two pyramids of Cheops and Kefren I found two 49-bar lines in parallel. Then carrying on to the west side of the Kefren pyramid, I picked up another running west with 49-bars. It ran through a modern villa some quarter of a mile away. We continued on in a wide arc until I picked up a 21-bar line connecting the village cemetery to Kefren on the north-south axis. My guide said that it was a modern cemetery. The tombs were not graced by carved stones or decorations, but by half cylinders of cement, carefully done as if to ensure that there was no chink for any soul to escape.

Moving onto the Sphinx, it was smaller than I had anticipated, but none the less enigmatic for that. It was on a 21-bar line coming from Kefren due east. For some reason, the access to it was locked, but some monetary negotiations with a gentleman claiming to be a watchman enabled me to go within 10 yards of it. The negative symbol was there, so I said the necessary things and it was replaced by the positive symbol. On checking I was told that this was OK, and the 21-bar line multiplied to a 49-bar line. We completed the circle of pyramids and, as we came to the north of Cheops, I found a 49-bar line running off on a north-east axis of the pyramid. It ran through the garden of the rest house, a neo-Egyptian building which had been the summer residence of King Farouk. I noted that, as it continued north east, it passed through a new looking mosque on the other side of the Avenue des Pyramides, which I subsequently checked on site. Also, noting that it ran off in the direction of Heliopolis, and thereby hangs another tale.

We had come full circle and were opposite the entrance of the King's Chamber. When I bought a ticket to go in, it occurred to me that it would not be advisable to enter if it was still being used for evil purposes, and this was confirmed by Elohim. So, I did the necessary, which seemed effective and I went in. For tourist purposes, I would have thought that the access to the King's Chamber would be made easy, but not so. The approach inside the structure is up a steep slope with a kind of duckboard to grip with one's feet, and I had to bend double all the way up. It wasn't helped that as you went further in, it got hotter and more humid. Not an easy climb, and as I arrived in the Chamber my clothes were as wet as if I had fallen into a swimming pool. People were in the Chamber, so I waited for my opportunity to dowse when they had left, finding seven concentric squares. Asking for the Elohim symbol, it came up with no bar to the double E. Mindful speculation about the nature of the sarcophagus, I dowsed it with the pendulum. It registered 91 on the first gyration, clockwise. I have not had time to work out the significance of the calibrations of the pendulum, but such work as I have done would indicate that this is a powerful force for good. The whole pyramid of course, has been well described by others many times. Suffice it to say that its construction is unbelievable, huge blocks fitting perfectly without mortar. No ordinary monument this.

I was about 400 yards from the pyramid on the lush green lawn of the hotel, and I went through the Grail procedure. The lines came out and then a maze symbol, or what I took to be one. It is impossible to dowse around a source as huge as the pyramid of Cheops. The Grail Stone is quite another matter. Anyway, I was able to detect lines which could have formed part of a huge maze symbol around the pyramid. If it were one, then it was infinitely more complicated than the Grail maze. I was assured that the pyramid worked in the same way as the Grail, that the 3,000 odd symbols I had recorded were more or less what was in the pyramid. "Give me the most important," I said. Which it did. "Need I dowse anymore?" "No." I lay down again in the sun, ruminating, and then a thought crossed my mind. I could see the logic of the double E symbol representing Elohim. But then I realised that the double square symbol was an indication of the fusion of the double E, when the Elohim influence was uncluttered. I'm not sure that it got me any further, but it ought to be a further clue in deciphering the symbols. Furthermore, the double square symbol might be the proportion of the double cube which is the shape of the altar of the Temple of King Solomon according to Masonic lore. All this was subsequently confirmed as accurate by a very experienced Kabbalist.

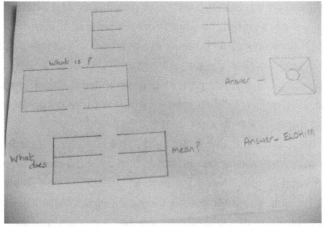

I went to Heliopolis later, on a fruitless visit, and I was able to stop and enter the Commonwealth War Graves Commission Cemetery there. A 6-bar line emerged from it. It was beautiful and everything was immaculate. The six line came from a large white stone in the entrance in the form of a double cube, not a particularly Christian thing. On it was engraved, "Their names liveth evermore". The Christian Cross was further down the cemetery. I had often felt before that the War Graves Commission had the task of considering the feelings of all the relatives of fallen soldiers, and that somehow it was a sign of respect that they were interred in beautiful cemeteries. Somehow it made war easier, more acceptable, less horrible. Perhaps there is also another reason, but I am not yet, not sure what it is. During various taxi drives in Cairo, I recognised the Citadel, with the huge Mosque of Muhammed Ali, the man who gave away the Needles to the USA, Britain and France. The Mosque is in the system.

That night I went up to the pyramids in the dark. There were few people about, and I wanted to check the work of the day. I was approached by a shadowy figure out of the darkness. He was not a guide, but the watchman of the Cheops Pyramid. We talked for a few moments. I explained to him that I was not an ordinary tourist but "doing professional work". This seemed to impress him, and he set off to accompany me on my tour. When I remonstrated with him, he explained that it was his pleasure, and he did not want me to come to harm in the dark.

Rome

Some-time before March 1977, the thought had been nagging at the back of my mind that I should visit Rome, and especially St Peter's. After an experience with Cleopatra's Needle and knowing also that the obelisk from Karnak in the Place de la Concorde was in the system, the fact that there is an Egyptian obelisk in front of St Peter's was a matter of interest, if not concern. A quick flight, a Hertz car, and I was in St Peter's Square two hours later. On the way to the Via della Conciliazione, the avenue, flanked with obelisks of this century, that leads up to St Peter's Square, I picked up a seven-bar line. This is odd because after the experience at the Great Pyramid I felt certain that St Peter's would be a 49-bar line and that it would come down the Via, but not so. Parking the car, I approached the obelisk. The north/south of the obelisk was on a triple line, and east west a seven-bar line. The obelisk itself is within a double circle. I could dowse the seven circles. However, when I enquired as to the name of the earth spirit, all I got was DE, and then when I asked for the higher intelligence, I was given an empty circle. In asking for the Elohim symbol, it came up barred. I enquired whether I should take the usual action.

I went to the Basilica itself only to find that it was closing time. However, on the first large area in front of St Peter's, I found in the stone the now familiar symbol. In the very centre were the seven circles again in dowsable form. It was then that I carried out the necessary invocation. The double square symbol came up at that point, and all around the square was the 49 square, square, the same one that had been produced in our flat in Madrid when the Pope pronounced "Urbi et Orbi" at Christmas 1975. I then asked again for the name of the presiding earth spirit and was given IFOR. It occurred to me that DE might have been the evil counterpart of IFOR, this was confirmed by Elohim. When I asked for the presiding superior intelligence, I was given TETRAGAMMATON, as at Silbury, and when dowsing the Spear in Vienna.

I returned to the obelisk and perused the inspirations.

SIXTUS V OBELISCUM VATICANUM

DIS GENTIUM

IMPIO CULTU DICATUM

AD APOSTOLOROM LIMINA

OPEROSO LABORE TRANSTULIT

MDLXXXVI

And

SIXTUS V CRUCI INVICTAE

OBELISCUM VATICANUM

AB IMPURA SUPERSTITSIONE

EXPIATUM IUSTIUS

ET FELICIUS CONSECRAVIT

MDLXXXVI

All of which adds up to the fact that Pope Sixtus erected the obelisk in 1586 and consecrated it with a cross on top, containing part of the true cross, to rid it of its impure superstition and the impious cult of the people of Dis, the land of the underworld. Well one might ask, why? What on earth is such a thing doing in front of the prime church of Christendom? And in the system? What did Sixtus V really have in mind? It can be used as a sundial as the northerly line has the signs of the zodiac measured out in the appropriate symbols in stone, the solstices of winter and summer being marked at the point where the noon day sun casts the tip of the obelisk's shadow. I returned to the obelisk. Thoth appeared which was not surprising and appeared pleased at what had been done. However, I still had not discovered any 49-bar line. I checked the obelisk again, and it was the same as before.

I took the car and drove around the walls of Vatican City. As I approached the southern sector of the Basilica, I found it. My slowing down the car to check the number of lines brought about my head the wrath of impatient Roman drivers. No walls fell down, Joshua did a better job at Jericho. As I went around the walls, I found various other lines of minor significance, but one certainly passed from the mast of Vatican Radio on a line to another radio or TV mast on the next hill. Completing the circuit, I did not find the other end of the 49-bar line until the very last moment. It emerged a few degrees north of the Via della Conciliazione. I parked the car again and checked it within the square. It fell within a sector I had not previously dowsed and, following it back, it went straight to the main entrance to join the 7-bar line just below the window where the Pope pronounces his "Urbi et Orbi". In following it the other way, it went directly to the Castel San Angelo or Mausoleum of Hadrian. In making the circuit I found it continued in a sharp southerly direction to the church of San Giovanni dei Florentini, from which I was able to follow the Piazza Navona, in which there is another obelisk of Egyptian origin, this one with hieroglyphs, the work of another Pope. It was in the system but not on the 49-bar line. It was blocked and I invoked its unblocking. The 49-bar line went to a fountain to the north, from which I was able to follow it to the Pantheon. There is another obelisk in front of this, but although it is in the system the 49-bar line does not go through it, but straight to the Pantheon. The obelisk was similarly blocked off, but I was able to clear it, hopefully.

As it was late, I had a beer and checked in at my hotel in the Via Veneto, a street which represents the other face of the Holy City. I went to a solitary dinner in a cafeteria and fell to pondering, particularly as the 49- square was all over the place. What on earth was I doing? Had I gone mad and was suffering from delusions of grandeur or some form of religious mania? Here was I wandering around the square of the principal church of the Christian world, making invocations producing apparent symbols all over the place, and interfering with the system, if indeed the system was not part of some huge convoluted delusion. Now half a bottle of chianti can be a comfort in such situations, although the cynical reader may consider it otherwise. I reviewed in my mind all that had gone before in the previous three years. Was it all part of some delusion? Was my apparent dowsing ability a wish fulfilment and the impatience I had felt as a would-be politician? Was it being manifested in some fantasy on a world-wide scale, in which I conceived myself as a significant figure, merely to satisfy these frustrations?

If the existence of the ley system were a fantasy, then it was shared by various people, some of whom had committed themselves to print on the subject. It was also shared by friends I had made during this period, most of whom had been able to independently to dowse the lines. On an empirical basis, I was prepared to be satisfied that the system had been proven. Too many tests had been made. But what of the Grail Stone, the Elohim connection, talking to earth spirits, and all the rest of it? This could stretch credulity too far. And if all this were fantasy, it was a better constructed fantasy than I had any right to expect of myself. It was a fantasy that continually received confirmation from people more expert in aspects of the occult lore than I. Indeed, after I gave the first of two lectures, an expert Kabbalist, now a firm friend, said, "I thought when you started you were telling a fairy tale, but since then my jaw has not stopped hitting the floor. Everything you have said, its symbology makes perfect Kabbalistic sense, it's incredible. I cannot fault anything." The feed-back that night had been extraordinary, people were able to supply correspondences with other things that made perfect sense.

Incidents flowed through my memory, and I became again disposed to the view that I was dealing with something real, if not the reality I had been accustomed to. Accordingly, I went to bed and rose early to visit the Basilica of St Peter. On the way, I found a 7-bar line from the residence of the Pope, whence he is accustomed to appearing to great crowds on lesser occasions on the north side of the square. It joined the main line out of the entrance. I had been to St Peter's twice before, but never with quite the same feelings or "knowledge". The 7-bar line went all the way down to the main altar above the supposed tomb of St Peter. As I began to explore the Basilica, there were various symbols repeated in stone all over the floor.

16 Point Star

Around the various side altars were circles with 8- or 16-point stars, and the octagonal predominated. Why I wondered, was 8 the key number of St Peter's in its decoration? The number of the infinite? The octagon, however, in my experience has something to do with power over people. It seems potent that 8 is the key number in the floor of St Peter's. All the circle symbols have 7 dowsable circles in them. 7 seems a less aggressive number.

I approached the tomb of St Peter and the Papal altar. Within the 16-point star that surrounds it I picked up a dowsable 7 circle configuration.

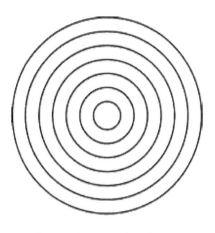

Seven Concentric Circles

As I ambled around following the circle, the rod suddenly opened, indicting a gap. Perhaps it was a labyrinth. I checked the other circles. It wasn't. An arc of 30 degrees of the seven circles was missing. I was shocked, it was the last thing I had expected. What it meant was that someone, at some time had interfered with the seven circles around St Peter's Tomb. (I also wondered how much I had missed in the past by not fully dowsing the seven circles). I asked Elohim about the circle and was told to take action. I invoked the Almighty and his legions as follows: "In the name of Tetragrammaton, Elohim, Metatron, Jesus and all that is good in the universe, let no evil enter or leave this place. Let it only receive and radiate good, and may it be restored to the form You wish. So be it." The circles were restored, and the missing segment replaced. I was told that this was OK, and the 49-square square appeared on the Basilica floor. I had noticed before that, the line from the missing segment to the "Altar of the Chair" in the apse was the 49-bar line, which was curious because the line down the nave was a 7-bar line, one of your lesser lines. But when the circle was restored, the 7-bar line became 49-bar line up to the entrance where it still split off to Hadrian's Mausoleum.

Before I left, I went to look at Michael Angelo's Pieta, now behind glass and safe from vandalism. In front was the 8-point star, but dowsable was a large spiral, the only one I found there. It was OK, that is to say, in the right direction. There are those who say that the Pieta and certain other religious works of art of the Renaissance contain an esoteric message, and those who wish to see the Seal of Solomon in it can do so.

Seal of Solomon

Suffice it to say that by any standard it is a work of sublime art. I do, however, feel that if what I am trying to say is true one might well look at religious art in a new light. After all, to be limited in one's imagery to the accepted religious figures of the day might well be a factor by which the great geniuses like Leonardo and Michael Angelo would not necessarily wish to be bound. The painting and sculpture of this period might well express something other than religious banalities, repeated many times over, however great the standard of artistry. One day someone must look at the works of Michael Angelo, Leonardo, Titian, Raphael and all of them, to see whether or not their paintings contain Kabbalistic symbols in their basic design. Why was Charles V, (Holy Roman Emperor,) so friendly with Titian and why did he insist on his "resurrection" being hung at Yuste? The evidence I have sought to gather indicates that Charles understood much. He would not be one for naïve imagery. There is great magical value in these works of the masters, who had a comprehension that could only be expressed in this way due to caveats of the day. But the circumstances of Pieta were good.

I went down to look at the Tomb of St Peter. You go down some stairs and a passage lead you around it, where the tombs of various other popes may be found. Nothing could be perceived with the rod except a powerful attraction to the tomb as one walked around it. It was clearly a power source. I noticed the eight-pointed star symbol prominent in the ornate access-way to the tomb.

Eight-Pointed Star

I was most impressed by the tomb of Pope John the 23rd "Good" Pope, exponent of ecumenicalism and general religious good sense. It was of simple, unornate polished granite, with his name and (P with cross) symbol, nothing else. No other Pope's tomb had this symbol that I could see, except St Peter and John. I wonder why? I dowsed the centre line again. Now a Grail labyrinth had appeared. All I can say is that it was complex, and dowsing a maze is at least an hour's work, and time was short.

I took the lift to the roof and could see how Hadrian's Mausoleum lined up on the bearing I had dowsed. From this vantage point, I fell to thinking "Why". What on earth did Hadrian have to do with the thing? The history books say that Rome was at its apogee during his rule, and the abiding theme of Hadrian was conservation and preservation, perhaps this is why the 49-bar line went there. But I had seen how the seven had become 49 down the nave when the circles, had been completed. Ought it not to continue in a straight line, instead of being diverted to the mausoleum? I was told that I was correct, and it ought to be changed, I asked the system to be restored to the form desired by the Divine Will. I later ascertained that the line had disappeared, and that the Via della Conciliazione was now a 49-bar line. However, the main entrance of the Mausoleum continued to emit a triple. What was the purpose of using his mausoleum in this way? Was it because he was conservative and an institutionalizer, and by injecting these particular characteristics into the Roman Church and obliging it to give pre-eminence to these considerations, its true spiritual mission could thus be obfuscated? I suspect this to be the explanation, but it is only a surmise. I had no more time, so I bought various official publications for later use. The history of the Vatican needs no elaboration here, other than that it is held to be on the site of Nero's Circus, where the early Christians who were alleged to have fired Rome were martyred.

The present basilica is the work of various architects, but mostly Michael Angelo, who obviously knew of a thing or two. The ceiling of the Sistine Chapel, was commissioned by the same Sixtus who had the obelisk moved, contained a profound story. Anyway, I noted that the Vatican Museum contains Egyptian mummies, which is odd, and I have heard some cogent remarks on the results of bringing mummies to Europe. Many other halls and buildings have the same symbols on the floor. In the throne room in front of the Popes throne, the design has 8 octagons on either side. Powerful stuff! In the Papal Consistory, where the cardinals gather, another symbol is found. The floor of the Sistine Chapel has a symbol which I have found in a fresco in the ruins of a church on the island of Comacine in Lake Como and in one of the floors in front of the Papal tomb in St Peter's it must mean something, The floor of the Hall of the Greek Cross does not look too good.

The Greek Cross/Cathar Cross

Its basic form is as above and pendulum dowsing the picture gave a huge powerful negative, the spin was so violent. I think that it is something to do with confining the Divine Light in a material prison. The Rotunda Hall has an equally- sided octagon. It gave a vestigial positive reading. Another point is the Baldachin of the Papal altar, four spiralling columns, two clockwise and two anti-clockwise. This theme is repeated in the church of Santa Maria Maggiore, of St Paul Without Walls and St John Lateran.

No one can go to St Peter's without the greatest awe, for its traditions, its exotericism and for the most extraordinary lavishness of its appointment. I wonder if Stonehenge cost as much in its day. I left St Peter's slightly dazed. I did not have time to recheck the new route of the 49-bar line, did it still go to the Pantheon? I suspect so, but by a new route. However, I had a feeling about the Piazza Venezia and the Wedding Cake, that huge, grandiose, glittering white confection, built by Victor Emmanuel II. This dominates the square where Mussolini, from the balcony of the Palazzio Venezia, used to harangue the crowds. I parked the car at the side of the Wedding Cake, haggled with one of the quasi-official attendants about parking on the pavement, an argument which ended when the transfer of a 1000 lire note was affected. In front a demonstration was in progress about the pensions of the war invalids, but no one seemed to be very interested. A 7-bar line came out of the centre, went across the piazza and up the Via del Corso. That seemed reasonable, but where was the 49-bar line. I walked down the pavement in front of Palazzio Venezia and as I approached the spot near the balcony of Mussolini, there it was, but coming out at right angles to the 7-bar line. I followed it across the square under the baffled gaze of a traffic policeman until it hit the 7-bar line. Then it stopped and so did I. I searched either side and there was nothing but the 7-bar line. I had never found such a thing before.

Looking around, however, I saw the spiralled column of Trajan to the east of the Piazza. Could this have anything to do with it? I went over, defying almost certain death from the traffic. Trajan's column is on a cross of lines, and I found a single line, how rare these days, going north. Then I found the 49-bar line again, narrowing to a single on the column, expanding again and carrying on to the east, this narrowing is a firm indication that the point is significant. I counted the spirals, 21. The 49-bar line went west to the 7-bar line. The Elohimic information was that all was as it should be. Proceeding to the Forum behind the Wedding Cake. A 7-bar line came through the Arch of Septimus Severus, down the Forum to the Arch of Titus. One of the Temples was loaded with the negative symbol, which was corrected, and then another.

On the way back to the airport, I was able to go around the Colosseum. The central line of the Forum went to it, and out the other end. I would have liked to go in, but there was no time. The 49-

bar line did not go through it. About 2 kilometres away in the direction of the airport, I noticed a small pyramid, half built into the wall. I suppose there had to be around somewhere, and it was on the 49-bar line, which had somehow come all the way around the Forum and Colosseum. It was called the Pyramid of Calus Cestius, but I have no more information about him at the moment. As I write this three days later, I wonder if I found the truth, and if I did the right things. How on earth does one know.

Jerusalem and the Golden Gate

The end of May 1977 was the occasion for a business visit to Bahrain. During the visit the feeling that I should spend 24 hours in Jerusalem became overwhelming. A quick visit to the El Al offices revealed that a flight was leaving shortly, and so on June 8, after huge security checks by some splendidly efficient Sabras, I arrived at Tel-Aviv, and one hour later I was driving round the walls of the Old City of Jerusalem. For some months before this, Jerusalem had occupied my mind, on and off. A colleague had come back with some maps of the city which he gave me. I studied these with interest, for the druids had spoken of the line, Tehran – Babylon-Jerusalem- Pyramids. I found the line at the Pyramids and, just before, at Tehran.

I had dowsed the large Mosque in the Bazaar at Tehran and found it to have a square pool in the courtyard in front. Each side had a 49-bar line. Indeed, a subsidiary system within the bar itself on a 7-bar line basis formed a cross under a dome with an octagonal inlet in the roof. Below in the confluence of four main souks was the 7-circle symbol, but the wedge was missing, I was able to restore it. The mosque needed some attention and south-eastern end of the city. At the western entrance, straddling the main road, is a huge, blue and white monument, built by the Shah recently, for the 2,500th anniversary of the founding of the Persian Empire under Darius. There is a blue octagonal projection at the top and the whole is a huge arch, much taller than the Arc de Triumph in Paris. I had noticed, driving in from the airport, that it was in the system and, before leaving, I had a chance to dowse it thus, all 49-bar lines.

Tehran was a huge avenue at its east-west axis, and it has a 49-bar line the length of it. It is crossed by other avenues with 7-bar lines, but I did not have time to study it much. The Iranian Parliament building is in the system. Somehow the Mosque and Monument connect up in some way, which I had not time to work out, but I felt satisfied that once again the Archdruid of France had been shown to be correct. Under the octagon of the Shah's Monument were 7 circles, complete which was encouraging, but the double E came up barred. This was put right.

All this strengthened the feeling that I ought to go to Jerusalem, and that the 49-bar line system was bound to go through it and probably through the Rock of Abraham. I wondered again whether the tragic history of the city and its region was not better explained by successive attempts by adepts to gain possession of the Rock for their purposes. What I had noticed was that on the eastern side of the wall, which forms the site of the Rock and where Solomon's Temple was, is a gate called the Golden Gate. The accompanying blurb stated, "The Golden Gate is sealed until the coming of the Messiah". I made some investigations into the traditions of the Golden Gate and found out the following information. The Golden Gate is a 7th century Byzantine structure over the earlier site of the Eastern Gate of the Temple Compound. The pillars of the Gate are said to have been given to Solomon by the Queen of Sheba, and Jesus is held to have made his triumphal entry into Jerusalem through this gate. The Jewish tradition was that the Messiah would enter by this gate. After

Islam had taken the city and imposed its rule for more than a millennium, the Arabs walled it up as they did not wish for any more Messiah's, Jewish or Christian, to trouble their rule. The general tradition is that its re-opening will herald the Millennium. The thought occurred to me that this legend might well refer to some profound interference with the line system, and that the physical sealing was an outward symbol of an occult act. The theory had been forming in my mind that much of the world's destiny somehow worked itself out in relationship with the line system and, here again, was an example where the public version of history obscured a profound inner truth. As I approached Jerusalem, I switched on the car radio. Almost immediately and unannounced, they played the opening bars of Richard Strauss's, "Sprach Zarathustra", better known as the theme music for Stanley Kubrick's "Space Odyssey 2001". It was oddly disturbing.

I arrived at the Old City at the Citadel, or David's Tower, and went around in an anti-clockwise direction passing Mount Zion on the left. The evening sun was brilliant, creating deep shadows. I found nothing until I passed the silver dome of the El-Aksa Mosque. From this came the 49-bar line, almost on the axis of the mosque, but slightly to the south east. I carried on round and, on the Eastern Wall, there was the Golden Gate. The road passes some 50 feet in front and below it. I could find nothing. I turned the car round and drove back to where a path leaves the road and goes up to the Gate. As I walked up, the evening sun cast a deep shadow on the valley below, but illuminated brilliantly the golden onion domes of the Russian Orthodox Church of Mary Magdalene, built by Alexander III. Some members of the Russian Royal Family are buried there. It is at the foot of the Mount of Olives. The path ran up through a Moslem cemetery, fresh palm fronds decorated some of the graves, a herd of goats was eating them with enthusiasm, tended by a small Arab boy on a donkey. I noticed some single lines coming in from the right, and down in the valley below I could see the series of tombs of the Valley of Jehoshafat or Kidron which, says a guidebook, are of special interest because of their distinctive shapes. The Valley is also known as the Valley of the Kings because David, Solomon and other kings of Israel are believed to have been buried there. It has been a favourite burial ground for Jews for thousands of years since, according to tradition, it is here that the Last Judgement (Joel III, 12) will take place after the trumpets of universal resurrection have sounded. On the left is the tomb called Absalom's Pillar, probably a misnomer, a large mausoleum surmounted by a tapering circular, but not conical, dome. There is Jehoshafat's tomb, and the Bnei Hezir tombs, a grotto in which it is said that James the Lesser hid after Jesus's arrest. The inscription indicates it was the burial place of a Herodian priestly family. To the right of this row is another free-standing mausoleum like that of Absalom, except that it has a pyramid-shaped roof. The Jews held this to be the tomb of Zecharial, the father of John the Baptist. The right and left mausoleums emitted single lines to the Eastern Wall, and I felt that if any major line were to be there, it might well go between them, just as at Blenheim or Fonthill.

I arrived at the front of the Golden Gate and I checked again, there was nothing. I enquired whether I should go ahead. "Yes", I was told. So I did and made the following invocation, "In the name of Tetragrammaton, Elohim, Metatron, all celestial hierarchy of light, Jesus and the Great Seven, and all that is good in the universe, if it is the Divine Will that this gate be opened and that a line should be here, so be it. Amen." I dowsed it and a 49-bar line was passing through it. I counted the parallels carefully, and the flow was from the east. Now, it may seem odd, but I was strangely unmoved by such an event. At the moment, it was as if one had carried out a routine job, just like mending a machine. I turned away and walked down the hill again to the car. The little boy on the donkey accompanied me and asked me if I wanted to photograph him on his donkey, declining politely, it did not seem quite the moment.

As I drove past the gate on the road below, it was difficult to gauge the direction of the line accurately at a functional point as it was expanding, and the angle of expansion is not necessarily an indication of its final direction. On the road in front, I picked up another line wider than any I had previously dowsed. I continued around the Old City and picked up another 49-bar line joining it at the Octagonal Tower of the Rockafeller Museum, just outside the Walls. Built in Templar style, it stands on the spot where Godefroy de Bouillon's Crusaders advanced on Jerusalem in 1099. It was built with funds provided by John D Rockefeller Jr and opened in 1938 as the Palestine Archaeological Museum. It houses treasures from the pre-historic periods till the Middle Ages, including reliefs from Sennacherib's Palace at Nineveh, the lintels of the Church of the Holy Sepulchre, carved doors from the El-Aksa Mosque and so on. Completing a circuit of the Old City I found no other line, and the first one I had found from the El-Aksa Mosque had disappeared. Of course, this mosque is held to stand on the original site of the Palace of Solomon and served as the headquarters of the Knights Templar. It contains the tombs of the assassins of Thomas A Beckett, who came to Jerusalem to serve with them after the murder. (Curious they should be so honoured after so foul a deed.)

By now it was dark, and I sought out my hotel, the Jerusalem Intercontinental. After several false starts and mis-directions, I found it, opposite the Golden Gate on the Mount of Olives. On the way to it, I found a new line from the Golden Gate. It seemed to go through a little octagonal church to another behind with a tall tower. I sat down to dinner with the guide to Jerusalem and read that the little octagonal church was the Dome of the Ascension, built encircling the Rock of the Ascension in 380AD, as a round structure. In 1187 the Crusaders replaced this simple structure with an octagonal form open to the sky. Moslems later took the shrine and covered it with a cupola, and this was the inspiration for the Dome of the Rock. The Tower of the Ascension, which is another claimant for the site of the Ascension, is of much more recent date, and contains a rock in an associated chapel on which the Virgin Mary is said to have watched the Ascension. Another church nearby, in the same complex, is the Pater Noster Church, which stands on the site of the Grotto where traditionally Jesus is said to have spoken of the destruction of Jerusalem and the nature of the coming Kingdom. It is also the place where the prayer, "Our Father" was first taught by Jesus. It is one of the earliest shrines on the Mount of Olives and was erected by Helena, mother of the Emperor Constantine, in 333 AD.

Later that evening, reading an account of the Ascension, I realised that a line had entered the Golden Gate that evening, "opening it" so to speak, and that line had come from the point of Ascension on the Mount of Olives. I was moved to the proudest depths of circumstances. Supposing I really had been the instrument of something important, supposing that I had stumbled across some fundamental truth I only half understood, that I might be meddling and rushing in "where angels fear to tread". I shivered. On the other hand, did one really have a choice? My recent experiences had shown me that I had much less free-will in my life than I had supposed. Indeed, I could now see that the whole of this story is a result of my having been led quite specifically along this route. At the same time, I could have refused to continue, I suppose, But I didn't want to. I kept being told through the Elohim symbol that everything was OK, and that it should be done, so I could absolve myself, to some extent. If you couldn't trust the Elohim, who could you trust? I suppose most people who had the opportunity of performing a small technical act which might just conceivably, on a million to one chance, make some contribution to a possible millennium, would actually go and do it. Anyway, it was done and there it was. It was appropriate, I suppose, that the waiter recommended me a half bottle of wine from Mount Carmel, the Vineyard of God.

After dinner, I walked around the Arab village on the Mount of Olives in which the Ascension churches are. It was a maze of narrow streets and I was unable to find a way to Church Tower itself. Making a complete circuit however, I could find the main line coming out the other side. At the same time, I was aware of many triples and occasional 7-bar line emanating from the central point. I was able to show that this was part of a gigantic sun-wheel pattern with the centre point where the church was. I eventually got to within 20 yards of the tower, the spokes were about 200 yards long, and I was able to dowse part of the circumference.

Awoke next morning at 5am, the sun was brilliant, and I rose to look at the silver and gold domes of the two mosques on Mount Moriah, the Temple enclosure. It was a sight full of wonder, the early morning sun tipping the domes with incandescence. No one was about and all was still. Such moments are rare. The coffee shop did not open until 7.30am, so I started out to visit certain sites before breakfast. On the way down I found another main line, a little further on from the one from the Ascension Tower, then realised that to the Golden Gate were going, not one, but two 49-bar lines! This accounted for the extraordinary width I had noticed earlier. Later, I confirmed this was the case. Looking at the map, there is only one possible site where the men of Galilee are said to have watched the Ascension, but I did not have time to go there and prove it. At the same time, I noticed another site on the east of the Mount of Olives which would probably be the continuation of the line through the Ascension Tower, the House of Figs. It is said to be the place where two disciples fetched the ass for Jesus to ride into Jerusalem through the Golden Gate on Palm Sunday. In 1883, the Franciscans erected a little church on the site of an earlier medieval shrine. Before construction, a cubic stone was uncovered which contained paintings and Latin inscriptions relating to the events that took place in that area. It is today the starting point of the Palm Sunday procession!

I proceeded to Mount Zion. It is from here, according to Isaiah's prophecy, "shall go forth the law, and the word of the Lord from Jerusalem". It houses David's Tomb, one of Judaism's holiest shrines, and venerated equally by Moslems. The tomb is contained in a thick walled, medieval structure, covered with an embroidered cloth, and was discovered by a Rabbi in 1173. In a Gothic chamber above is the site where the Christians believed the "Last Supper" took place. It was built by the Franciscans in 1335. It is also held by some to be the place of the Pentecost where the Holy Ghost appeared to the Apostles. According to Jewish tradition, the Messiah was to come from the House of David. The ram's horn is still blown regularly in order to awaken the sleeping king, as he is the one to open the Gates of Heaven to prayer and hasten the advent of the Messiah. There is also a Basilica of the Dormition, built at the turn of the 20th century and served by the Benedictines. It is held to be the site of Mary's death. Also, there is the Cellar of the Holocaust dedicated to the six million Jews who were exterminated in World War II. Thus, it is a site of veneration to Jew, Moslem and Christian alike. I visited Mount Zion just as people were stirring. In the area of David's Tomb sweeping up was going on, but it was not open. However, some of the associated vaults could be visited. In two chambers, one which I took to be the Cenaculum, or "Last Supper" room, I found the seven circles, but with a wedge missing. I was able to replace it. A sweeper pressed two lit candles upon me in one of the grottoes. My end of the transaction took the form of 10 Israeli Pounds, (about 60p) which seemed to please him. Outside the Cellar of the Holocaust was the square stone pillar dedicated to the Jews who died in Bergen-Belsen. A triple line ran from it to the complex David's Tomb. Walking around Mount Zion, however, I could find no other indication of activity.

I returned to a hearty breakfast, and by now the city was stirring, and I went down again to visit the Temple Compound. I entered by Dung Gate inside which is a narrow ramp to the Temple Compound alongside the Wailing Wall. After paying for my ticket and evading the solicitations of various guides, I completed the circuit of the Compound. The first thing I noticed was that the 49-bar line connected the El-Aksa Mosque with the Dome of the Rock. The Dome itself was on a cross of lines, all 49ers, but the one to the east was running some hundred yards to the east of the Golden Gate. It ran through a wholly unidentifiable square of concrete about 15 metres by 15 metres, then north where there was another slab of a similar size, then east to the Gate, some sort of re-routing was occurring. There was no official information about these slabs, but each had a ventilator, and my surmise is that they might be underground water tanks. I followed the line to the Gate or the steps leading down to it. They were blocked by barbed wire. Evidently, even today, no chances were being taken about a Messiah coming through that gate even if the stones were removed.

I went back to the El-Aksa mosque, left my shoes and socks outside and went in. I would not call it one of the great mosques of the world, but it was redolent of history. It is mentioned in the Koran in a vision of the Ascension of Mohamed and means, "the distant place", far from Mecca. It is Islam's holiest shrine after Mecca and Medina and is thought to stand over the area where Solomon built his Palace, south of the Temple. As the guidebook says, "As such it is a special interest to Freemasons." It was built between 709-715 by Caliph Waleed, son of Abd-el-Malik, who constructed the Dome of the Rock. It was destroyed at various times by earthquakes and not much remains of the original structure, most of the present structure dates from 1034. In the 13th century, it received a distinctive entrance porch with seven arched doorways corresponding to the seven aisles within. After the Crusaders captured Jerusalem, it became the headquarters of the Knights Templar. Saladin rededicated it on his recapture of Jerusalem in 1187. In 1951, King Abdullah of Transjordan was assassinated at the entrance, and a pillar still bears the scars of the bullets. It is a focal point of Islamic religious activity in the Holy Land. As I said, it is not an object of great beauty. I padded over the carpet floor. The 49-bar line ran the length of it to the point below the dome which was roped off to visitors. This must have been the line whose continuance I noted the previous evening, but which did not now continue. Coming out, I continued on bare feet across the stone slabs, now warming up in the morning sun towards the Dome of the Rock. Directly between the two, on the connecting 49-bar line, is the circular El Kas fountain, surrounded by taps and stone chairs, at which Muslims will sit to wash their feet before prayer. This fountain is connected to the 34 cisterns in the Temple Compound, which are estimated to contain 10 million gallons of water.

Onto the Dome of the Rock, it was a breath-taking building from the outside and exquisitely beautiful from the inside. It was an octagonal form surmounted by a Golden Dome. The story goes that Caliph Omar, on capturing Jerusalem in 637, was shocked at the filth and rubble that lay about Mount Moriah and, as a punishment for neglecting such a holy site, he made the Christian Patriarch Sephronius grovel in the muck. Then he set about clearing the site with his own hands and built a wooden mosque. The present most beautiful building is the work of his son, Abd-el-Malik, who based it on a 4th century shrine on the mount of Olives, commemorating the Ascension of Jesus as we noted earlier. It must be one of the most beautiful buildings in the world, and certainly the most beautiful octagonal building. The Christians used it as a shrine after the Crusaders captured Jerusalem and it was served by the Knights Templar, who dubbed it the "Templum Domini". Saladin, again, rededicated it on his recapture of the city. The outside of the building is covered with blue and white tiles from Persia, and inside is the Dome, and here the guidebook cannot be bettered, "is a glorious blaze of red, black and gold stucco". It contains many beautiful stained-glass windows, the whole decorated with those marvellous interweaving patterns essential in Islamic art. A thing of beauty to rejoice the soul! All this is to sidetrack one from its real purpose, the placing of an octagonal structure over the Rock of Abraham. And, inside, with a circular wooden surround, is the Rock itself, the very pivot of three great cultures and religions of the world. In Judaeo-Christian and Islamic tradition, it is the Rock where Abraham offered Isaac, his son, in sacrifice to Jehovah, to be told that such barbarities were no longer necessary. An indentation on the Rock's surface is held to be the footprint left by Mohammed when he lept to heaven. It was the sanctuary for the first and second Temples of the Jews. God instructed Solomon to build his first Temple there. What is striking is that this rock is central to the mystical dramas of Judaism, Christianity and Islam. The 49-bar line can be dowsed coming into or going out of the Rock itself. A final piece of evidence for me is that the line system is crucial to all valid forms of religion, apart from its other significances. Maps of the Medieval world show Jerusalem as the centre of the World. They may not have been making a geographical point.

There is a stairway leading down beneath the Rock. It contains grottoes which are the traditional places of prayer of Elijah, Abraham, David and Solomon. Muslims call this cave the "Wells of Souls", and the dead are supposed to meet there twice a week to pray. When I went down, there were only American tourists. I waited for them to leave. On the floor in mosaic is a circle. In the centre is a small star with a hole in the middle. I dowsed the seven circles within it. They were complete. I stood alone and, touching the Rock above, made a prayer, identical to the one I made outside the Golden Gate with the following exceptions or additions. "Let the Millennium begin, if it is Thy Will and then, so suddenly that it startled me, because the thought was never further from my mind, "Let Satan be banished forever from this Planet". At that moment occurred what I took to be a sonic boom from an Israeli jet fighter training somewhere above. I left the cave and, above in the Mosque all hell had broken loose, if you'll pardon the expression. People were shouting and running with fire hoses. I asked an official what was happening. "A routine fire practice," he said. Somewhat bewildered, I went on my way. I noticed on going out that the Mosque itself had many symbols on the extension and on the floor of the entrances.

I returned whence I came and went in search of the Via Dolorosa. A small boy took charge of me and said he thought that I was looking for the church of the Holy Sepulchre. I let him take me there. A small contribution sent him away smiling. The Church of the Holy Sepulchre is a chaotic mess, architecturally and theologically speaking. Today's chaos arises out of the fact that when Saladin took Jerusalem, he allowed Christians to continue to use the shrine but retained the right to grant entry, and so it is still today. Moslems have, apparently arbitrarily, apportioned rights to possession of the shrine to Roman Catholics, Greek Orthodox, Armenians, Coptics, Syrians and Abyssinians on a rotational basis. Since reconstruction can only arise from possession, and knowing that Christian sects never agree with one another, the present state of disrepair can be readily comprehended, it is in a sad state. I entered and wandered around, within the area of the Seven Arches of the Virgin (the remains of the 11th century construction,) one could dowse 3 circles, empty.

I entered the Holy Sepulchre itself, but it was well guarded, and one could not do anything untoward. It was not beautiful, but it was moving. Going around the back of it, I was assailed by a man in some unfamiliar religious garb, who was a tout, and quick as a flash, he had me inside, on my knees (no choice for it was only a few feet high,) in a small enclosure. In broken English, he told me here was the Tomb of Jesus, and opening a small door there was the edge of a tomb on which were placed many religious artefacts, and notes of various denominations. He pressed upon me a crude crucifix, a small metal of the baby Jesus and a bottle of oil. I succeeded in pendulum dowsing the oil in that cramped space, under the guise of some private devotion, and received a good indication. I asked for another and was given it on condition I made a further contribution to the 20 Israeli Pounds I had already placed on the Tomb. Someone else was waiting to enter and I was quickly urged out. This strange little room is referred to as the Coptic Chapel. I dowsed it with the rod and found that a 49-bar line was emanating from it.

Somewhat bemused by this experience of religious husting, I came to the Chapel of Mary Magdalene, next to the Holy Sepulchre to the north. Clerics in different garbs were going to and from. What took my eye was the black and white tiled floor. There were two circles. I dowsed the seven circles within them, entire. In between the two was the following motif,

I was overcome, there it was in black and white stone, in the church of the Holy Sepulchre in Jerusalem, the double-cube symbol, the resolved double E of the Elohim, the first time I had seen it anywhere (Other than dowsing it), and a new dimension I had not worked out, two of them together make an equal armed cross of the Cathars and the Knights Templar. Of course, more importantly, it was also the symbol on the Grail Stone.

Intact Double E Symbol – When Barred There Is a Vertical Line,
Giving Four Squares

The Via Dolorosa is really made up of five streets in a step formation
and following them back, I dowsed a 49-bar line from the eastern
end of the church of the Holy Sepulchre. It did not follow the route
but out through it, in a straight line, finishing at Station 11, at the
Chapel of Condemnation. I picked it up at the appropriate points on
the way through. It passed through Station V where Simon of Cyrene
was forced to carry the cross. There is a huge underground cistern in
the area. I have no doubt that the original Via Dolorosa followed a
different route from the present one, but it was extraordinary to find
that this fundamental drama of the Christian faith appears to have
been carried out on a 49-bar line, once again. I reflected on how
history and the line system are inextricably interwoven. At this point,
I went off to lunch completing a circuit of the walls again. Two
things had changed. There was now a 49-bar line coming out of
Mount Zion and another out of the Citadel David's Tower at the
Jaffa Gate, which gave me much to ponder about.

One of the things that had struck me most forcibly about the tourist
leaflet on Jerusalem was a picture of the Shrine of the Book, where
the Dead Sea Scrolls are housed. It is brilliant white, and its shape is
exactly like the accepted shape of a flying saucer. It was as if one
had landed in Jerusalem in the grounds of the Israel Museum.
Everybody knows the story of the Scrolls at Qumran on the Dead Sea

104

in 1947. The shape of the Shrine is based on the form of the lids which sealed the jars in which the scrolls were found. It is white because the Qumran Sect, whose scrolls they were, regarded themselves as Sons of Light while everyone else were Sons of Darkness. The Shrine is close to the Knesset, the Israeli Parliament, which was built with the funds willed by James de Rothschild in 1957. It was put into service in 1966. Anything built by the Rothschilds, as we know, is worth investigating. By the time that I arrived at the Shrine of the Book it was closed, but I was able to dowse around it, and what I found at first confused me. Between the Shrine and the Knesset were two parallel 49-bar lines! The only other place I had dowsed such a thing was between the Pyramids of Kefren and Cheops. On the other side was a single 49-bar line and following the angle it appeared to run to a similar building to the Shrine. This again was white and circular, rather like a huge white onion, upside down in the earth. This was the Israeli Goldstein Synagogue in the grounds of the Hebrew University. I drove round the Knesset Building and noted a 7-bar line joining it to the main buildings of the Hebrew University. Round the other side, the twin 49-bar lines could be found again. It was not possible to get nearer to the Knesset Building.

I returned to the citadel, parked the car and dowsed on foot, so that I could see what had happened. Because of the fact that these very large lines taper down at a functional point, I had passed across the two which were coming together and narrowing down and giving the impression, on a quick dowse, of being one. At the citadel itself, they diverge. One went to the Church of the Holy Sepulchre and would have been the one that I had earlier dowsed at the supposed Tomb of Jesus. The other went to the Dome of the Rock. The flow I noted was from the Shrine of the Book to the Knesset. Now the principal monuments of all these cultures and religions could all be shown to be integrated within the line system. The 49-bar line system in

Jerusalem could be shown to link the site of Jesus' Ascension, the Dome of the Rock, the Holy Sepulchre Church, a new synagogue, the Shrine of the Book, the Knesset, David's Citadel and the El-Aksa Mosque, indicating the common nature of their religious mysteries. Yet Israeli schoolteachers, taking their broods through the Old City, were armed with sub- machine guns, and everybody is still threatening everybody else with fire and destruction. A bomb went off in the new city that afternoon, happily doing no damage.

In the evening sun, I drove around the walls one last time. I stopped at Mount Zion. The flow of the line was outwards. Returning to the hotel, I stood on the terrace overlooking the Old City, and enquired what more needed to be done and elucidated that switching on the system would be a good thing. So, I prayed in the established formula that the light might now go forth into the world from Jerusalem according to the Divine Purpose. I expected this to produce the double-cube symbol everywhere, instead it produced the 7 circles. Never had this symbol been produced when switching on before. I felt it to be good. On the early drive to Tel Aviv the next morning, the symbols were there all the way. Through the El-Al security checks. "Hope you enjoyed your stay", said the passport man. Shalom! The 7 circles were in Rome Airport where I changed for Madrid, and in Madrid I could dowse that the whole Mediterranean was covered.

What I have written here may well strike the reader as a reasonably well-written travelogue of a day in Jerusalem, by a religious megalomaniac who ought to be put out of harm's way. I would not be surprised. All I can say is that it is a scrupulously truthful account of what I saw, felt and did that day, and I hope that I have earlier provided the reader with some logical basis for why I did the things I did. It may all be rubbish, high class rubbish, at least. You need a bit of ability to produce rubbish of this calibre! As I recorded it after the

106

visit, I did not feel myself to have indulged in delusions of religious megalomania. I prefer to think that the reasoning is the same as that which makes one call the doctor in the middle of the night because a child has a high temperature. I suppose that I could not take the chance that, faced with the possibility of making the most terrible fool of myself, I neglected to do something that just possibly might improve our lot on this planet. Anyway, it is done. What the results might be, time alone can tell. I cannot believe any harm will result.

A New Main Line from Brighton To High Rocks

In May 1977, I was returning home late one night and passing the Neo-Gothic church of St Peter's, the parish church of Brighton. I had dowsed this from the very beginning and found nothing. I concluded that in some way it was "graceless". Later, I had established that the architect was Sir Charles Berry, architect with Pugin of the new Palace of Westminster, and therefore "knowledgeable." I had reflected, some years ago, that perhaps he hadn't got one thing right, and thought no more of it. However, on that particular night, the thought struck me that perhaps here was a case of interference. I made enquiries of Deor, the local earth spirit, and was told I was right. I had never asked this question before. I did the necessary invocation and suddenly the church was in the system, manifesting single lines from each side on it longitudinal axis 14-bar line.

As I went home, I was able to discover that the southern line from the church, a 14-bar line, went straight to the octagonal room of Prinny's Pavilion, and thence through the Old Town Hall of Brighton, a neo classical structure, and then out to sea. In subsequent days one could see how this line moved northwards, in and out of the Wolstenbury area and on in the general direction of London, creating new lines in an area with which I was very familiar. It appeared that one had opened up an entirely new circuit of indefinite distance, just as one presses a button on a map of the London Tube or Paris Metro and lights up a particular route. This line ran through Preston Park, through a late 19th century clock tower, a fruit of the munificence of a local worthy, and thence to a neo-gothic church and on up to Wolstenbury. The clock tower is an octagonal construction on an octagonal plinth. After a week or so, the 14-bar line subsided into a single.

Driving past this area of Brighton each day a further thought suddenly struck me. From St Peter's down to the sea run a series of gardens in a sort of avenue, culminating in the circular area with the gardens and fountain called The Old Steine. Outside St Peter's is a white obelisk war memorial and at the other end, just before the fountain of the Old Steine, is a dark red granite obelisk, a war memorial of the Royal Sussex Regiment. I had seen examples of black and white, or dark and light, obelisks at Blenheim Palace, at the Katyn Memorial at Gunnersbury and at the memorial of the Polish Air Force at Northolt. I further noticed that the dark obelisk was in conjunction with another municipal war memorial, mosque-like in style, a dome above an octagon, and I recalled the tradition that the Old Steine referred to the ancient stone circle that was once there. Indeed, on Radio Brighton, a "white witch", self-proclaimed, had stated this to be the case, also that the original megaliths are the stones to be seen today around the base of the fountain. Furthermore, in a garden between the two is a tree circle, and a notice says, "It is an offence to enter this area".

Shortly afterward by the eastern entrance. No line could be found but coming out of the main entrance was a 7-bar line. My brother, David, came to stay at the weekend and we went to have a closer look. In front of the doomed war memorial the 7 circles were complete, and behind them was a triple line leading into the square pool associated with it, but not emerging the other side. We got it going, and a 7-bar line emerged joining the memorial to the fountain and to the dark obelisk. The dark obelisk put out lateral triples, one to the octagonal room in the Pavilion and another that eventually went out to sea, but that was all. We noticed, too, that on either side of the tree circle in the forbidden area were two rectangular plinths about 50 yards apart, with erased inscriptions. They reminded me of Beckford's plinths at Fonthill and whatever had been on them had been removed. Further up towards St Peter's, in the same garden, was a large octagonal fountain, whose octagon was not readily apparent, but set in a sunken octagonal pool, only visible from being very close to it.

At 2.00am that night, I moved into the forbidden area. A triple line ran from each plinth to the tree circle in the centre. Within the tree circle were the 7 circles with the wedge to the north missing. With due permissions and invocations, I was able to complete them. What surprised me was that a 49-bar line now embraced all these points, from the fountain at the Old Steine all the way to St Peter's, narrowing down at the fountain, war memorial, obelisks, tree circle, octagonal fountain, etc, thus indicating them to be critical foci in the system. By any test this system was one of the most deliberately contrived which I have ever encountered, circling me via Tunbridge Wells. On one of the neighbouring rocks is engraved the following inscalithic stone, war memorials, obelisks, tree circles, double plinths, octagonal fountain and a neo-gothic church. I went home, puzzled, to my couch. I confidently expected the 49-bar line to wane with time, as the 7-bar line had done, but it didn't, and it was there 2 months later. This, from previous experience, indicates it to be permanent.

I expected it to follow, more or less, the track of the London Road, but it didn't. From St Peter's it went off north-east to Lewes, via a dew pond on the Downs. At Lewes, it arrived at the Priory, where it turned north to the parish church. Then on, in surprise to the isolated Hamsey Old Church, the church where we had taken the strange photograph three years before, and which we found to be in a diamond of lines passing through strange holes in the buttresses. From there the line goes to Newick Parish Church, Maresfield Church and again, a surprise, through the Commonwealth Radio Communications Station near Crowborough, whence it joins the main line from Pevesey at High Rocks, near Tunbridge Wells. On top of one of those huge Cyclopean rocks, I found the point where the two incoming lines narrowed to a focus of minute dimensions before continuing on to Penshurst Place via Tunbridge Wells. On one of the neighbouring rocks is engraved the following inscription:

"Infidel! Who with thy finite wisdom

Wouldst grasp things infinite and dost become

A scoffer of God's holiest Mysteries.

Behold this Rock, then tremble and rejoice.

Tremble, for He who formed the mighty mass

Could in His justice crush thee where thou art.

Rejoice that still His Mercy spares thee."

March 21st, 1831 J Phippen

High Rocks is an awe-inspiring group of huge blocks of sandstone, 50-60 feet high and wide, with strangely wrought fissures between them, and well-cut sides. It is said that this place was first brought to public attention by King James I, who visited it when he was a guest of Sir Philip Sydney at Penshurst, and it was opened up as a public beauty spot, not surprising as the Stuarts were interested in such places.

The questions raised by this experience are huge, and I believe the correct answer contains the truth about the whole ley-line system. Why had someone or some power turned off a line which ran from megaliths, war memorials, tree circle, fountain, double plinths, obelisks, neo-gothic and medieval churches, dew pond, priory, radio station and Cyclopean stones? Who was responsible for the building of the elaborate system at Brighton, the war memorials and obelisks, etc? Could there be a group of people with "Masonic" knowledge in the Public Works Department? What purpose is served by switching it on? Why were the inscriptions on the Brighton Plinths erased? How on earth does the Foreign and Commonwealth Office Radio Communications Station get in on the act? There is not easy answer, but the real answer will unlock the mystery. This particular case is central.

I later discovered that the garden with the plinths and the tree circle is set in a "diamond" of lines, as is Hamsey, to which the line went on to. "The Diamond is in the form of the Vesica Piscis", said Bob Cowley who was with me, and he pointed to a statue of Queen Victoria in the same complex. My later enquiries showed that the missing statues were two of a set of five, which had come from the Mayfair home of Sir Barney Barnato, a self-made millionaire, who had committed suicide in strange circumstances. The house had been brought by the Sassoons, who owned much of Brighton, and it was their behest that the statues, five of them, were set up in the Queen Victoria Park. There was a public campaign against them, and they were removed, nobody knows to where. Three plinths were distributed to mark the entrances of other parks in Brighton and two were left, inscriptionless to mark the potential passage of the line through the tree circle. I have an old postcard showing the statues in situ. They were worthy subjects, like grace and charity. Why there was a public outcry against these objects of worthiness, I cannot understand. A deeper mystery lurks underneath, and it is another of those extraordinary side lights that illumine the whole of the story.

The Earth, as Mind, is controlled by lines of force, its nervous system. The Manichean struggle is carried out on earth through the operation of that system. It depends on telluric, celestial and spiritual node points. Informed people on earth can create focal points through working to increase the lines. Subliminal influences can also inspire people to do certain things in certain places. Knowledgeable people with good or bad intent can manipulate the system. I see the multiple line patterns on important sites, (at that time 49-bar lines), as Messianic in nature, carrying out the Divine Plan. Much more was to evolve from this in subsequent years, including increases in the numerical ratios, as we will see later.

Churchill, Bladon, Blenheim and Chartwell

In May 1977, I had occasion to visit Oxford, and I was able to go onto Blenheim which I had long planned to visit. We drove to Woodstock and approached by the eastern entrance. No line was found but coming out of the main entrance was a 7-bar line. This line was on the main avenue of Blenheim, it goes straight to the tower of Bladon Church where Sir Winston is buried. Blenheim was named after a little village on the Danube where Marlborough won the first of his victories. It is said that the Queen herself chose the architect, Sir John Vanbrugh, creator of Castle Howard and Greenwich Hospital, passing over her chief architect, Sir Christopher Wren, in the process. Vanbrugh as his pupil and, in view of Wren's intimate involvement in Operative Masonry, one may suppose that his pupil was well-informed. Sir John Vanbrugh appointed as his assistant Nicholas Hawksmoor, who is responsible for much of the detail, including the ceilings in which the octagon figures frequently.

112

Hawksmoor also assisted Wren in the building of St Paul's Cathedral. He also designed and had built the west towers of Westminster Abbey and was responsible for various university buildings at Oxford. Wren's comprehension of the sacred dimensions of the ley system seem obvious. Equally obvious from the evidence is the fact that this cannot be separated from his Masonic and Rosicrucian connections. He communicated his knowledge to his pupils and associates, and they applied it to both religious and secular monuments. Blenheim is one of the latter, and it appears that it was deliberately and specifically built into the ley system.

We joined a party to tour the apartments of Blenheim. The Great Hall had a triple line running east-west through it, and it was something of a "Frisson" to find, to the west, that the line ran through the bed where Sir Winston Churchill was born. "At Blenheim," he once said, "I took two important decisions: to be born and to marry. I am happily content with the decisions I took on both occasions". He proposed in the Temple of Diana! Interestingly, the guidebook includes the comment by the late Duke: "We can look back now on the pattern of Sir Winston's life and see, or think we see, a pleasing inevitability. His birth here at Blenheim, his proposal of marriage here beside the lake, his burial at Bladon, these things form a mosaic which seems almost too neat to be true." The guidebook goes on: "Vanbrugh's north to south axial line through the Column of Victory, the Great Hall, the Saloon and the Great Tower of Bladon Church, which may be seen from the Saloon, and beside which tower Sir Winston is buried. This physically and symbolically linked the places of his birth and burial." One wonders if the author of the guidebook, David Green, was unconsciously inspired or consciously aware. The fact remains that a 7-bar dowsable line runs down the main axis. I checked it from the south side as well, as it left the house to go on down to Bladon Church.

We were taken around the sumptuous rooms of Blenheim. I noticed Hawksmoor's ceilings particularly octagons and ovals. What struck in my memory was the Long Library, a magnificent Vanbrugh design, with Hawksmoor's detail, at one end, the great organ installed in 1891 by the 8th Duke, with above it a remarkable octagonal ceiling. I took a look outside. The water gardens are the life's work of the 9th Duke, who died in 1934. The key to their design, says the guidebook, lies in the Bernini river-gods fountain on the second terrace. This was interesting, because Bernini was the elderly Italian sculptor who was working in the Louvre and who permitted Sir Christopher Wren to see his drawings on his visit to Paris. This scale model for the famous fountain in Rome's Piazza Navona was given to the 1st Duke and revered by the 9th, who determined to give Vanbrugh's palace the majestic, formal setting he knew it deserved. What the guidebook fails to mention is that there are two of these fountains, and that one is surmounted by a black obelisk and the other by a white one. I was able to dowse that a 49-bar line was coming in from the west and was bounded by these two obelisks. The line narrowed substantially to be bounded within a smaller compass by two fabulous beasts, reminiscent of those at Beckford's Fonthill. Two reclining sphinxes, but with female heads on longer necks than that at the Pyramids in Egypt. From there the lines disappeared into the second terrace of the water garden to re-emerge the other side, to the south of the Woodstock Road entrance, where I was able to check it.

Blenheim was, as I suspected, on a main line, all was in order, according to Elohim. The last year at Bladon seemed to have worked, and the line from Churchill's tomb was now a 7-bar line. That could only be good. I noticed before leaving that the Marlborough Arms are based on the Hapsburg double headed eagle with a halo around each head. This was because the House of Hapsburg had benefitted from Marlborough's activities. I wondered whether that is the source of the family's occult knowledge? I look at Charles V (Holy Roman Emperor,) crest now, on a Toldeo plate on my wall, and find it identical in general terms to that above the monument to the first Duke and Duchess of Marlborough in the Blenheim Chapel. I left in pensive mood, finally noting that the grounds had been laid out by Lancelot (Capability) Brown, a man whose activities I determine to investigate on another occasion.

Our next visit was to Chartwell, home of Sir Winston Churchill. As a good friend of mine lived just up the road, I had been able to dowse it in passing and show an important line running through it, but that had been year earlier. I picked up the first 49-bar line running from the house to the round pond. One was able to notice that the fishponds, insofar as one could dowse over them, showed evidence of the 7 circles. We approached the main entrance and I could see the line I earlier detected on the road outside. It came through the front door, but there were two lines! In the library, one cannot penetrate too far, but it was enough to dowse the double-square rectangle. Upstairs, one could visit his study, where he used to write, rather than in the library. Here another double squared rectangle could be dowsed. Churchill used the study for the best part of 40 years. It was an essential part of his life. There were majestic views across the gardens to the lakes. The bedroom contains a four-poster bed from which may be dowsed a triple line, but nothing else is available for dowsing within the house.

The garden is a place which really tells all. On the front lawn, there is an ancient yew tree. The line from the bedroom loses itself in a spiral around this tree. The 49-bar line on the round pond does not enter or depart from the house, as a circuit of the lawn showed. I moved to the south and around the croquet lawn. There was nothing. At the southern end of the croquet lawn is a curious, circular saucer tumulus, which serves as a garden waste dump. Access to it is through a narrow channel. Inside are the 7 dowsable circles, though they were incomplete. I was able to restore them. It reminded me of a similar construction with similar dowsing phenomena at the Rothschild Villa at Cap Ferrat in the South of France. From there one can move into the rose garden, through whose avenue I picked up a 49-bar line. In the centre of the avenue is a sundial. The whole area was a kitchen garden, the greater part of whose walls were built by Churchill himself between 1925 and 1932, but its transformation into a rose garden was a gift to Winston and Clemmie in 1958 to mark their Golden Wedding Anniversary. The 49-bar line through the rose garden makes a circuit to come back to the house at the base of the railed garden. The other comes in from the Chart and leaves from the base of the garden via the round from the Marlborough Pavilion. Built at the inspiration of Lady Churchill in the twenties, this is a temple to the 1st Duke of Marlborough. Four Terra-cotta plaques on the wall represent rivers associated with his campaigns in the War of the Spanish Succession, and a frieze evokes the wars in particular Blenheim. On the floor, great flagstones form an octagon, albeit not equilateral. Elsewhere in the house itself, above his study, is a kind of turret or bell-tower with a weather cock. It is octagonal.

Leaving Chartwell, I was pondering the fact that it was not only a 49-bar line, but had a secondary 49-bar line as well, and I reflected that Churchill had been born in a focal point of the 49-bar system in England, and had lived the major part of his life on a similar line. When I related this to my brother, David, he said, "What about that 49-bar line from the north door of Westminster Abbey. We know it does not go through No 10 Downing street, why not?" I replied, "I think I know where it might go, the Admiralty Block House where Churchill had his War-Room deep below." It was some weeks before I could go there. On a hot July afternoon and, under the watchful and puzzled stare of a London bobby, I walked onto Horse Guards Parade and there it was. So far as I can tell, the line goes through the

Treasury, changes direction slightly through the Foreign and Commonwealth Office, misses Downing Street and goes across Horse Guards Parade to the Blockhouse. The circle, if you like, complete, birth, domestic life, public life and death, all directly involved with a 49-bar line.

The question is, what does it all mean? Was Churchill a very superior puppet manipulated by the force that manifests through 49-bar line? Or was he conscious of the magical world and able to work quite deliberately with it? We know that he was an intimate in his youth of Wilfred Blunt. An Oil painting by Blunt's son in law hangs at Chartwell. Churchill was a Mason with United Studholme Lodge. We know he employed Dennis Wheatley as a Special Adviser during the War. We know he employed Walter Johannes Stein, that Grail Adept who fully understood the diabolical machinations of Hitler and his henchmen. We know that map dowsers were employed by the Admiralty with his approval. We know that he forbade reference to Hitler's occult activities at the Nuremberg Trials. We believe Churchill personally designed the octagonal pill boxes still to be seen in the cornfields of southern England. They are fed by a triple line and contain 7 dowsable circles complete within them. As one who was once trained as an infantry officer, I could never understand why these all stand out in the open in the middle of fields, instead of at the edge of copses, woods or some other form of natural camouflage or protection. Now I can only conclude that their defensive function was not military.

We know too that Churchill laid out and built much in the Chartwell garden with his own hands. Was his exile and retreat a magical retirement during which he was preparing some occult power source for the struggle he knew was coming? What was the nature of his reverence for Blenheim Palace? He must have understood something of the sacred architecture. In all his speech's he singled out Hitler and Nazi-ism as a monstrous theological evil, making the struggle a Manichean one. Of course, for me, the dowsing evidence is conclusive, but for others I can only produce circumstantial evidence. Let those who can dowse go and find the same. Did he give us vital insight when he addressed the Combined Senate and Congress of the United States during the Second World War in the following words? "He must indeed have a blind soul who cannot see some Great Purpose or Design is being worked out here below, of which we have the honour to be faithful servants."

Lourdes and the White Goddess

Lourdes, Pyrenees, September 1977. What was it that drew hundreds and thousands of people every year to this place? For some time, I had wanted to go and see the primary shrine of Mary, and eventually we did. In August, I had been discussing the ley-line between Santiago de Compostella and Rosslyn. Using map-dowsing, I had found it to go through Lourdes and as other parts of the line had checked out on the ground with the rod, my interest in Lourdes had quickened further. When we arrived, my first impressions were contradictory. The Chapel of Our Lady of Lourdes was beautiful, but the town was a desert of souvenir shops. I had never seen so many. The story of St Bernadette of Lourdes is well known, and the cynical would have been forgiven suggesting that a more profitable business enterprise for the town could scarcely be conceived, it was a timely hit in the arm for the Church, in an age in which its fortunes had not exactly prospered.

A preliminary tour of the town hardly diminished the cynical view, for there was nothing in the town, not even a line, nothing from the Chapel or the Grotto. We had driven right around the grounds. As I went down to the Chapel precinct, I tried to get the Elohim sign up, it came up barred. A little further on, that soft "phut" I had first heard or been aware of at the Pyramids, and there it was, the negative symbol.

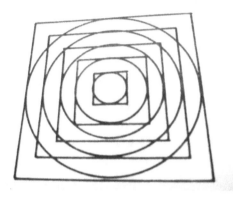

On the face of it, therefore, whatever there was at Lourdes wasn't working. I proceeded down the hill, taking a side-road which passed the house where St Bernadette was born, nothing. One re-joins the main road across a bridge, which aligns with the main axis of the Lourdes Sanctuary and Chapel, but there was nothing. It was just before midnight and the gates to the Sanctuary were still open. I went down the double avenue that leads virtually east west to the Chapel and Basilica. The Chapel is neo-gothic in style and, although it is beautiful and flanked by two octagonal towers, it does not have the true gothic majesty of the medieval cathedrals. Two sweeping rising colonnades like embracing arms reach round to take the visitor up above the Basilica to the Chapel standing on the rock above it. Within its embrace lies a piazza and the surface is of polished stone in different colours in which a motif of a rood cross is implanted. There was still nothing!

I moved across to the right under one of these colonnades to where the Grotto was, and there were signs of activity. Apparently, a Mass had just finished. I could see the Grotto with a blaze of candles around it, but clearly things were over, and so I went to the front of the Basilica and stood on the steps and went through the mental prayer I have detailed elsewhere. Now, I say that with odd feelings, as these feelings are always with me on these occasions. What am I, the product of modern rationalist, humanist education, doing on this spot, praying in this way? The arrogance of it is enough to give one gooseflesh, and the fancifulness of it enough to make one laugh, or weep in self-ridicule. But once again, I did it because the whole of this strange experience, demands that one does it, and one's reason says that, if this is rubbish, no harm is done and, if it isn't then one would be failing in neglecting to do it. Anyway, it was done. I have prayed in the past, but routinely intoning the Lord's Prayer or Creed in the School Chapel is not real prayer. Since I learned the trick of dowsing, and since the whole experience of the Elohim Communication, prayer has become an act wholly dissociated with words. It becomes a total submission of the consciousness to a series of images involving the celestial hierarchy, and a huge leap of the spirit into another dimension. It only takes a few seconds, but it is an enormous journey and it involves a state of mind unlike any other I have had until I learned to dowse the Grail and its wonders. Call it a "plugging in", if you will. A flight of fancy, perhaps, but I can only compare it to a huge expansion of awareness to take in for a moment the whole of the universe. I suppose megalomania is not necessarily any different, but there you are, that's what happens.

The whole place changed. A 49-bar line ran out of the Basilica, down the central axis of the cross, but keeping within the boundaries of the coloured stones. The arms of the cross had 14-bar lines. As I walked back, a 7-bar line now connected the two statues of St Bernadette. At that moment, the Chapel clock chimed 12am, preceding it with the "Ave Maria", I could not help breaking into a dance in time with it. I enquired whether I might additionally get the place going, and although many recent requests of mine to do so had been turned

120

down, this seemed to be in order. So, I did it. In all vacant spaces, the twin double-square symbol in the square appeared. I was the last one out of the Sanctuary. The 49-bar line continued across the bridge, expanding as it went. The streets were full of symbols. When I returned to the hotel, my companions had already retired for the night.

The next morning was cold, snappy and brilliant, and one had to walk briskly to keep warm. The symbols were still there. I walked down to the Sanctuary at about 9am, to find it already crowded. I made straight for the Grotto, where Mass was already in progress. It was a sizable Italian pilgrimage. For the first time, I could stand in front of the Grotto, and stayed for a time, moved by the expectations of the terminally sick arrayed in front of the priests. A purple skull capped one, started on a lengthy address invoking the Virgin's aid for the sick. Nothing happened. The crowd dispersed, and the stewards hustled everyone away for the next group. One did not know what diseases were represented there, presumably terminal cancer, chronic arthritis, paralysis and the like. One was struck by the fact that the vast majority were aged, but of the younger element the majority had learning difficulties or afflicted in similar ways. As they were dispersing, I moved on up the path which enabled me to overlook the scene. It was a moment to reflect. A little girl who had learning difficulties played around my feet. Her ugly features were full of gentleness rarely seen in those whose bodies and faculties are whole. Would she be any happier if she were made "normal", I wondered? The look of profound sadness on her mother's face and the resigned, but total patience, with which she treated her child, certainly deserved to be removed, but Lourdes never did that sort of thing anyway. From the vantage point, the whole sordid but beautiful mixture of Lourdes itself in poignant relief – the brilliant morning sunshine, the chestnut trees with the conkers just ripening and the leaves turning to their autumnal hue, the rush and sparkle of the river, the hopes and disappointments of so many, the vestments of the priests, the hundreds of candles the earnestness of those who accompanied the sick, the cynical officiousness of the stewards, who saw it all every day, day in, day out. God knows how depressing it would have been, had it been raining. Yet a 49-bar line was coming from that Grotto. "Cure them all," I cried inwardly in anguish. Nothing happened, and I turned away.

On one side of the Grotto are the baths, where those who can, bathe themselves in accordance with the Lady's injunction. The 49-bar line on the east west axis goes through them. On the other side, still on the line, are the taps through which the Lourdes water flows, people drink it constantly. It is the best tasting water that I have ever drunk. I wandered back to the hotel, going to the Chapel and the Basilica en-route, where Masses were being said in abundance. What struck me in the Basilica was that its interior was faced with some small slabs of marble, hundreds of thousands in total. Each one was inscribed with a vote of thanks in gilt letters from persons who had had their prayers answered by the Lady. This was the most eloquent witness of Lourdes.

A visit to the Grotto revealed that its sides have been worn smooth by constant touching and kissing, rather like the worn toe of the statue of St Peter in St Peter's, Rome. I dutifully placed in a crack, one or two medallions, of Our Lady, I had brought earlier in the Supermarket of the Rosary. Pendulum dowsing showed them to be highly charged, presumably as a result. As we moved round, however, I was able to establish something far more important. Within the Grotto, the 49-bar line began in the Ram's horn spiral, and out of the rock to each spiral ran a 7-bar line. At one side is the spring, suitably enclosed in glass, where a fairly powerful flow of water emerges, a far cry from the muddy patch found by Bernadette. Above the Grotto hang twenty or so abandoned crutches blackened with age. In an enclave within are half a dozen, apparently new, their stainless-steel glistening in the candlelight. Re-joining the crowds, one noted an air of almost jollity about the quickness. The lame had been quickly wheeled away. Black suited priests moved about, some earnest, some plainly bored, others distracted – Irish, English, Italian, Spanish, French – all clucking about their various flocks. A German bishop signed autographs with a hearty panache worthy of a manger of a successful football team. People asked blessings of passing priests. But the Grotto was emitting a 49-bar line and it had a ram's horn spiral, each horn receiving a 7-bar line from the rock. This was the crux of the matter.

Across the river, immediately in front of the Grotto, I noticed an open space with a raised altar of approximately double cube proportions. It was an overflow area, primarily designed for the younger pilgrims when things in the Grotto got too crowded. I crossed the bridge to it and found that the line went to it. One was able to approach the altar, indeed young boys were playing on it. From the altar, the line changed direction and went towards a distant hill, which appeared to be hollowed out in a manner reminiscent of Wolstenbury. However, I did not have time to investigate it further, but the flow was from the Grotto. I took the family to the Basilica and Chapel from which, with the compass, I confirmed their orientation was east-west exactly, with the flow from the east. This corresponded with the map dowsing results. Around the Chapel, I detected no other lines, just the east-west line and the line from the Grotto forming as it were, a Tau Cross. With mixed feelings about Lourdes we left. One was left with the fact that Lourdes was clearly within the ley system and the Grotto contained a ram's horn spiral with two 7-bar lines attached. I remembered the strange photograph of the halo effect at Wolstenbury, that had shown up on the film but which I was not able to see. That also was on a ram's horn spiral.

Might it not be that it is through the spirals that the system gathers its terrestrial energy and that to those viewing the site of a powerful source of telluric energy, its presence may be made manifest in various ways. These could be by dowsing the spiral, by feeling the energy as intense cold, or by seeing Mary, the Earth Goddess herself, particularly when one's whole conditioning was to see things in terms of Christian iconography. An ancient Greek girl might have seen Demeter, a Roman – Ceres, and Egyptian – Isis. I perceive things through the rod as geometrical shapes but is it possibly all the same thing. All phenomena have their origin in the basic aeonal forms of the cosmos, the language of God, as Pythagoras would have it. The essential duality of the cosmos is expressed in the opposition of the mother-feminine-earth principle with the son-sun-celestial-masculine principle. The ley system seems to draw on both where particularly felicitous conjunctions are achieved. The Earth temples of Sussex are terrestrial and celestial in their functions. Thus, it may be held that the cult of Mary, which in the Pyrenees predominates over the worship of Jesus, is nothing more nor less than the continuation in a Christian guise of the ancient cult of the Earth or White Goddess. I suggest this is what Lourdes is about.

In Andorra, the patron saint is Our Lady Meritxell. A church was built to her in medieval times because, says the legend, local folk noticed flowers blooming out of season in a particular spot and on investigation found a wooden statue of the Virgin and Child amongst them. They bore it off, but overnight it vanished, and they found it next day in the same place amongst the flowers. They took it away again, but it kept returning, so they felt there was nothing for it but to build a church on that spot to house the miraculous statue. There it remained until 1974, when an unfortunate fire destroyed it. Now a new, larger, finer basilica is rising next to the burnt-out church, and it dowses. It is on a 21-bar line and a 14-bar line – the 21-bar line running through the centre of Andorra. It is interesting to note the message of the Lady to Bernadette is to get the priests to build a church in Lourdes. The villagers in Andorra decided to build a church in a particular spot because the miraculous statue kept returning to the same spot.

In all parts of England similar legends abound, indicating the inevitable choice of the site of churches being out of man's hands. In Sussex, stones kept being removed at various sites in the night and placed elsewhere until the masons gave in, in desperation, and built on the site indicated by this supernatural power. Oxen which lay in the form of a cross dictated the site of others. In France, similar stories abound. What lies behind it all is the suggestion that the siting of churches is not random, but dictated by factors other than simple human caprice, that certain sites are "good" and that the divine force requires a church or similar religious monument there, be it stone circle or Delphic Oracle. As Louis Charpentier says of Chartes, *"it was a powerful point of the confluence of telluric currents recognised in pre-Christian times, and the building of the finest medieval cathedrals there is witness to the particular forces operating at that point. And so, the Earth Goddess appeared to Bernadette and demanded a church on that site and she got it. Is it any different for the Meritxell phenomenon, or the oxen, or the stones that moved in the night?"* I think not.

One is struck also by the presence of the sacred spring. Holy water has always been important in Catholicism, as have sacred springs. So, were they in Greek mythology? One is obliged to note that springs and underground water, whilst not following the ley system, do emerge at points in the system, or at points where they burst through or are capable of doing so with a little help, eg Underwood's blind spring, and Bernadette's scrapping of mud. The line is attracted to that point. Lourdes, Chalice Well in Glastonbury, the hot springs at Caldetas, the well at Tunbridge Wells, Abraham's Well at Shipley,

Sussex and many others are all in the system, and, in some way or other provide some sort of land vital. Certainly, all such water reacts positively to the pendulum, whilst London tap water seems lifeless by the same tests. Taking the waters in Britain, has seen a decline in the great spa towns. Not so in continental Europe, particularly in France and Germany. Spa towns abound in the Pyrenees, advertising the various springs for different complaints. The Druids point out that stone circles, dolmens and the like are all different in their healing properties, and a true Druid knows how to identify the proper place for particular complaints, and I think that we may accept that blind springs are also involved.

To that extent, what should we expect of Lourdes? I did not have a chance to study the 22 cases or miraculous cures, maybe they have something in common. I venture to suggest that this might be worthy of some study and that Lourdes be identified for what it is. Lourdes may well have been overblown and oversold, achieving the cures within its powers, and disappointing thousands who should never have been there in the first place. That is not to detract from the sanctity of Lourdes or Bernadette's experience. It is only to point out that there are many other unsung spots of equal value for certain cases, and very likely many other cases of people seeing things. Most of them would never dream of telling anyone else, let alone prefects and priests. What on earth would the neighbours think.

The cult of the Earth Goddess persists, cloaked in many guises. It may be seen in the stories of the Quest for the Holy Grail, where knights forever rescue virginal maidens from dragons and other diabolical manifestations. I take this to mean that he who would truly worship the Earth Goddess, or seek to understand the ley system, or carry out the purposes of the feminine principle of the Divine, must protect her from the seriousness of evil, keep her paths straight and bind the dragon. The chaotic, turbulent, spiral primal earth force into straight, controlled, creative channels. Thus, may the essential biorhythms of the Earth proceed without let or hindrance in the unfoldment of the gentle, loving, cradling, nursing influences of the Divine Feminine principle, and a Knight of the Grail be worthy of his calling. For the Grail is the cup, the chalice, the creative stone, and in that sense, as Emma Jung forcibly points out in! *"The Grail Legend is phallic, vaginal, womb-like, the cornucopia, the bountiful matrix. Not for nothing is the other Grail symbol the spear, the male phallus, the solar force, the instrument that slays the dragon and pierces the side of Jesus. For the male principle must find its true reconciliation with the female, not dominate and obliterate it and permit it to proliferate in all its gentleness. As in all things in this Manichaean universe, equilibrium in the eternal duality of things is the prize. The whole Grail story illustrates this perfectly. The pagan traditions of the White Goddess were also kept alive in the rules of courtly love sung by the troubadours. Their songs should not be seen as trite invitations to platonic adultery with the ladies of the court, but a survival of the cult of the Earth Mother. Their message could also be an attempt to preserve it from the hand of the Church which had become obsessed with dogma, fine points of obscurantist theology and an institutionalisation which set its own survival higher than truth. The reality of Earth Magic had been assumed by the early Christian Church and practised. By the end of the Middle Ages outward forms had overtaken the inner truths, to the extent that death awaited those who practised the ancient religion, like the Cathars on the Camp des Cremats at Montsegur."*

As a postscript. Emma Jung further points out that, in Robert de Boron's version of the Grail, when Joseph wishes to use the Grail as an ocular symbol for the first time, the voice of Christ tells him that when he requires counsel he should call on the three powers that are one, and the Holy Woman who bore the Son. Then he will hear the voice of the Holy Spirit in his heart. This means nothing less than that the Grail really forms a quaternity in which the blood contained within it signifies the Three Persons of the One Godhead and the vessel can be compared to the Mother of God, as in a Victorian hymn: "Salve, Mater Salvatoris, Vas electrum, Vas honoris, Vas caelestis gratiae." This would lend further weight to what I tried to say earlier, namely that Mary, the White Goddess and the Grail are effectively the same thing, and that the ley system is a manifestation of this aspect of Divinity.

This is borne out to some extent by an anonymous Grail contribution called the "Elucidation" which recounts how the Kingdom of Logres was destroyed. *"At one time, there were living in that land in certain puis, (burial mounds or grottoes of springs) maidens who used to refresh tired travellers with food and drink. If one went to a puis in need, a beautiful damsel would appear carrying a Grail vessel or cornucopia from which all kinds of food would emerge. And so, it was until a king named Amangous ravished one of them and stole her vessel. His people emulated him, and the maidens never came out of the grottoes again. From that time on the land went to waste. The trees lost their leaves, grass and flowers withered and the water receded more and more. In King Arthur's time, his knights took it upon themselves the duty of finding the puis again and of protecting the maidens that dwelt within them, and they swore vengeance on the descended of the villain that had insulted them. But they did not succeed, until Gawain and Percival found again the magical court of the Fisher King, which had been lost after the rape of the damsels, and the land grew green again."* This again I take to be an allegorical reference to an abuse of the ley system and the White Goddess who manifests through it. The attempt to restore it, which is still yet to be achieved, is designed to re-establish a direct harmony between masculine and the feminine principle. This, while it remains disrupted, creates desolation, disequilibrium and all the jagged edges that the contemporary human psyche exhibits, not to mention the vast ecological problems that we are facing. Bernadette's experience was one step towards achieving that objective. Vastly misunderstood, exploited and abused, but nonetheless evidence that all is not entirely lost. The damsels just occasionally do come out of the grottoes to provide for the innocent supplicant. This may well be the most fundamental truth of our times.

Close Encounters of the Fourth Kind

Around the time of Christmas 1977, a group of friends who had shared an experience in 1976 in Wells Cathedral Chapter House, began to talk about following the message received at Wells. Accordingly, we looked for the date of Easter 1978, and specifically Good Friday, which in that year was 24th March. "That's early!" someone said. Then other facts began to emerge. At 16.20GMT there was to be a lunar eclipse. It was also a day of the Full Moon, and the Spring Equinox. These facts alone seemed significant enough, without looking at the planetary conjunctions. What had been a job filed away in the subconscious, now began to be a positive, conscious mission. My mind began to examine in a more serious way what it could be about. As New Year started, I began to receive information through the Elohim Channel, through mediums, through chance encounters and from books that just happened to turn up. So far as the Elohim were concerned, I cannot remember the day that I first began to ask questions, but the following information began to emerge:

1) That the Arsinal Grail should come to Glastonbury and be "turned on."

2) That this was to mark the end of one era and the beginning of another.

129

3) That things would begin to change.

4) That the role of the Elohim would end, to be replaced by another whose name was Chloe and whose symbol was the letter "C", but with a narrow opening on the upper right-hand quadrant.

I was puzzled at the information. I reasoned thus. The Jehovah Elohim was that aspect of God, which was concerned with spirit and form, ie matter. If the new Aquarian Age were to be concerned with the beginnings of the return of "matter" to spirit, then the raising of earth-bound man's perceptions was the key objective. The age of Pisces, associated with the Christian era, had certainly been a landmark in the history of mankind. It had instigated the first glimmerings of individual consciousness, and therefore individual responsibility. Previously the law of the Old Covenant had prevailed. Whole tribes and races had been following their group karma, lemming-like, and individual consciousness was the exception rather than the rule. Jesus had given the New covenant, which meant that individuals were responsible for themselves. He had preached a doctrine of individual morality, which removed the individual from the guilt of the group sin on the one hand but made himself reliant for virtue on the other. It was a real step forward in the recorded history of the consciousness of mankind. Of course, the rise of religious institutions stultified the psychic joy of the early Christians, who had rejoiced in the awareness of the spiritual gifts brought at the Pentecost and preached by St Paul.

About the turn of the first millennium A.D. the process began to deteriorate, due to the attitudes enshrined in the Roman church. This institution apart from denying the existence of the etheric body of man, began also to remove from the ordinary person that inner awareness of God which had been enjoyed formerly. This privilege was now allocated to the priest and, later on in the second

130

millennium, was attributed rather to the institution itself, or at least to that institution as represented by the Pope and his cardinals. This outward form came to replace personal awareness, so, at the present time, the spiritual pilgrim can only view the church as a museum through whose corridors the soul may wander without stirring even an echo. Christ had said, "Where two or three are gathered together, I am in the midst of them." But the true understanding of his words has become totally lost in the panoply of priest craft, pomp and circumstance, and the temporal considerations of wealth and power.

As the knowledge of the Divine receded from the ordinary person, so too the knowledge of the sacred architecture, the telluric and celestial forces, and the whole awareness of the earth as a living organism disappeared. This had been known previously by all those who danced around the maypoles or standing stones, and it had reached its finest expression in the sophisticated sacred architecture of the great Gothic Cathedrals. This knowledge became restricted to an ever-decreasing number of people. This suggested, on the one hand, that the Church followed a deliberate plan to withdraw it and, on the other, that there was an attempt in lay circles to preserve it, in groups and sects which were to become victims of the Inquisition. Some of these groups were motivated by the hope that better days would return, and their knowledge used again for the good of mankind. Others were motivated differently, perverting the knowledge for unholy ends, both private and political.

It is strange that the last 150 years has seen the burgeoning of the spiritual gifts of St Paul almost without exception outside the Church, such as gifts of healing, speaking with tongues, mediumship and so on. This is ironic, since the founding fathers based their teaching and practice on these gifts. The retreat of the Church into establishment and outward form, whether by accident, weakness or deliberately contrived, has gone hand in hand with the rise of the lay materialistic dialectic. The result is a handful of priests with personal awareness and a dissatisfied membership increasingly endeavouring to forge its own links with God and deal with spiritual matters on its own account. However, the message of individual consciousness got home. The attempt to destroy the ethic was nearly, but not quite successful. Enough individual moral and spiritual awareness remained for the people not to surrender completely before the wave of materialism. We had seen the new power of the State attempting to manipulate the masses in an unprecedented way and, it was successful. Was that, I wondered, what it was all about?

My friend, Joyce had been increasingly taking me into her confidence. I had come to know her, as a result of a remarkable intervention in a talk I had given at Trevor Ravenscroft's. She was a medium, an astral traveller, and a remarkable woman in the best sense. She knew all about the Grail. For some-time she had been writing automatically, and much of this had to do with the vibratory nature of the universe. Although some of what she produced was pessimistic, forecasting cataclysm in common with other mediumistic material available at that time, it was clear that she was producing information relevant to our work on the ley system. This was, that the then biorhythm of the earth was based on the number 7, (as we had ascertained) and that in order to raise the consciousness of mankind further, the factor of 8 had to be introduced. I discussed with her the idea of whether a cataclysm was inevitable, citing Prometheus and Jacob as examples. I argued that that if it were true that man had the Christ within him then, if he were sufficiently informed, he had the power of changing his destiny. Indeed, it was his destiny to have that power. She did not resist the argument too strongly even though it was at odds with what she had accepted earlier.

About that time, I had become aware of the work of Andrija Puharich, an old friend of hers, and the mentor of Uri Geller. He had given a lecture in London in November 1977, in which he had given his views on the purpose of the new 40-megawatt transmitters, which the Russians had built. They were, he said, nothing more nor less than the practical application of Nicola Tesla's theories and experiments. Tesla was an electrical genius who had effectively revolutionised the industrial age, by making it able to utilise all the advantages of alternative current. That he was a mystic also seems clear from his writings. He certainly understood that Moses was an expert in the use of electrostatic electricity, affirming categorically that the Ark of the Covenant was an electrostatic generator. Michael Bentine and I conducted some experiments with such an apparatus. We were able to show that the electrostatic field could be directed in a beam by holding a dowsing rod above it and rotating it. Pot plants shivered each time a rod pointed at them. We were also able to show that the electrostatic charge could be "leaked" to a seven circle dowsable configuration, causing it to expand into a full Grail symbol, leaving the generator fieldless. Thus, we reasoned, the fields formed in the symbols could absorb the electrostatic field in certain circumstances, permitting the hypothesis that the unified field theory was correct. This meant that the human psyche was capable of functioning within the unified field, whether it be called "ether", "prana" or what you will. Moreover, the operation could only be carried out through the human psyche. It followed that the human psyche could dominate or be dominated by the electrostatic field, and probably also the electromagnetic and radio-active fields within the unity of all things. We recalled the ability of Uri Geller to make a Geiger counter scream at a pitch indicating fatal radioactivity in John Taylor's laboratory in London when no radioactivity was present. We had also noted another phenomenon which we felt to be important, namely, that when a pendulum held between the finger and thumb were introduced into a dowsable line or symbol, it went 5 degrees out of plumb and remained so. What was more extraordinary still was that when we conducted tests with symbols which I produced mentally the pendulum was affected equally. This provided us with a hypothesis for telekinesis, and the possibility that the pendulum had moved in someone else's hand because of an act of will on my part. This is not an experiment which is repetitive, but it is repeatable. It seems to depend on the persons present rather than on a set of physical circumstances. But this is in keeping with the hypothesis of the relationship of the unified field and the tuned human psyche. One had created gravitational anomalies!

It was in King's College that Andrija made his presentation. What he had to say was this. Working on the Tesla theory, the Russians had built a stupendously powerful transmitter to transmit energy wirelessly through the earth, for weather and seismic control, the sinister aspect, was that these could also be used to affect the human psyche at any specified point of the globe. By the juxtaposition of earth waves transmitted through the core of the globe and air waves beamed to and from the ionosphere, a marriage of the two could be achieved at predetermined points, and a resonance set up. According to the frequency, specific results could be achieved. Andrija himself had conducted certain experiments, (limited by concern for the volunteer human guinea pigs,) with extra low frequency transmitters, but had satisfied himself that there were frequencies which could produce in the subjects, depression, nausea, elation, violence, quiescence and so on. I found none of this surprising. My own training in military intelligence, in particular in the case history of Cardinal Mindszenty in Hungary, had demonstrated that the exposure of human beings to certain frequencies of light and sound could produce psychological changes, especially in weak subjects. What was startling to me was that whole communities could be affected at long range, as had happened in Canada? Andrija said there was no defence against it. But he did concede privately that a person trained in alphagenetics could be proof against such a practice. This is a technique of controlling one's own brain rhythms, as a yogi does. However, there are not many of these about.

A question we arranged to be asked at the House of Commons certainly obliged the Government spokesman to concede that such transmissions were taking place, "although" (and I quote) "they were not a matter of concern." Therefore, it appeared that there were now technological means of invading the human psyche or, to put it another way, magic and machines had come together. We speculated about this concept further.

Much of Joyce's freestream material was about this point. I select here certain extracts which convinced me about what she was producing. After a statement confirming the existence of ley lines, the source implied that there were methods of defence against the system, firstly using colour rays, and secondly:

"It is disturbing these beams through curves and angles, but never 90 degrees, that you will deter their thrust. It will be possible in the near future to so recurve these beams that you will be able to send them back to those who have sent them out. The symbols which are coming forth through your ley lines are exactly the symbols that will be used in redirecting the light beams."

"It is imperative for you to have proposed ways of stopping and redirecting these magnetic waves."

"We have impressed upon you repeatedly that the basic cycle of your Earth dimension is governed by the 7-cycle. When you begin to work with an inter-dimensional breakthrough you are operating on the 8-cycle, your well-known infinity sign... the magnetic beams your Russians are sending wrap themselves around people and are held together by the 7 spiral turns above and below."

"These magnetic beams you are concerned with operate on a current of their own, in the same manner as the crystal substance."

"There are those on your plane who will feel no effects from any of these penetrations. They are individuals so encased and coupled with their etheric body that the beams will, so to speak, curve around those beings... These beams will not affect your entire peoples, only those who themselves operate upon fears and frustrations."

"It will soon be possible to project massive healings through your TV networks, if you beam through the ultra violet ray (the spiritual essence of its radiation) and couple it with the magenta ray, which is massive love rather than individual love. Using this energy, you will in fact cancel very swiftly that which the Russians are projecting.

"Do you not see that these beams are available to you for creativity on a world-wide scale that your Earth has not yet experienced?"

"These beams will always fan out from a central point. In this case the central point will be a "channel" reinforced with a device containing a crystal...It is important for your "channel" to visualise the energy as it travels first the ultra violet frequency, and then into the broader mass spectrum of the magenta vibration, seeing them as they span/fan outwards from the focal point. Begin to project of mass healing, as it is a positive tool against the beams coming from the Russian area..."

"Yours is a battle of the few, but what you achieve will be the vibrations for the beginning of the next Earth cycle. It is only through the vibration of the spiritual core of the universal system that there is any hope for your planet."

"As you know, there are places on your Earth where several dimensions meet together. These will be the cross lines of your veins.

They are the gathering points of energy and therefore will attract other energies by their very concentration."

"The spiral... is the basic energy pattern of your Earth...If you have many ley lines converging at a point, it is from this point that inter-dimensional connections can be made... If you place yourself on these energy points, you will be within a connecting link of two worlds. Your dowsers know of these meeting points and are beginning to understand their significance."

"Your concern at this present time is to find these central spiral points. They are obvious places at first. These are the old ones. Then there are the new ones which are the most important to find. These will indicate the places of 8th dimensional energy. The former is 6th dimensional energy. Seven, the balancing point has governed your Earth. You will be moving into the 8th pattern."

"The Earth is being prepared to receive higher energies... If we are raising your planet to an 8 vibration, then many changes must occur on your plane. The 8 vibration will require change in the body itself, therefore many of your people are understanding foods, etc"

These transmissions started in May 1977, and the last one was February 1978. I was very struck by this material because it coincided with and amplified many points that had emerged in the study of the ley system and the finding of the Arsinal Grail. It also began to give a series of specific objectives to implement earlier instructions "to turn on" the Grail – that is, to perform that trick of the mind that seemed to activate it. I had given copies of the symbols to various people who had expressed and interest. But thus, far we had elicited comprehension of only a few of them, and a hazy understanding of their basic nature. I was satisfied that Andija's statements were correct, and I had looked further into the writing of Nicola Tesla. Joyce's transmissions indicated that the symbols were somehow important, and the idea (always in the background) that colour, form, number, frequency etc, were and are related in table of cosmic correspondences. The idea formed in my mind that one of the objectives on Good Friday must be to block the entries into the human psyche which were available to these transmitters. This became a conviction, and I thought that it might be achieved by projecting the appropriate symbols.

At the right moment, (naturally!) Joyce introduced me to John, space traveller extraordinary and expert in alphagenics. As I said earlier, alphagenics is the use of yogic techniques which enable the individual to control his own psychic state as a deliberate disciple. John showed me his "space-ship". A quite beautifully designed room in which he had incorporated, in the appropriate colours, various spirals and octagons which enabled him to go "space travelling" whenever it suited him. By the correct use of these "parcels" he could move at will through certain dimensions and "fly". I dowsed the room and found it to have 7 circles under the octagon in the ceiling and the double square rectangle in another part of the room. We talked at length about the form and frequency, he produced some tapes of some frequencies involved in the Russian transmissions. The first, he said was at a good frequency. It sounded horrible to me, and the negative symbols came up. "It sounds bad to me," he said. "There is something wrong. It is playing at a different frequency." This is interesting because my theory was getting support in an unexpected way. Then he ran through a tape in which the pulse was decreased to a level equal to the brain waves associated with the state of meditation together with a commentary. As this was proceeding, I recorded a change in the symbols of the room. Now this room was a functional point for two reasons, one because he made it so by what he had done there, and two, because there was already a single line coming into the house from the nearby church. This I had already dowsed, and when I went into the church it went into new, shining white, double cube altar in a side chapel. On the front of this, in crimson, was inscribed a "chi-rho". Par for the course, as Michael would say.

The dowsing of the symbols during the tape was reminiscent of a long-range dowse. The seven circles under the octagon in John's circles were replaced by another symbol on a small scale. These went on to become larger, and eventually produced the combination of the two symbols, resulting in yet another symbol, (as in the Church of the Holy Sepulchre, Jerusalem,) when the meditative state was reached. All this I found Corroborative, and once again it seemed to confirm a relationship between the symbols and sound, in this case highly specific. The tests which Michael had done showed that electrostatic fields could be introduced into the dowsable symbols, and I felt we had now a basis for some sort of operation involving the transmitters. I later enquired through the Elohim channel as to whether this was correct and, receiving the affirmative asked how many symbols were necessary. The answer was 12, and the symbols were then transmitted. They meant little, but I was struck by the fact that there were those which I had associated with beneficence. Moreover, there were 12, a number I had come to associate with Grail Activities, for example, Jesus and the 12, Arthur and the 12, the 12 associated with Charlemagne, Joseph of Arimathea, the 12 members of the Arundic council, and the 12 signs of the Zodiac. I felt sure it was correct to project these symbols on Good Friday, during the operation.

I noted that Joyce's transmissions were full of reference to crystal and its significance. The Grail was a crystal device. I noted also the statement about the Earth being on a cycle of 7, Traditionally related to the ley system, in the sense that 7 was a crucial factor in the parallels in multiple line, also that it was going to move to an 8 factor. "Does that mean," I enquired of the Elohim, "that the ley system will also move to an 8 factor." "Yes" was the reply. I remembered something that Trevor had said at my first talk in his flat. "There are 7 Elohim. They are sun beings. They are concerned with the creation of identity and form. Six remain on the sun, but the seventh remained on Earth as a sacrifice, and took away all those influences on Earth which would have stopped them being sensitive to the other six solar influences. He was the greatest and associated with the Moon." Based on this and similar statements. I have come to associate the Jehovah Elohim with the number 7 and the form of matter, and I retained the notion that he has a specific mission in human evolution. If a transition from a 7 rhythm to an 8 was intended, would that involve the end of his mission? As I said earlier, (I was told that this was so, and that a new entity would be called "Chloe" based on the (C with a small opening on the righthand side,) symbol. We had now established two objectives for the operation, the protection of the human psyche against psychotronic invasion, and a transition to a higher frequency, which involved the end of one era and the beginning of another.

I had to go to Spain in February. Whilst I was there, I had an urgent communication from Mary, a medium and healer whom I had met only once, and whom my brother, David knew better than I did. I was to attend a circle for an important communication. I had attended one earlier and found it interesting, but undramatic. In that occasion, I had mentioned the finding of the Grail and other associated matters. This call had some urgency. What was interesting was that she lived in a house called Avalon on St George's Hill. David and Michael,

Clementina and Fusty Bentine attended with some others of Michael's acquaintance. As before, Mary made me sit at her right, with Michael opposite at either end of a horse-shoe formation. I had received the Grail stone from Paul, who had brought it to me from Andorra. Bearing in mind Mary's heart condition, we left it in the room secretly in its container. On the first occasion, David and I noticed that, as the circle opened and developed, the 7 circles appeared, later to be surrounded by the Grail symbol. We had also noticed that a 14-bar line was running through the property, and all seemed to be well in terms of symbols. That afternoon a substantial depression had overtaken me, a fact confirmed by Michael and David when I joined them. When we joined Mary, she said the same, namely, that she had felt some form of psychic attack that afternoon. David and I went around the house, "doing our thing". The 14-bar line reappeared and the good double-square rectangle symbol. As so we began.

The first half hour was concerned with matters of a trivial and gentle nature. I took out a fragment of the Grail and placed it in Mary's hand. "Oh, that burns right through my hand!" she said. (It must be recommended that psychic heat has nothing to do with kinetic heat.) As on the previous occasion, Mary felt the room to be full of Knights Templar and Cathars. When I dowsed a place where she had previously seen a knight, I found a double-square rectangle. "Jesus is here!" she said and, addressing a Jesuit novice and an Anglican priest who were present, received their confirmation. "He is in a robe of rusty red colour and going around the circle in turn taking people by the hands." Some confirmed a feeling of cold in their hands as He came to them. He came to me. "He says you are His brother and doing His work," said Mary. "He is now putting your armour on. It is chain mail and you will need it for the further work you are to do." I looked at my hands and saw them to have a luminous "coating" over them. I have been short on psychic experience, but one or two things had been happening of late which had at once disturbed and elated me. The first had been in January at Joyce's house. She and John had gone into a "transmission condition" and for some reason had asked me to dowse the Elohim channel in response to the questions. As I stood up to dowse the answers, I shook my head, for it was as if I were in the middle of a golden snowstorm. I had closed my eyes, and when I opened them, it was still there. It was a beautiful experience. I had told Michael about this later. "That's grace," he said. "You lucky chap!"

The other time had been in Barcelona. One night, as I was going off to sleep, my vision was affected by cloud-like effects at its perimeter. At the centre of my vision, key symbols then appeared in magenta – 49-square, the spiral, the 7 circles and a whole kaleidoscope of firework effects, which were a pleasure to watch. I kept opening my eyes and shaking my head, but they persisted both with eyes open and shut. Then to the right I had seen a group of white-robed figures. I am not sure whether there were three or four, but they were certainly there. I thought about how much alcohol I had drunk that night, in case that should account for this experience. I decided that I had not had enough, and anyway it was an experience without precedent for me. Later on I had told Joyce about this, and she had reassured me that all was well. Having said all that, here I was now in Mary's circle, seeing points of luminosity over my hands and wrists, when she said that Jesus was clothing me in chain mail. By any test, I needed it. But what in earth was going on? When that phase was over, she announced that there was a giant figure in shining armour present. Others saw it too, but not me. "It's Arthur," said someone. "That's right," said Mary. Through her, Arthur said that he was calling his knights together for an important operation for England. Those present on this occasion represented and were re-living the roles of the ancient knights and were to swear their oath again.

Mary went around the group, asking each their Arthurian identity, assisting them if they were in doubt. David had brought the sword which I had bought for him in Spain, a replica, made in Toledo, of the sword of Alphonso the Wise. He had laid it on the table, at Mary's request. It was pointed, though not deliberately at Fusty, Michael's eldest daughter. During this phase, she was on the point of going into trance but abandoned it, confessing later that she had felt a very deep urge to "go off", but was somewhat scared. Mary asked me to take up the sword and take it around the circle. "Who are you, Colin?" she asked. "I have not been told," I replied. "Colin is Parsifal," said Michael. "That is right," said Mary. "You found the Grail. Now take up the sword and take it around the circle and re-swear your oath." We, did, although I must say I felt a "bit of a Charley". However, I did not want to deny the process at this point. So, I went around. She designated one member as Lancelot. Guinevere was identified. David was Sir Bedivere. The Anglican priest was Merlin's assistant, and so on. "Who were you, Michael?" asked Mary. With a gasp, Michael replied, "Mordred!" This, to say the least, was staggering as Michael is one of the gentlest and kindest souls I have ever met. He re-swore his oath. Arthur made some further remarks about the task ahead, and I returned thoughtfully to my seat, wondering what sort of ceremony I had taken part in.

What happened next was on a more mundane level, but it was still quite extraordinary. Mary's voice took on a very masculine timbre, and a wholly distinctive accent, as if she were a 1940 RAF officer. "Donald Campbell here. Arthur lets me speak. I gather you are trying to do something for England." "Hello, Donald," said Michael, for he had known him well. "How are you?" "Not too bad." "Donald, do you remember what you wanted to show me that night you took me back to your flat?" "Oh, the CBE. Well, that's not very important." "No!" said Michael, "It was something else." "Oh, the guns! Yes, Tonia sold them later. No hard feelings. She didn't feel the same about my things!" After these exchanges, he said that Arthur was saying he was taking too much time and bade us goodnight. Through Mary, Arthur re-iterated the importance of the event and what we had in mind, and the circle broke up. Michael was astonished. "No-one here could have known about that night," he said. "Donald took me back to see his father's hunting rifles." He was less impressed about his being Mordred. "I couldn't say anything else," he said. "There was this black entity behind me, and I knew it was him. "As refreshments were served, David and I did the usual survey of the gardens. I found a 49-bar line, where earlier there had only been a 14-bar line. The party relaxed, I did not know the Jesuit or the Anglican priest, but I did inform the former of my dowsing of Loyola, where the founder of his order had experienced his first vision. He did not know what to say about this, although he admitted that, at one stage in our recent proceedings, St Ignatius had been present.

Some of us went to Michael's house, where I was staying the night. Michael opened a bottle of claret, as the proper sustenance under the circumstances. Fusty explained how she had felt like going into a trance. Clementina said, "I never see things like other people! Except this dragon..." "Oh yes?" we said. "Tell us about that." "Well, there was this dragon behind me, all green, with webbed feet and breathing fire. That was when I complained of feeling cold, and Colin came over to dowse what was going on." In fact, I had dowsed around her and found a solid square which I had asked to be dispersed. "So much for those who see nothing," we said. I felt "cheesed off" because I had seen so little, except for the golden rain again and also, when Arthur was present, a sort of magenta mass which I could only describe as being like the Catholic representations of the Sacred Heart. That was the thought closest to my mind. "What about Mordred?" asked Michael. "After that everyone seemed to move away from me." I thought about that and the other events of the evening.

I had felt, before we left Mary's, that it was alright to get the Grail stone out of its box and I gave it to Mary. "Yes," she said. "You found it. This is what you have to do. At a suitable point in Glastonbury Abbey, (I had told her it had to be Glastonbury,) there is a flat place of significance." "You mean Arthur's tomb," I said. "Yes," she replied. "You will raise this stone first to the West, then to the East, then to the South and then to the North. First you will sprinkle each corner with Holy Water. Do you have any?" "I have Lourdes water," I replied. "That is alright. When you raise the stone, you will project a great arc across the sky, sealing that point as it were. But you will spend more time sealing the North. That is the critical area. Do you understand?" "Yes" I said, somewhat taken aback. "God go with you," she said. "You really did find it. At the same time, you will put one of the seals on the four horsemen of the Apocalypse."

Now we were discussing the whole affair back at Michael's. "Shall we take it seriously?" asked Michael. I thought for a moment. "I think so," I replied, "for what we have been witnesses to was not a manifestation in form of the beings concerned, but of their archetypes…. At the same time, the presence of the evil archetype of Mordred was not sad news. It was necessary. For, if we are sincere in all this. Someone must carry the diabolic archetype in preparation for the operation." Indeed, I felt happy that is was Michael, because he was the very best person to deal with it. I reasoned as follows. The whole Grail business was almost impossible to accept on conventional terms. The "Colin is Parsival," bit failed to get me into the street, grabbing passers-by by the lapels and informing them of the good news! It made me think, for that was an objective dowsable message. Certainly, we had learned a lot over the years and, if you like, learned to "draw Excalibur out of the stone". For the Grail stone had shown David first and then me how to use the weapon of light as a purely psychic weapon. But the business of "group reincarnation" did not impress me too much. What I preferred was Tom Bearden's analysis of "other world", where he made (for me at any rate) a successful attempt to align modern physics with other dimensions. Inter alia, he had made the point that you could probably reincarnate as whom you wished if you give the right wavelength. I liked this explanation, because there was no element of aspiration in it. If dear Michael was lumbered with Mordred, I could not accept that the Old Covenant was operating in his case. Indeed, I had the fancy job and he had the tough one, and if anybody deserved a fancy job, it was he.

Andrija had made a cogent point during his November talk in London, along with Tom Bearden. It was about group mind-linkage. He told us that he had been instrumental in training a group of young physicists in group mind linkage, and they had travelled together in the astral. Some very odd experiences had occurred, including unwilling teleportation, happily with no lasting effects. Some of the group had been tempted by a very real "devil" who offered money for their disaffection, again to no avail. But he made the point that a large enough group, perhaps only 100 or so people, could invade the collective unconscious and rid it of its rubbish. That is to say, they rid us of this diabolic archetype of ours, by doing some cosmic spring cleaning. Meanwhile we could replace this archetype with others of a more beneficial nature. Instantly, as he was speaking, I saw this role of the Grail Knights, not as killers of physical dragons and protectors of earthly maidens in the forests, but as highly developed psychic travelling into the great unconscious and rooting out the archetypes of evil. The "killing of the dragon" is the mythological representation of the directing of the ley energies into disciplined channels. In the same way, the Grail mission would be to change the archetypes that dominate our human subconscious. It appears possible for a well-disciplined group to travel through the great unconscious of the human race. I wrote on this theme to Andrija and Tom. I learned that a group had been disbanded which disappointed me. I felt it had to do with the Grail mission and drew Tom's attention to the points made above. When I discussed this with Andrija the possibility of a cleansing operation, he said that the members of the group had gone their separate ways, which left me with an idea, but no way of implementing it. The thought persisted in my mind that a further objective of the Glastonbury operation could be an "astral raid" of this sort in order to "sort out" the archetypes. To this extent, the experiences at Mary's had a curios validity.

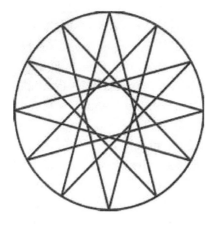

12 Point Star

Arthur appeared to be relevant. It is my view that Arthur is an aspect of the solar archetype which appears as Christ, as Albion, Frederich II, Hohenstaufen, Charlemagne, etc. It is zodiacal in the sense that most of these archetypal figures are associated with the number 12. The prophecy of Balek about the New Jerusalem in England, the re-awakening of Albion, the promise of Arthur's return and the anticipation of the Second Coming could conceivably be part of the same concept, ie the lifting of the enchantment which had fallen upon Britain and therefore upon the rest of the world. Mary has said in her sanctuary, "By doing what you are doing, you are preparing for the Second Coming." I heard her words with mixed feelings. The lunatic asylums have done a steady business in people who get involved in Messianic affairs! Yet Mary did not know that I had been to Jerusalem and "opened", under instruction, the Golden Gate, connecting the Rock of Abraham with the Mount of Olives again. If there were one chance in a million of us doing something relevant, we should all be willing to take it. Now, Blake, and Bligh Bond and others had always slightly worried me because of their predilection for Britain as being of prime importance in these affairs. It was some time before I came to realise that this was not based on some crude nationalism, but a recognition of some definite and little-known facts about early Christianity. We have seen elsewhere a claim by the Archdruid of France that the Celtic Druids, far from being bloodthirsty barbarians that Julius Caesar would have us believe, were in fact a religious group within the same tradition in which Christ manifested in Jesus. That is to say, they were Pythagorean and Essenian. As I have been able to test the Archdruids claims with respect to the ley-lines and their functions and have found them to be correct in every respect, this provides me with a basis for accepting other contentions of which I am unable to test. I have also come to accept that legend should never be dismissed. It always has something factual and important to say.

Briefly, the point I find important about the legend concerning Joseph of Arimathea are as follows:

1) Joseph of Arimathea had trading connections with the lead mines of the Mendips, had visited these islands and, on at least one occasion, had brought Jesus with him.

2) Avalon had been a centre of Druidic sanctity of which he would have been aware. It is said that after the crucifixion the first thing he did was to return to Avalon.

3) Joseph was presented with 12 hides of land, each 160 acres by (?). This was the basis of the refusal by the Celtic Church to accept papal authority later. It was claimed that Britain's bishops had unbroken apostolic succession.

One conclusion from all this would be that Avalon was a place of cardinal importance after Jerusalem in the mystery of Christ. Just as the ley-line system of Jerusalem showed it to be of prime importance, so the contention that the New Jerusalem is at Glastonbury ought to be taken seriously, with all the Bligh Bond and William Stirling implications. And here we were, under instruction to perform some sort of Grail ceremony at Glastonbury.

As I said earlier, Good Friday 1978 was not an organised event. But it drew the people who should have been there. And thus, on Maundy Thursday there arrived in Wells myself, Nick, Tammy, David, Eric Bosshard, (who had flown over especially from Washington), Michael, Fusty, Suki, Pesky, Joyce and John, to be joined in the following morning by Harold, Jill and Nancy, Bob and Veronica, Chris and Marcia. They all came because they felt they had to be there. After dinner on Thursday night, (which was devoted to human irreverence and minor hysterics), we felt it right to meet the following morning at Wells Cathedral. We were welcomed by the Cathedral staff and clerics as friends of Michael, who had done a BBC television appeal on behalf of the Cathedral the previous Christmas. In the Cathedral, I was seized again by the utter peace which that place gives me more than any other. All functioning well. I returned to the Chapter House. The vesical came up, and the fish, and I was given total confirmation to go ahead. The name Jesus surfaced. We continued round the Cathedral, as if we were being

149

prepared. As we said later, the final stage of this long-awaited event started there. It was a pretty good start to the day.

We had beer and sandwiches in the hotel lounge and drove to Glastonbury. On the way David and I noticed that we moved into a zone of continuous energy just before the hump-backed bridge which marks the border of Avalon. We came out of it on our way up to Chalice Well, where John suggested we went first for purification. We drank from the well, and John felt that the Grail stone should be washed in the well water. This we did, and thereafter no one but me touched it. It was about 3pm David and I tried to make contact with the Elohim channel, finding it extremely difficult. For a moment, I could not understand. Then I thought of the Chloe symbol. I was getting this instead of the Elohim symbol. "It's already happened," I said. David knew nothing about the shift that had been predicted, because I had forgotten to tell him about it. However, he concurred with my findings. As we approached the Tor I noticed that the symbols of two years ago were no longer there at the foot of the hill. "I expect there will be different ones there tomorrow," I said. We pressed on up the Tor. At the top there was a mighty wind which penetrated to the soul and marrow. It bore a relation neither to the ground level wind nor the overhead clouds. It seemed almost the rushing mighty wind of biblical days. The dowsable circles were functioning inside the tower. We returned to the foot, dusted ourselves off and retired to a teashop.

As we sat there it began to dawn on me that I was about one hour away from the operation towards which all the work of the last three years had been leading. I went into a "brown study", thinking of the mental projections I had decided to do. I rehearsed in a very positive way. Michael had been to the Abbey shop and had presented me with a present which I will treasure to the end of my days, a replica of a cross which had been found on the tomb identified as Arthur's. On it were the words; HIC JACET SEPULTUS IHCL ITUS REX ARTURIUS IH SULA AVALONIA, which roughly translated means, "Here lies the tomb of Arthur, King of Avalon", On an earlier visit, Michael had asked the shop to make an English silver replica of the cross and, as they had made two copies, he kindly gave me the second one. We had completed several circuits of the Abbey walls in the car and found that the huge energy field was changing, and that it changed with every circuit! The continuous zone we had noticed earlier was no longer continuous, but there were very wide areas of dowsable energy shifting around the Abbey. We tried to make sense of it. "It is a huge rotating spiral, centred on the Abbey," suggested David. I tested his statement and agreed with him. We assembled in the car park and moved into the Abbey grounds, a motley and rather dis-organised group of men, women and children. My thoughts were somewhat confused, although I was aware that, at that moment, we were not masters of our own destiny. Those who were there were volunteers in a way, but we had made no definite plans of any sort. I felt a mild sense of panic. The time was getting near, 5.20pm British Summer Time. What on earth was one to do or say? We had no established pattern for such as occasion.

The group coagulated as if by mutual consent on the Galilee, a point which John maintains is the most important in England. We stood in a circle. At that point I had promised to summarise the purpose of our visit for those who had not taken part in all previous preparations. What I said was roughly as follows:

That the objectives of the operation were -

1) To secure the proper transition to the New Age.

2) To project, through visualisation and penetration into the racial unconscious, a re-affirmation of the Grail archetype, the concept of Christ, Arthur, Albion, whole idea of solar

logic, (however it had been expressed,) as a predominant influence in the New Age, and the elimination of the evil archetype, Mordred the destroyer.

3) To protect the replacing of the seals of the four horsemen of the Apocalypse, who had unleashed demoniac forces, manifesting in the violent images in the racial consciousness.

4) The protection of the human psyche from technologically produced influences.

I made the point that if anyone did not feel able to take part in such an act, we would quite understand. No one left. I exhorted all to put on their spiritual armour. So, saying, I asked Michael to say a prayer. He asked us to join hands and he made a prayer to the Archangel Michael and all his counterparts in the celestial hierarchy, to bless our endeavours. It was the most appropriate prayer. I asked Michael to join me in going forward to the area of Arthur's tomb, in preparation for others to come and join us. I asked John to go out of the precincts of the building and seal it off. I do not know why I did this. It just seemed right.

Michael and I walked forward from the Galilee together, myself to the left and he to my right, John left to go outside. Michael and I separated by about a cricket pitch and focused on the two great columns of the ruined arch. My own sensations were ones of absolute certainty as to the validity of what we were doing. Michael and I seemed to be walking in step. I felt tall, almost as tall as the pillars we were approaching. We passed the pillars and entered the area of the tomb. I went through the discipline of purifying the area, that is to say, visualising a beam of white light from the forehead and sweeping it around the area. Michael and I then returned towards the columns and took up station by the side of each. Michael had a blackthorn walking stick with him, which he placed point down

152

between his feet, both hands on top, for all the world like a knight at vigil. I fell into a similar stance, both physically and mentally. I gave the signal for the others to join us, and they came forward. We had agreed not to speak a word during the operation. Wordlessly, they fell into a circle around Arthur's tomb. I stood to the east end, for no premeditated reason. Michael was to my left and Joyce to my right. I sprinkled Lourdes water at each of the four corners, and Harold, Jill and Chris chose to stay outside the circle. I took out the Grail stone and went through the procedure Mary had outlined, precisely, projecting the sealing of the four points of the compass, spending more time on the North.

Joyce had said earlier that day, as a result of her particular perception, that she was quite certain that as a starter to the operation we should visualise a counter clockwise spiral of energy revolving outwards and upwards from the centre of the group, that is from the stone, placed on the centre of the tomb. I therefore placed the stone on the tomb and the spiral projection commenced. I went through the projections I had rehearsed, taking the items from one to five. My sensation was of departing into some infinite region of the cosmos, a very high, and long way away. Each projection and visualisation was made. I am aware of no other recollection or impression than of doing them. I do not know how long it took but probably two or three minutes. I came back to earth and stood there in a neutral condition for a while. Tears came to my eyes and blurred my vision for a moment. I looked at Michael and he nodded. Without a word, we broke up.

As we walked away something happened which was the most moving experience of my whole life, second only to the realisation that the new line from Jerusalem's Golden Gate went to the point of the Ascension on the Mount of Olives. "Look!" said John, pointing upwards. On the centre point of three arches on the southern side of the Abbey sat a white dove. It was cooing most enthusiastically, we all watched him in a poignant moment of credulity and incredulity. "I think he approved of us," said John, "for he joined us at the very beginning. When Michael said his prayer on the Galilee, he was there above us, and two feathers fell in the centre of the circle just as we broke up. He followed us up the church and as we formed a circle, I watched him form a victory role to take up position on the arch. You know," he said to all and sundry, "that the white dove is the symbol of the Holy Spirit." "Yes," I replied, "and in every Good Friday Grail ceremony described in medieval legends, the White Dove comes down on the Grail.

We broke up into smaller groups and left the Abbey. Driving back, David and I noticed great energy bands occurring as we dowsed our route back to Wells. "I am quite sure it is a gigantic spiral," he said. We drove in a curiously voided frame of mind and drew up outside the hotel in Wells. It was in front of the Market Cross and we knew that earlier it had had a 7-barline. I dowsed it. One-two-three-four-five-six-seven, and then as a quite excruciating look of attempting the control of the rod appeared in his face…eight. "You were right," he said. So, two startling things happened that day, the arrival of the dove and the transfer to the eight.

After dinner, we all sat down to give our own versions of what we had felt and at that moment. John took notes. Michael and family left for dinner in Bath. "It's an old show business adage," he said, "take your money and run." Later he, Fusty, Pesky and Suki wrote down their versions. It is fitting that these should be recorded here. Michael confirmed by telephone that night my impression of being a knight. "I felt as if I had on a rough jerkin and chain mail, not plate armour." He had sealed off the area. Going through the columns had been like going through a portal into another space. "I also felt this was not the first time this had been done by me. There had been no rehearsal, but everyone present had known precisely what to do. I relayed Michael's comments as we sat around in a circle in the hotel lounge, before a log fire. I dowsed around the group found an 8-bar line entering from the direction of the Abbey. There was a symbol in the centre of the group. It was like the double square rectangle at first, but it continued. It was a trapezium thus:

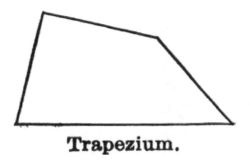

Trapezium.

Bob then told of his experiences. He had tried to go through his Kabbalistic ritual to help the proceedings. "But do you know," he said, "however hard I tried, I could not remember a word of it." All he could do was project a pentagram to the four cardinal points and a circle of fire. He received no return images, but during the high point he had felt a very cold wind on his back. David then spoke, saying he too had felt it to have been a military exercise. It had taken a very long time to walk up to Arthur's tomb. Everybody had seemed to be in step. Although it might have been suggested by earlier discussion, he had felt St Michael energy to be present. Towards the end, distinct impressions had come into his mind. The first had been a huge sword held upright over the group as if in a victory salute. The second had been of a spiral energy shooting out of the circle and circling around the earth. He felt that he had left his physical body. His spiritual armour literally felt like armour, it was smooth and soft like a space suit. It didn't come out like medieval armour, but like a space cadet armour. Eric, our man in Washington, then spoke. He felt himself to be the dummy of the group. He had felt happy on the Galilee and had

155

felt lines coming into that point from all directions. He had been the last to join the group at Arthur's tomb. He felt he would rather have stayed in the Lady Chapel. He had felt changes in the energy fields and had spinal shivers and couldn't help shuddering. He had been expecting a manifestation. (At this point, as he was speaking, I saw the "golden rain" effect in the room.) He also felt we should have linked hands around Arthur's tomb as well, but I pointed out that we had already formed the link at the Galilee. When he returned to the Altar of the Lady Chapel after the ceremony he felt, "an incredible pulsing energy." It was good and he was pulled into it. As he walked through the car park he had felt as if he were walking through a loop of a spiral which was then expanding.

Veronica, who had not really taken part in the pre-match warm-ups, had no preconceptions as to what might happen and therefore her testimony was most interesting. She too, had the strong impression of a military operation. John, whom she had seen moving off to the side to seal the exterior, had been standing very erect. She felt the approach to the tomb to have been very light, almost like flying. She had really felt and seen the spiral of light. It had emerged from the Grail stone and spiralled upwards from within a circle around the group. There was a downward spiral from the heavens which met the lower one above the church like an hourglass. The stone looked light in weight, etheric and timeless. This happened more than once. She had been impressed by the youngest group member Nancy, (Harold and Jill's daughter,) who had joined the circle. She seemed perfectly still within herself, and radiant. She then felt a strong energy come in, a neutral one, but then it joined up each person in the group and gave a great sense of well-being, with a strong movement up and down her spine. The base had become warm and this had moved up to the heart area. She had felt the sudden cold wind blow, but it had blown through her, not around her. She felt as if her body elements were separated. Then she felt her trousers flapping and she came down to the earth. Tamsin said she felt as if she were in a spiral, warm and as if she had gone on a long journey. Nick didn't seem to see or feel very much. Chris confirmed an earlier comment by Michael that he had seen the grass on the tomb change to lime green, the colour, as John pointed out, of the 8th dimension.

Joyce then gave her feelings. She had noticed there had been 17 (1+7=8) people present. There had been a processional energy and as I had walked forward it was as if I had been lifted into the air. An energy stream had arrived to fill the void in the Abbey and then moved back. When the spiral energy had started, it had been the fastest group spin she had ever seen, and she had seen a few in her day. The stone had gone rose then taken on a yellow glow, and then annex ion with another dimension had been made. Above she had seen a sort of planet in the sky with a disc around it. Its axis had been tilted. Then she had seen a pentagram, then a pyramid, then a planet like object, rather like a UFO mother ship, with open ended tubes coming out of it. She had felt very warm at that point. Then had come the cold breeze, which Bob remembered had been exactly at 5.20pm. She had dreamed of Nancy the previous night as being an 8th dimension representative.

John stated that he had been aware of a light barrier all around Avalon which, in the road from Wells to Glastonbury, is on a particular hump-back bridge. There he had noticed David and I had first started to complain of solar plexus problems and had dowsed a major energy field. He felt strongly we should go to Chalice Well where auras had been cleansed and he had had an overwhelming desire to wash the Grail stone, giving it to me thereafter, so that no other person should touch it. When we had gone up Glastonbury Tor, he felt great "Merlin" energy. He himself had balanced the energy, projecting it into a great white crucifix. While he had been alone in the tower on the Tor the powerful wind had, as it were, lifted him up.

At the Galilee, he had felt strong St Michael energy coming in from the cardinal points. He noted the white dove and the feathers falling. After we had linked hands, he had felt a procession of medieval knights on horseback coming in from the Abbot's Kitchen and going on up the Tor. He noticed that what was coming in was from the animal, vegetable and mineral kingdoms. The "Merlin" energy came from the animals, and it was as if the little animals from the woods, had gathered to watch what was going on. He too felt it wrong to go on to Arthur's Tomb, but now felt on reflection that it was probably right. As I had put holy water on the four corners, he had seen a shooting white light, after which four white horses came to appear at the four corners of the precinct where we were. They stayed only for a short period. The stone was the focus of the light. He then went "out of body", feeling very tall and looking down on the group from a great height, in company with a great congregation of the "etheric church". The spiral occurred and went on revolving. He was aware of an energy shift, as it were, tilting the earth. He saw UFO like objects in the air connecting to the Grail stone. This connection left, leaving a blue light. The stone changed to rose and gold. The Arthurian energy he felt had been closed. Then he felt that a great "thank you" had been said.

Fusty told her story thus. She remembered that in Wells Cathedral that morning she had had a distinct smell of burning wood. Later, as we moved to Arthur's Tomb at Glastonbury, she had a vague impression of being a man, that she was taller and her shoulders were slightly hunched, as happens when people are taller than their fellows. Whilst standing around the tomb, she was very cold, (a feeling only shared by others at 5.20pm when the wind blew,) and shivering violently. It was just before the circle broke up that she felt warm and at peace. As we all left the feeling of peace was emphatic, but for the next two days she was plagued with feelings of migraine and sickness. She did not feel or see things as strongly as she might have, but then due to her incipient mediumistic tendencies, referred to earlier, her subconscious was deliberately blocking out these feelings.

Suki to whom I had given the stone to carry into the Abbey grounds, said that Michael, on entry, had said he felt great power. She moved over to him and "as usual I felt nothing. Then I got a sort of tingling in my nose and mouth and I could not breathe. It was as if my throat had completely closed. I moved away and I was alright again." She said that when Michael and I moved forward to check the ground we seemed different. We walked like taller men, and when we halted, we looked as though we were on guard. Michael, she recalled and as I remembered, held his blackthorn stick down, but she said that although I held nothing that I recall that I looked as though I was holding a stone stave horizontally with arms extended downwards. When we were standing in the circle, I moved in front of her when I was putting the stone to the four points of the compass. As I stood in front of her, again she could not breath, and it reached the point where she felt she had to leave, then I moved on and it was alright, many of the others had seen her sway backwards at this point and were afraid she would fall over. She was not aware of swaying in the physical sense, although she felt it mentally. When all was normal again, she started to project the spiral, as requested, and kept feeling she was falling asleep on her feet and each time she jolted herself awake by cutting off the thoughts and opening her eyes. "When we moved away, I was really floating and just wanted to smile," She joined the group which went to the Abbot's Kitchen and, like all of them, felt it was too much and had to get out for lack of breath. "For the rest of the day I felt sleepy but really happy." She explained further that she never "sees" anything. She can distinguish the dream state, and that night as she was falling asleep a picture exploded into her mind in a flash. It was brilliant. It was a clear summers day, and there was a white castle on a green hill with a bright blue sky. Not a fairy castle but a military fort with a square tower at each end. On one tower a pennant was flying. The hill was higher than the horizon so that it was silhouetted against the sky. When she told me about it and asked me what it was, my immediate reaction was "Camelot".

Pesky shared the impression that Michael and I had been very tall men as we walked forward. It was as if to military figures had been superimposed over our persons. He too had had the impression that Michael held his blackthorn as if he was on guard. He noted Suki swaying, "as if she were in seemingly semi-trance," and twice he had thought she would fall. His last impression had been of a pastel blue light over everything. It was all pervading and cold, but not in a sinister way. After it was over, he had felt a compulsion to return to the altar of the Lady Chapel. "I am not a particularly religious person, but it seemed important to pray there. I removed my shoes and knelt with my forehead on the altar saying, "Let this be good. Let this be right." As I knelt thus, I felt warm and happy, and the stone against my forehead was warm. I felt one with the stone as with the beginning". Pesky did not know that this altar, according to John, is the most important spiritual place in England.

These are the impressions of most of the people who were present at what, on the face of it, had been a gathering of gentle, religious, occultists cranks but which, when examined in depth, may well have been and probably was a religious and spiritual act without parallel for possibly 2000 years. I do not say this out of any fanciful or "inner" awareness. My conclusion is based on results or changes that took place that day and seem, four weeks later, to be permanent changes in the ley system.

1) The 7 is now 8,

2) The line system functions on a 2-4-8-32-64 basis instead of 1-3-7-14-21-28-42-49 basis.

3) The spirals in the earth temples in the South Downs changed to a circle containing 7 circles. The spiral has disappeared. The dragon had been slain.

4) The symbols I had dowsed two years ago, at the foot of Glastonbury Tor had changed.

The next day in Glastonbury we went to the Abbey grounds and checked everything out. As we moved near the altar in the Lady Chapel, John again pointed out its significance and the fact that one should only move behind it with permission. I sought and obtained such a permission and noted that there was a 64-bar line in that confined space. Oddly enough, above and going to Arthur's Tomb was a 16-bar line.

We went onto the Tor and while John and Eric went up, I dowsed the symbols at the foot, having noticed that the previous morning there had been nothing. John then felt he should go up Wearyall Hill, where Joseph of Arimathea rested on his way to Glastonbury. There he planted his staff on the ground and it grew and leafed into the Glastonbury Thorn, which botanist say is a type of thorn that grows in the Middle East. This was where he felt a new energy coming in. Certainly, I could dowse it, a broad swathe coming down the hill. We went to Wells, noticing again the huge spiral effect that seemed to be emerging from Glastonbury. On the way, back to Brighton, I stopped to check the Wolstenbury lines. The singles were all double and the triple a four, so it had reached there. Later Eric reported similar phenomenon from the U.S. and Fred the same from Spain. I found the changed the ram's horn effect, but the 7 circles in the flat remained the same. The Elohim symbol had definitely gone to be replaced by the Chloe symbol.

So, what had we done? Apart from the inference that we were an innocent band of pleasantly harmless folk fantasizing an occult romance, one had to face the fact that the dowsing results showed everything to be different. Therefore, my conclusion is that at least some of the objectives of the exercise were achieved. It is arguable that we had little free will in the matter, and we might as well have been hired hands performing a cosmic puppet show which was inevitable, with a script written by others. I wonder. I had often felt this to be the case, but I had never any doubt that we were going to go through with it, and the question of what would happen if we didn't go through with it seemed both apposite and irrelevant at the same time.

I reasoned thus. The shift from a factor 7 to a factor of 8 had taken place. On the face of it, human consciousness had moved one stage up the scale. What did it mean in practical terms? We had to bear in mind that occult tradition in general, and the Revelation of St John and the account of Genesis in particular, had indicated that the basic rhythm of the earth was on a 7 frequency. What would happen if it were now on an 8, 8 being the number of infinity, a good number for the Aquarian Age. The first thought that occurred to me was that, whereas the basic bio-rhythms were on a 7 in the past – the 7 days a week, no one could expect this to change – however, perhaps the fact that the ley system no longer reflected this indicated that man's higher self could escape from this rhythm. I also reflected that whereas I had at last made sense of the Elohim symbol, now one had to cope with the Chloe symbol, a circle with the 1.30 to 2.30 section missing. What could this mean? I do not know, nor can I surmise. The significance of this symbol will become apparent in the next Age. It is no wonder to me that David was having problems with his old friends in the Celestial Hierarchy. On Kabbalistic level their numerological function had been changed, consequently even their names might change. Perhaps a new Revelation is necessary and a whole new nomenclature and identification of Function. Perhaps

David has to do this. A whole new divine cosmology may be necessary.

As to the other objectives of the operation, time alone will tell. I hope and pray they work. Perhaps the new age will spark off a new and general awareness of the Christ spirit in everyone which will bring to an end the current struggle between Marxism and a democratic freedom which is purposeless. Perhaps the time has come when political leaders can lead men to the stars instead of to the trough or the dole queue, when the subjugation of the individual to the state bureaucracy or the search for material satisfaction can be replaced by a conscious search for spiritual fulfilment in a new relationship with the cosmos. Fervently I hope so.

Tuscany, The Tibetans Have Come

"The Tibetans have come," Joyce said to me one day, her eyes lighting up with excitement. "They have come to Pomeia, just up the road from my house in Tuscany. They are setting up a Buddhist Monastery." She asked me to map dowse the area, which I did. "Your house is on a double 64-bar line," I said, "and it connects to your new Buddhist neighbours. There are a few places in the world that are on a double-64. I'd better come down and look at it all." Our Italian company was having it's A.G.M. which I was to attend, so I was able to spend the weekend before the meeting down there. I fell out of a cloudy, grey and damp London to a cloudy grey and damp Pisa. Joyce met me. Firstly, we went to Pisa Cathedral. I wanted to check that it was functioning as I had left it the previous autumn. It was. However, in the Cathedral as we were wandering around, we were looking again at the black and white symbols on the floor. For some reason, we were drawn to one symbol. It was very charged up. It was the only one where I got a reaction on the outside square. It

163

was one of perhaps 50. Joyce with her particular way of seeing things, said, "There is something going on in this one." I tried to enter it and found myself somehow dislocated each time I tried to go in. It was as if one were suddenly dizzy. I made three attempts and finally burst into the centre circle. It contained the 7 circles. Joyce joined me. "What's all this about?" she asked. "I think I know," I said, "and its why I wanted to come to the Cathedral first. We must have these 7 circles moved up to your house (about 40 kilometres away). I'll tell you why in a minute. Please join in an invocation and visualisation with me to get it shifted." We did it and it was dispersed.

I should add in this context, that according to my map dowsing, the line on Joyce's property was from Siena Cathedral to Pisa Cathedral, so we were sending the 7 circles up the line, as it were. When I had map dowsed her property and found it to be on a double 64-bar line, this had struck me forcibly with some significance. The other places where I had found it were between the pyramids of Cheops and Kefren, between the Citadel of David and the Shrine of the Book at Jerusalem, and along the Dragon Line of England. As I also dowsed that the double-line was only in the immediate vicinity of Joyce's property, and elsewhere continued as a single 64-bar line, what could be the significance of Joyce, Tibetan Buddhists and our association with her? Then it came to me. Of course, Mount Pamir was the terminal for this line. Mount Pamir in the Himalayas was the Mount Meru of the Buddhists, from which the Sacred Knowledge flowed, and where the 33 gods of the Buddhist Tantric system dwelt. I had often wanted to conduct a long-range operation to cut off the Ahrimanic influences from that mountain which flowed into the ley system, but I was always told "not yet". I remembered that the time was quoted by the Elohim as the Spring of 1978. I enquired of Chloe if the operation had to be carried out at Pomela during the visit and was told yes. I discussed this with David, and he agreed to join in at 11pm on Saturday, 6th May 1978,

Earlier that week, he and I had conducted some apparently interesting experiments. Ever since he had sent me the 7 circles as a result of the projection of the triple line from Beckenham to Brighton, and we had learned how to use the 7 circles without using any artefact, we had simply used it in this way. The weekend before, however, he had come to stay at Brighton, and we had been discussing the Radive experiments in recording spirit voices out of nowhere and I had idly switched on the tape recorder to see if we could get anything. I played the tape back and there was nothing. I dowsed around the room and said to David that the operational lines we had been working on from the 7 circles all seemed bigger. When we switched off the tape they returned to "normal". I didn't think too much of this, but David seized on it and pointed out to me later that week that I had unwittingly demonstrated something of vital importance. Whereas we had shown over a year before, to our own satisfaction, that a sequence of symbols could be recorded on tape and replayed so that they were dowsable around the recorder, it now appeared that recording in the presence of a line affected that line when the recording was replayed.

David phoned me to give me some indication of this and, before telling me the whole story, asked me to take part in some further experiments. He asked me to dowse again the line that was coming from him in Beckenham to me in Brighton. It started its life as a triple, then after Glastonbury I had noted it had become a 32-bar line, although neither of us could give a reason. In order to check that it was the same line, David had run an earlier test to boost it to a 64-bar line which I had dowsed, and which had satisfied us to its provenance. He had done this by invocation. When I checked this again at his request, it was a double 64-bar line with a single line on

165

either side of each 64. He asked me to check again, and it had become a triple 64, each with a single line on either side. I reported this to him, remarking that the only other place I had found such a phenomenon was when I had done a survey of the U.S. Air Base at Torrejon, Madrid, where nuclear weapons are stored. The combination of lines converging on what I took to be the nuclear arsenal had this single line on either side. "Anyway, what were you doing?" I asked. He told me that he had recorded a blank tape on the 64-bar line and replayed it. This had doubled it up. He had then played another similar recorded tape, which had been the apparent cause of tripling it. We did not know what this meant, but once again I felt we had made another fundamentally important discovery, which we would doubtless come to understand later.

Anyway, there we were, Joyce and I, on our way to her property in Pomeia in Tuscany. We arrived in the early evening. She lived in a modernised farmhouse with a great sweeping view of the Tuscan hills. The first thing I set out to do was check out whether the map dowsing of the double 64-bar line was correct. On the way in we had passed the Buddhist monastery and I picked up that the lines were certainly passing through it. I took the angle. Joyce's house had a 64-bar line at the either end of the rectangular shape. The house faced east-west. Thus far, the map dowsing had again shown itself to be correct. I went looking for the 7 circles. Eventually I found them, superimposed over a triangular table at which she wrote her books. Neither line passed through the circles. 11pm was soon upon us and we prepared to join David in the operation. I checked the 64-bar lines and found a single line on either side. I concluded that David was operationally with us. We made the invocation, which followed the usual form, and with the objective of ensuring that only love and light flowed down that line from Mount Pamir, which aliments Europe, the Middle East and Africa. I immediately dowsed the house again. The double 64-bar line had come together on the 7 circles.

166

The next morning, I set out to find why Joyce, who had had visions of the Grail stone and its function and was impelled to come to the talk at Trevor's, had acquired a property in such remarkable circumstances, and why the Tibetan's had come to this particular place. I checked the garden and found that she had two spirals going for her, which was a unique in my experience. But Joyce had always stated that when she went on her "trips" she "spiralled". Anyway, here was some correlation. I checked the alignment of the 64-bar lines. From the garden, one could see the Buddhist monastery, a neo-Renaissance castle on a hill about 500 metres away. However, the lines did not go exactly in that direction, neither did the direction of the lines from the monastery go towards Joyce's farmhouse. There was a "dog leg" somewhere. I spotted a conical hill which might account for it. We set off across country to explore, follow up the lines and call upon the Buddhists. Between Joyce and the Buddhists was a valley and a large country house. We followed the lines and eventually they diverged from my roughly observed alignment to the conical hill. We had lost them. Then over to the left I observed, at the end of an avenue of pines leading from the country house, an octagonal building. "On no," I said to Joyce, "here we go again." We moved over to it and noted that it was a Christian monument with a cross on top. It was on two levels. The top level was closed by wooden doors but the bottom level was accessible to the eye through a metal grill door. Faded flowers and a crucifix indicated it to be some sort of chapel. The lines were on it, uniting at that point to indicate some functional nature. They continued on to connect to the Buddhists.

We set off across the valley and eventually arrived at the Instituto Lama Tyong Khapa. We walked up the drive and came to a large castle type construction clearly in the throes of renovation. Sounds of luncheon came from one room, and a little child played in some sand. We took advantage of this to check the lines coming in, which they did, and on the other side in a sort of the courtyard they came together on a large pool of water, a well or a fountain in a state of disrepair. They separated to converge again within a high walled garden where the circular foundations of an earlier construction, which I took to be a gazebo or summer house, could be seen, the 7 circles were perceptible. The lines then separated and went through a new, but not quite finished, villa. We wandered a bit more and then a girl in a type of nun's habit came out and courteously enquired our business. We explained that we had come to visit them as Joyce was a neighbour and we were interested in their coming to Pomeia. Joyce explained she had spent time in a Tibetan Buddhist monastery in Scotland and that she was into transcendental meditation. The girl's face lit up. "You'd better come in." We entered the temporary refectory to find a group of about a dozen finishing lunch. They were all Italians with the exception of an American, the mother of the child and wife of the leader, Massimo. We were made welcome, offered tea, and sat down to talk, they explained that they were Buddhist converts who were setting up a monastery to which Tibetan Lamas would come to live. They expected the Dalai Lama to come and see them soon. The new house that we had seen was for the resident Lama.

Carol was a gentle, peaceful girl, and a perfect complement to her husband. Both radiated an inner peace and tranquillity which made me envious. They showed us around, taking us to their meditation room, a temple where one took one's shoes off. It was lovely, a golden statue of the Buddha and a side altar on which food offerings were placed. Cushions indicated the place at which each neophyte attended service. I dowsed it. In the centre was the symbol, the new Elohim resolved symbol. Massimo took us into the gardens. Joyce explained that I was a dowser, a fact that left them puzzled but relatively unmoved. As I explained a little of the line system, it was quite apparent that they had no idea at all about it, even when I said that the line they were on could be traced to their Mount Meru. However, one thing struck me as interesting. Massimo indicated that the circular foundations we had noticed in the garden, where I had dowsed 7 circles, was the place they had chosen to build a meditation centre or oratory. I explained to him what I had found. "Why did you choose it?" I asked. "It just feels right," was his reply, which perhaps may be a good piece of evidence to suggest that the ley system and symbols are perceived in different ways by different people.

When they came to tea at Joyce's, I asked Massimo why they had chosen this particular property. "Well" he said, "we had several possibilities in the general area, but we asked the Tibetans, they said that although the others were OK, Pomeia was a situation we could never better." They had been to look at it the previous year and approved of its acquisition, which made me think that the Tibetans knew a thing or two. They had chosen to come to Pomeia and chant on the double 64 line there, the line that ran from Mount Pamir – Tehran- Babylon – Jerusalem – Cyprus – Rhodes – Santorini – Delphi – Athens – Eleusis – Corfu – Brandisi – Rome Vatican – Siena – Pisa – Genoa – Nice – Marseilles – Arles – Narbonnes, splitting into three, one via Barcelona to the south of Spain via the huge modern pyramid at Figueras, the other via Rennes le Chateau – Seo de Urgal – Saragossa – Madrid – Escurial – Yuste – Tomar – Cintra, with a branch at Seo to San Juan de la Pena (Grail Monastery) – Pamplona and on to Santiago de Compostela. It would be interesting to see the results.

As we talked later, Joyce pointed out that the Tibetans were directly concerned with changing vibrations and their objective was to advance this process as far across the earth as they could. "I'd be delighted to work with them," I said, "We seem to be in the same business. I would like to talk about it to the Lamas when they come." "Oh, they won't talk to you about it," she said, "You would have to communicate telepathically. They will talk about the weather and the crops, but never about these things. Telepathy is the means of keeping the whole matter safe from profane minds." I look forward to such a meeting and seeing if I scored at all on the telepathic wavelength.

So much for close encounters with Tibetan Buddhists. That night some odd things stated to happen. As we stood on the terrace in front of the house, with a clear sky and bright stars, we fell to talking idly of UFO's. "Why don't you arrange for one to land here?" I said, "I have many questions I would like to ask." "Have you seen one?" said Joyce. I once saw a light moving high and fast across the sky, shortly after the launching of Sputnik I, I took it to be another satellite, but it might not have been. Why don't they send another one now?" I said laughingly. Within seconds, a similar light moved across the sky from right to left. "It was just like that," I said. We watched it. I do not believe it was an aircraft. It was a single continually glowing light, with no noise, and apparently higher than aircraft fly, and therefore moving pretty fast, just as I suppose a satellite does. "Well that was nice," I went on, "What about another in the opposite direction?" It appeared on the same trajectory but from left to right. "How obliging," I said, "Thanks, friends." Then I said, "Could we have a shooting star now?" Within 15 seconds, it burst over our heads. Fortunately, there was no feather available to knock me over with. "Satisfied," said Joyce. I thought about this strange encounter, and reflected that coincidence was a strange thing and we had seen two satellites. After all there were plenty up there. The next evening, we stood in the same place. "How about another show?" I asked. The first one appeared again within seconds. I thanked them. "Next one, please." It came from left to right. It seemed identical to the others, with one notable exception. As it flew into the box of Ursa Major, it disappeared in the centre. I looked carefully. There was no cloud behind which it could have gone. It simply disappeared in the centre of Ursa Major, the Grail Constellation. "Fair," I thought. And the possibility of these having been satellite sightings began to recede in my mind.

The following evening, we were in the same place discussing the symbology of the Grail, particularly in relation to the odd photograph with the orb I had taken at Hamsey at the very beginning. "The Grail on the one level is a dynamic but balanced opposition of masculine and feminine energies." It was a cloudy night and as I spoke the clouds parted for a brief second to reveal the faintest sliver of a crescent moon. "There you are," I said, "the female Grail symbol." A convenient cosmic visual aid. Then I realised that the new moon lay exactly in the trajectory of the UFO's (in the literal sense) we had seen on the previous two nights.

Our penultimate expedition was to look closer at the adjacent country house and octagonal chapel to see what reason there might be for its being a functional point in the double 64 arrangements in the area. The lady who "did" for Joyce also "did" for the lady of that house and she was away. Adriana was only too pleased to show us around. We followed the lines into the garden. They converged onto a circular pool. "Par for the course," I observed, thinking of Michael. From there they went into the house, most of which was closed, so we could not see too much. I noticed a 4-bar line coming out of the front door, and when I followed it for about 20 yards, it ended in a rough-cut cubic stone. "Another bogey", I thought. We followed the lines away from the house, down the avenue of pine trees to the octagonal chapel. Adriana had the key. We entered. It was a mausoleum. The family tombs were there above the chapel below. I checked if we were not welcome. It appeared we were not. I noticed that the principle tomb indicated that the occupant had been a Knight of the Order of the Crown of Italy, an order I knew nothing about, but resolved to find out more. We thanked Adriana and left. On the way, Joyce and I pondered what the family knew and why they had locked themselves thus into the system. We had no answer but resolved to investigate further in due time.

Our last expedition was to the Sleeping Dragon. I had been looking over the landscape in front of Joyce's house. The back of it was on to mountains, but the front gave on to rolling hills. The first of which was a long ridge like the Hog's Back near Guildford. "You've got a Sleeping Dragon there," I said to Joyce, thing of Stephen Feuchtwang's "Chinese Geomancy", "I think that we should wake it up." I figured the head to be very much in the area of Joyce's property and we resolved to walk down the spine to see what there was. About the point that would equate to the 4th vertebra, we came upon an excavation which reminded me of a dewpond, except that it was square. I went down and in, for it was dry. The symbol was evident, and a 4-bar line was passing through it. On the other side was a most strange square tower, about 4ft each way, and 6ft high. It was surmounted by a pyramid about 3 ft high. This I rated a "birdie". It topped a shaft down which one could look and see the bottom of the sluice gate. "This is part of some old water system," I remarked. From the pyramid tower the 4-bar line split into two. "Come on," I said to Joyce, "Let's wake up the Dragon," for I checked earlier with Chloe that this was desirable. We made the necessary invocation. The two 4-bar line became 64-bar lines, one proceeding down the spine, the other to the left and down to a tower which we could not investigate. It was reminiscent of waterworks towers in London – rectangular. We later established that this line went to an alabaster mine, still worked but dating from Etruscan times. It bounced off the face and came out again. What this had to do with a pyramid capped well shaft and the 4th vertebra of a Chinese Dragon I may one day learn. We felt that we had probably done as good a job as we could in activating that area for the Lamas when they came. We took aromatic plants on the way back for Joyce's garden. A long black and yellow dotted snake uncoiled itself from its morning slumbers in front of us and made off.

The last night of my stay Joyce, at my request, went into trance. As she was counting herself in, it was announced that a new group of intelligences was communicating. The burden of their message was as follows. Things had gone well at Glastonbury, but even more energies were going to come in – a new wind came from the north which we could recognise when it came. We were doing pretty well in our conclusions and efforts. In the next six months, my life was going to change dramatically, ("Oh no, not again," I groaned inwardly.) Will that be bad?" I asked. "No, but demanding", was the answer. There were other things I should have taken notes but didn't. Things seemed to be going according to the Glastonbury exercise. The Tibetans were good news. Several Delphic remarks were made, and Joyce counted herself back in. She was interested that a new lot had communicated and that a new mind was to enter. We ate and pondered.

The next morning, I left for Milan, reflecting that Joyce's path crossing mine was no accident. It was equally no accident that she had acquired property on a double 64-bar line before she had any inkling of the significance of such technicalities and that the Tibetans had come, which was probably the most important thing of all. We had established most friendly relations with the advance guard. UFO's had appeared in the sky on request, as well as a shooting star. We were on the brink of a new dimension of a great adventure that had no end. It was good.

The Americas

A TWA 747 took me, in November 1979, to New York. Over the Atlantic on the Great Circle route, I dowsed at regular intervals and found nothing. Having been wished a good day at various times and asked how I was, by every member of the cabin staff, we flew in over Long Island. Instantly one was aware of active line energies. This was fascinating for, although Eric had told me about the ley system in Washington, this was the first time I had personally dowsed the American Continent, although this was not my first visit. It was very busy but I noted nothing special. On the taxi ride into New York, I found nothing. I had thought about New York for some time and one thing had struck me. The twin obelisk of Cleopatra's Needle in London was in Central Park and, bearing in mind the relevance of the European obelisks to key sites, I was certain in my own mind that Central Park obelisk should be integrated.

Having installed myself in my hotel, I telephoned Hilda, a friend of Joyce's, whom she said I should meet. She greeted me with enthusiasm. I took her to dinner, and we talked at length about subjects of mutual interest. I explained to her how I had found New York to be dead, like Lourdes. We concluded that it was the flagrant commercialism, as I have sought to describe elsewhere. Having established our mutual credentials to each other's satisfaction, I asked if I might go to her flat to say the invocation on her terrace. She agreed instantly. It was on the 19th floor overlooking the centre of Manhattan. I am sure all the film shots of the city must be taken from there! It was perfect. It was 10.30pm local time. We said the necessary invocation and at that moment a puff of smoke appeared opposite. Hilda was quite taken aback. We were pretty certain it was from a conventional source, but it was on cue.

As it was 5.30am for me, I fled back to the hotel. On the way I noticed that there were lines where they should be, including one big one coming out of Central Park. Next morning, I went for a walk in Central Park to find the Obelisk. One notices in Central Park outcrops of rock and some individual rocks standing free, very large ones. On a knoll within an octagonal surround was an octagonal building some 20 yards across. People were sleeping in it. It seemed to be s shelter for the homeless. It had 8-bar line in it. As I progressed through the Park, it became apparent that certain sections were laid out geomantically – octagonal fountains, avenues, bandstands, etc. Finally, we arrived at Cleopatra's Needle, the twin of that in London, all the way from Heliopolis. It was functioning on a cross of 64-bar lines. It checked with the one I found coming out of the Park the previous night. The other axis was on the Metropolitan Museum of Art, where in a new wing a whole Egyptian Temple had just been erected, the Temple of Dendur. Indeed, the Museum has over 45,000 objects from Ancient Egypt. I asked for the name of the presiding entity and came up with Thoth as in London. I moved on. "Some people get mugged here, even in the morning," said a driver of the taxi which took me back to the hotel. Anyway, there is was, the obelisk of Heliopolis was functioning in Central Park.

That evening I telephoned Hilda. "Hey, what did you do?" she asked. "All my friends are phoning up and telling me that they had strange dreams last night. One of them even passed out. I had some very odd dreams too and slept badly." I pointed out that, as Athene Williams once commented, "You can't tweak the devil's tail and not get a backlash!" and this operation of ours had been somewhat more than a "tweaking". Hilda seemed pleased by it all and promised to observe events in the next few weeks and report to me. Time permitted little further observation in New York, but I did notice that St Patrick's Cathedral, a pleasant neo-Gothic edifice, had now got itself on a 64-bar line which passed through the Rockerfeller Centre. There was not time to determine where it linked with the systems on the obelisk. Many of the main thoroughfares of New York City now had fairly heavy lines running down them. It all seemed good. I was told everything was OK and the Chloe sign came up. It was time to go.

A flight from La Guardia took me into the near heart of Washington, where Eric was waiting for me. He levered me into his Volkswagen, and we were soon in his house on Capitol Hill, drinking white wine. It was evening by now and on the way in I had seen, illuminated, the great obelisk that is the Washington Monument, and also the Lincoln and Jefferson Memorials. All were emitting lines. The Capitol itself was pushing out a big one. Obviously, Washington was functioning, and in a way which one might have expected. Now we had to see how. Eric started briefing me on the situation and we made plans for the following day over dinner. We would have breakfast with Christopher Bird, co-author of "The Secret Life of Plants," and commentator on dowsing affairs generally. Then, in the few hours available, we would tour all the places in Washington which we held to be important. Next morning, we drove over to Georgetown, where Chris lived. Washington was a far more beautiful city than I had imagined, and Georgetown is a delightful period suburb. I met Chris before in London at Trevor Ravenscroft's. They were like twins – both heavy set and bearded, with deep voices. Trevor had let Chris read some of my writings and when we met in London he had looked at me with curiosity, puzzled at the sort of person who had written the strange material he had read. We met again with pleasure. He observed "This man has written the craziest material I have ever read!" We exchanged pleasantries and went to a good American breakfast at a nearby "eatery."

Then we went through the great park at the edge of the city to the first point on Eric's itinerary, the new Mormon Temple, some twelve miles from the centre. It was pure Walt Disney, a huge hexagonal iced cake! We entered the lobby. A white suited official was behind the desk. He carefully explained to us that we could not visit the

Temple as we were non-believers and not "Elders" of the Sect. Elsewhere I have tried to enter Mormon temples and always received the same reply. It was on a cross of 64-bar lines. We moved round it until we came to a flower bed at the rear. There, picked out in the flower beds with little shrubs as a border, was the double rectangle within a raised octagonal platform. It was prominent and obviously deliberate. This was not an idle fancy. The Mormons clearly have an architect's department in Salt Lake City that has some comprehension of our subject. I have dowsed two Mormon temples in London, and their U.K Headquarters in Lingfield, Sussex, and they all exhibit important lines, depending on their size. They are building many such temples in many lands. We noted the direction of two of the lines on the Washington Temple. One went on the Walter Read Army Centre and the other to the U.S. Navy Medical Centre. Why?

We drove back into Washington, and circled the White House, where I was able to pick up a 64-bar line emerging in an oblique line with the Washington Monument Obelisk. Lesser Lines emerged at right angles. One went to Blair House nearby where, at that very moment, Israeli and Egyptian delegations were still locked in their epic struggle for peace. I went through the necessary disciplines and a 64-bar line replaced the smaller. We remarked that it was now nearly lunchtime. "Fine," said Eric, "we will lunch in the cafeteria used by the House of Representatives." I noticed that this building was connected to the Capitol by a minor line. After lunch Eric and I went to the Capitol, where I found at each corner a double 8, a heavier version (I assumed) of the double 4. This had replaced an earlier line, noted by Eric, which had been a line of unfortunate influence. Down the main axis of the whole central system of Washington (laid out by the French Architect, Pierre L'Enfant,) we established that there ran a double 64-line, merging from time to time into a single. From the Capitol, it emerged as two 32's which focused on an octagonal fountain on the near side, continuing as a 64 down the main axis. The double 8's followed avenues which approached the Capitol in the form of a St Andrews Cross. We went inside and wandered around. It is a beautiful building. Wren himself would have been proud of it. Its proportions are satisfying. In the galleries, the mosaics on the floor incorporate motifs which may be found in the cathedrals of Europe – zodiacal and esoteric. When one looks into its architectural history one finds it laden with Masonic overtones. George Washington and Pierre L'Enfant selected the site and at first their choice was much criticised. But one morning in 1791 they rode around the swampy area on horseback and L'Enfant declared, "I could discover no one situation so advantageously to greet the congressional building as is that on the west side of Jenkins Heights. It stands as a pedestal awaiting a monument." The senior Mason, George Washington, agreed with him, and a competition was launched for a design for the building.

What the official records do not state is that they had chosen a sacred site of the Indians and that it contained a sacred well, conserved to this day. Another interesting thing to note is that the stones of the building reveal the same Mason's marks as those found in European cathedrals. A design by Dr William Thornton won the contest, and on 18th September 1793 the cornerstone was laid. This was done with due Masonic ceremony by George Washington, as President and acting Grand Master of Maryland's Grand Lodge, together with representatives of other Grand Lodges in neighbouring states. George Washington wore for the ceremony a Masonic apron said to have been made for him by the wife of General Lafayette, (himself a Mason,) and conducted the ceremony with a marble headed gavel and a silver trowel. The ceremony ended with prayers, Masonic chanting Honours and a fifteen volley from the Artillery. Through various vicissitudes and professional bickerings the building progressed. So did the building of the White House, sited by

L'Enfant, and on 22nd November 1800, President John Adams addressed the Senate for the first time in the completed Capitol. It was shamefully burnt by the British in 1814 and the destruction would have been complete but for a rainstorm which extinguished the fire. The windstorm that followed killed 30 British soldiers and blew cannon off their mounts. This coupled with the accidental explosion of the gunpowder store, so demoralised the British that they left Washington, never to return. Jefferson's chosen architect, Latrobe, another Frenchman, began work of reconstruction, and it was an American born Charles Bullfinch, who completed the designs of Thornton and Latrobe, including the central rotunda. The cornerstone for the Capitol's central section was laid on 24th August 1818. On 24th October 1824, it was completed in time for a gala reception for the Marquis de Lafayette.

We went to the rotunda and found the eight circles with a section missing in the direction of the Washington Monument, just as we found with the dome of St Peter's in Rome. We went through the necessary discipline and it was replaced. Walking around the building afterwards we found that the double 8's had become 32's and we felt things generally to be in order. From there we went to the great obelisk of the Washington Memorial. Having noted that Amon-Ra had provided the obelisk in New York, it was interesting to observe that this Washington one was an entirely modern creation. While the Washington obelisk is on a cross of 64-bar lines, it is not geodetically central to the White House, although the line does connect the two. At the point where logically, the Monument should stand is a small markstone which also connects to the White Hose by a 4-bar line. All was in order and we left. However, one or two historical facts about the Washington obelisk ought to be pointed out. The cornerstone was laid on the 4th July 1848. Benjamin French, Grand Master of the District of Columbia Masonic Lodge, consecrated the cornerstone, wearing the same apron and sash that

George Washington wore at the Capitol ceremony 55 years earlier. The new Monument was paid for by public subscription and the amount took some years to raise. It was apt that a man of such Masonic associations should have an obelisk for his monument although, of course, no modern capital city should be without one. It is odd too that Washington's home at Mount Vernon should have been surmounted by an octagonal tower and that his so-called simple tomb should have a Gothic arch as its entrance and be surrounded by obelisks. Benjamin Franklin and Thomas Jefferson would have understood. Another interesting point to note is that the Great Seal of the United States has on its reverse side the pyramid with the all-seeing eye.

The Washington obelisk is the largest in the world. From 1848 onwards stones were sent from various states in the Union and from other nations, Greece sent a piece of white marble from the Parthenon. A group of Chinese Christians sent a stone covered with oriental characters. Pope Pius IX sent a slab from the Temple of Concord in Rome, but this oddly was stolen from the site in 1854 and was never recovered, The Sultan of Turkey contributed a stone. So did Brazil which has its own obelisk in Sao Paulo. When Eric was an engineer for the Washington Metro, he recalls there was a standing order for all those engaged in the tunnelling to report any odd slabs of marble they might find. Work on the obelisk was halted during the Civil War, but it was finally completed in 1884. It is 555 ft high. We left this impressive monument and proceeded to the end of L'Enfant Grand Avenue, passing the Greek temple, which is Lincoln Memorial, itself on a cross of 64-bar lines. From here there is a bridge across the Potomac diagonal to the Monument. This is the Arlington Memorial Bridge, leading to the Arlington Memorial Cemetery. Thence we went, our intention being to visit the tomb of John F Kennedy. The 64-bar line from the cross on the Lincoln Memorial crosses this bridge.

It was late on a chilly evening of the Washington fall. Eric had been there previously and had expressed himself unhappy with the energies he had dowsed there. We arrived at the simple tomb with the permanent flame. Kennedy is one of my heroes, a regard which has not been dimmed by the later reports concerning his private life. This is not the place to enter into a profound diagnosis of his presidency. Suffice it to say that, for me, he was a solar figure, bringing light, hope and panache to the world. John Kennedy brought light into the affairs of the United States. He did initiate a process which has given reality to the citizenship of the black minorities. He did restore dignity and honour to the Presidency and re-establish its ideals, in the eyes of its foreign friends at any rate. He did open up the energies of pride in country rather than nationalism, decency in the world instead of domination. Interest in art, not the hamburger. He brought glamour, in a very real sense to an otherwise gloomy institution. The U.S. President can release good or bad energies. John Kennedy released good ones. Thus, the world mourned his death as for no other leader. When he was killed, as Jules Feiffer has commented, something died in the American psyche. And he has an eternal flame over his grave. Why? How? We were pondering this as we proceeded to the spot.

The simple grave of John F Kennedy reminded me of the apparent simplicity of that of Winston Churchill, (whom Kennedy so graciously received before the joint Houses as an Honorary Citizen of the United States). Churchill's grave which he chose himself, is on the main axis of Blenheim Palace and thus the discerning can see that the whole Blenheim complex is Churchill's monument. We do not know exactly how Kennedy's grave was chosen, but it is on the main axis of the Arlington Memorial Bridge which goes directly to the Lincoln Memorial. Thus, likewise it is no simple tomb, and it lies on the 64-bar line to the Memorial. It was thus that we approached it. It is flat within a shrubbed compound and with a sort of circular piazza on the wall of which are engraved some of his better-known sayings. "Banalities!" said Eric. "I don't know," I replied, "They strike plenty of chords around the world." Eric dowses somewhat differently from me and he found some three-dimensional pyramidal forms in front of the tomb. I noticed that the line stopped on the piazza and did not enter or leave the tomb. Where Eric had found the pyramidal forms, I found negative symbols. We went through the disciplines and the positive symbol appeared. The line now entered the tomb. Eric reeled from the energy, for he feels it more in the body than I do. Time was running out, but we had time to notice Robert Kennedy's grave nearby, and that of Pierre L'Enfant above and in front of Robert E Lee's house, (now part of the cemetery). We left, musing as to what qualifies a U.S. President for burial in that spot and how the whole history of Washington was Masonic in its overtones and its forms.

Soon we were en route for Miami, out over the sea and into the dreaded Bermuda Triangle. I could dowse nothing until we came in over the coast at Miami Beach, when we entered a zone of energy wider than any I had previously encountered, running parallel to the coast. After a few days in Miami, I was en route for Mexico City, which I did via Dallas, where a change of planes was necessary. On the way we flew over the Everglades, and I could find nothing there. I wondered, therefore, were the lines evidence of human civilisation? From Dallas, where there were plenty of lines, we flew across the Bay of Mexico to Mexico City, where there were none that I could find by casual dowsing. As we went on into Mexico they started again.

Our agent collected me at my hotel the following morning to take me to one of the major objectives of the journey, the pyramids of Mexico City. Elizabeth Maas, a gentle and courteous lady, drove me out to the pyramids. We had not met before, but we had a long-standing commercial relationship. I thought I had better explain why it was that my hand was moving across my body from time to time for no obvious reason. She took it all in her stride when I explained my method of dowsing. "I shall have an interesting day!" she said. As we approached the general pyramid complex, I noticed a 64-bar line coming off in the direction of Mexico City. We went on and alighted so that I could do work on foot. It was hard work as the area is large and it took most of the day. The main axis was a 64-bar line and the so-called Pyramid of the Moon was on a cross of such lines. I was unable to go completely around the Pyramid of the Sun, but it too was on a 64-bar line entering and disappearing into the main axis. I climbed both pyramids, a fairly demanding task, somewhat apprehensive as to what I might find on the summits of the two places, where history tells us that human sacrifice was carried out on an unparalleled scale. To my acute surprise, I did not find unpleasant symbols, nor did I have any unpleasant sensations, but rather ones of peace and tranquillity. On both places, I performed the necessary invocations and in each case the group of 8 circles within one square was replaced by on 8 circles, without a square. Perfect, but what was there before was not so bad.

The pyramid of Quetzalcoatl was interesting. As it had not really been restored one could not climb it. Behind it are the heads of the Plumed Serpent. At ground level four project, 16-bar lines came from each. What was especially interesting was that the lines came precisely from their mouths focussing into a precise point. They went through the pyramid and came out the other side to focus on a raised platform rather like an altar. On top were five circles. Then became one after the invocation and then continued on to the main axis as a 64. This site was an example of deus ex machina, if you like within the Aztec pantheon. Basically, the legend of Quetzalcoatl was that one day a white skinned and bearded god arrived in Mexico, taught the indigenous population the arts and sciences, had a lot of aggro from the local gods and withdrew in indignation, swearing that he would one day return to destroy them all. He was called the Plumed Serpent because of his general attributes. (A parallel with Thoth-Hermes would be permissible here.) What was interesting to me was that the energy lines in China associated with dragons, as they were in England and here on another continent one could dowse energy lines emanating from the dragon heads in the sanctuary of Quetzalcoatl. The serpent-dragon phenomenon occurred over large areas of the globe, including Greece and Rome.

I left the complex weak at the knees, literally, for those who climb steps of these pyramids at such an altitude will find entirely unsuspected muscular weakness. I felt weak headed too, for my dowsing had revealed an evaluation of the complex in total disagreement from that which history had led me to expect. I speculated on this as Elizabeth Maas drove me back to Mexico City. "In any event, we know very little," she said. "A very rapid destruction of an evolved civilisation by a handful of soldiers was accompanied by the destruction of all their records. We have only the chronicles of those who accompanied the Conquistadores to rely on". She dropped me at my hotel. We passed on the way the Shrine of Our Lady of Guadalupe. "I don't like the new building," she said. Idly I dowsed it. An 8-bar line emerged across our path. I thought little of it. I was still reflecting on the reason why the energies at Quetzalcoatl had been good rather than bad. Later on, I developed a theory on the subject, a theory which had remarkable repercussions. I also noticed that certain main thoroughfares in Mexico City had multiple lines – 8,16, and 32, and the general situation (according to Chloe) was O.K. The great Memorial to the Revolution, more or less in the centre of the city, is a square triumphal arch, in a mixture of Western and Aztec styles. Its octagons are slightly rounded in deference to local style. It had the eight circles underneath it and a cross of 64-bar lines on it. I did not have the time to do a complete analysis of the city, but it seemed to be functioning well. In looking cursorily into post Cortez Mexican history, one finds Masonry and the family of Bonaparte and Hapsburg involved.

I spent the following afternoon in the fabulous Museum of Anthropology. It was odd that an energy line of 64 bars came out of it and united with a line emerging from the Palace of Maximilian I, and the statues of the ancient gods in the museum and the famous stone Aztec calendar were all emitting lines into this one. The Museum was, so to speak, loaded! Also interesting was the inscription inside the vestibule which indicated that the purpose of the Museum was to do justice to the destroyed civilisation, an odd thing to do if that civilisation had only been concerned with human sacrifice and bloodlust on the grand scale claimed by the conquerors.

My next stop was Brazil. Guatemala is in the system as, I believe, is every inhabited area of the globe. My route to Rio de Janeiro was at first over water and I found nothing but coming in over Caracas the system started again. When we took off from Caracas and flew over the Amazon jungle, we ran out of lines again. That is not to say that there was nothing there, but only that it was not on a scale that would reveal itself by casual dowsing from an airplane in bursts of a few minutes. Rio had lines. I changed here from Sao Paulo. We waited in line interminably to no avail. Only one of my bags had arrived, the little one with my shoes in it. I can tell you that a way to reduce one's morale to zero, is to arrive in a strange land in a rainstorm to one's clothes, (and presents for the children) gone, and two days in which to do one's business. My bag never turned up. Pan Am gave me 100 dollars, and I bought myself some underwear. Fortunately, my business friends in San Paulo were sympathetic about my turning up in jeans and a safari jacket. Sao Paulo was business all the way, except that I was with friends. I had a chance to take a brief look around. It was functioning well. There was a huge obelisk, not quite as big as the Washington Memorial, but reminiscent of it. This was a memorial to the Constitutionalists who had put Brazil onto a relatively even keel and made it independent of capricious monarchies and colonial overlords. It was on a 64-bar cross. Sao Paulo is a lovely, lunatic, chaotic city. It drives you mad but makes you love it. How people live in it I don't know, but it has a frenetic fascination. According to Chloe it functioned well. I abandoned such thoughts and concentrated on my business friends and their charming hospitality.

The Sword of Michael

There are various great swords of legend which were wielded with apparently magical powers. They were used to kill dragons, rescue maidens from wicked men and generally do good. Even Joan of Arc was credited with one, and when it broke, she lost her magic powers. The great sword of Charlemagne was used by Roland, we are told, to cut a valley through the Pyrenees through which the greater part of his army was able to retreat. A great confluence of dowsable lines passes through this valley. In one legend Roland used Charlemagne's sword to open the pass, in another version he used it to open the pass at Monte Perdido. Other passes bear the same legend. In Vrrog there is a great fragment of rock which, people say, Roland tore away from the heights of Roncesvaix. The shrine at Roncesvaux is dedicated to the Virgin Mary and I suspect this to be the place of telluric significance within the general context of the cult of the Earth Mother, or the knowledge of the ley lines. Associated with the monastery and chapel is a pyramidal building said to mark the foot of the rock split by the sword, where the great heroes of the battle are said to be buried. It is not on a line of any consequence as these are diverted away from the monastery and associated buildings by a wayside cross of some antiquity, the so-called Pilgrim's Cross, on which multiple main lines, unique in our experience, converge. The

186

pyramidal form however is curious, yet it is not the original form which was a cupola on a square base. Today's pyramid is made of corrugated iron.

At the end of our search we are left with an apparent connection between the divine sword, great heroes, ley lines and the cult of the Earth Mother. It is impossible to overlook Excalibur. We are all aware from earliest childhood of the story of Arthur, the Pendragon, established his right to the throne by drawing a sword from the stone. Nobody else could do it. There are also strange connections between Arthur and Charlemagne. The Sword of the Stone however did not last long, it was broken in battle. Arthur received Excalibur from the Lady of the Lake, in the company of Merlin. It was given to him by a hand rising up from the lake, to which he knew it must be ultimately returned. The Lady of the Lake might be held to be an aspect of the Earth Mother, that aspect has to do with water, the spiritual side of man, the Gemini aspect of the Grail. There seems to be some confusion as to whether the first of these swords was in an anvil on the stone, or in the stone itself. T H White in "The Sword and the Stone," has it right through the anvil and into the stone itself, in the mouth of King Pellinore. On the sword were written words, "Who so pulleth out this Sword of this Stone and Anvil is the Right Wise King Born of all England." This Arthur first obtains the sword of masculine, brute strength, to be replaced later by a more subtle one.

One cannot help but feel that the Grail legend and the reality of alchemy are one and the same thing. The de la Warr "Black Box" and other similar devices depend for their efficacy on the abilities of the operator as a dowser. The operator must also be able to visualise correctly the objective or patient, be it to cure of some malady or remove objects from fields at long range or, as Tom Bearden has suggested, even to destroy submarines under the sea. Assuming all these phenomena to be correctly observed, the human operator

187

creates an essential link in the circuit. In the same way, the alchemist adept insists on spiritual change in the alchemist being attendant upon great work. As a teacher and instructor of alchemists, de la Warr, for all his elusive reference to the Holy Grail, does appear to have instructed his operators on the basis that he was dealing with technology rather than an alchemical phenomenon. My opinion would be that a radionics operator to be genuinely and constantly effective requires all the disciplines of the Western and Eastern ascetic and mystical traditions.

Thus, when we are dealing with the Sword of Michael and dragon killing, sacred stones, grails and the like, we see also that it must be wielded by people of certain spiritual qualifications. There is an important truth hidden in these allegorical accounts, just as in the alchemical treatise. Studies of the effects of pyramid energy by Patrick Flanagan confirm that we are dealing with etheric energy, as it is known to mystics, alchemists and esoterists of the past, that energy which makes the material universe stick together. He discovered that a three-dimensional pyramid functioned equally well when reduced to two-dimensional form. Von Reichenbach demonstrates that sensitives can see the odic energy emerging from the tips of various crystals and, after some experiment, it seemed to us that the fact that crystals produced this form of energy was due to their form rather than their intrinsic nature. For the same reason pyramids, whatever their material, seemed to produce the same energy as long as the form was the same. Cardboard, stone, even aluminium struts with no infilled area, performed in the same way. Wilhelm Reich's work fell into the same category. Clearly, he was operating in the same area as de la Warr, trying to use the energy for healing. It was the same with T Galen Hieronymous. Interestingly, both de la Warr and Reich had noted odd effects when they created too great an ambient "charge" of this energy. Jean de la Foye, in his book, "Ondes de Vie, Ondes de Mort," admits that drawn symbols have effects and gives a list of them, analysing their respective influences. Many of them are well known occultist symbols. This could be described as "magic", but we must also remember Pythagorus and his sacred geometry.

Elsewhere I have sought to describe how we found the seven circles within octagonal forms in religious buildings, either complete or with a segment missing, which we seemed to be able to put right. The missing segment apparently indicated that the particular energy aspect, represented by or manifested in the seven circles, was not functioning correctly. Important though we recognised the seven circles to be, I had thought that the accompanying physical octagonal form was necessary, or even a circular form. It had not percolated through me that such forms of dowsable energy could exist without an accompanying physical form. I have tried to show how significant the seven circles are as an esoteric symbol, but we were beginning to get the message that it was significant functionally. We had learned from the Grail Stone that this appeared to be an important symbol of the Elohim function and, after the de la Foy experiments, we noticed too that if you drew it on paper it produced large lines. I do not say that, if anyone does it, this will happen. I was struck by the reports of Ostrander and Schroeder, "Psychic Discoveries behind the Iron Curtain", where they described the psychotronic motors of Pavlita, strange forms of organic and inorganic material which produced energy to rotate pin-wheels when Pavlita and his daughter charged them by concentrating. What this seemed to indicate was that, whereas form was important, its function depended on a human activator. Thus, the seven circles had to be drawn with intent, rather than just a pretty picture.

The fact appears to be that not only does three-dimensional form produce energy, but also that two- dimensional form does the same. I was forcibly reminded of the so-called follies of "Mad" Jack Fuller, erected in the 18th century in and around Burwash, near Kipling. Not content with an obelisk, he also built a cone, called the Sugar Loaf, within whose chamber one can dowse seven circles and he had himself buried there. Here we have the juxtaposition of cone, obelisk and pyramid, by a man who plainly was not mad. Moreover, his introducing oboes into the services in Brightling Church instead of singing is not eccentric as it might seem, Herein, perhaps, lies another clue. We have noticed earlier how various forms of chanting affect the line system. The basso-profondo chants of the Tibetan lamas produce the seven circles around the tape player, and they claim publicly to be capable of charging places and objects with positive spiritual energy. Jack Fuller certainly got his pyramid tomb charged up in many ways.

A curious confirmation of this phenomenon was provided by a visit to a northern Buddhist monastery at Chateau de Soleils near Digne in the French Alps. They admitted, that they had placed themselves on a key Templar site and have a great rock crystal on top of their temple. They were generally being forthcoming in explaining what was going on to the extent of providing a map of the grounds. However, the one thing they did not talk about was the white bee-hive construction in the woods, about 4 metres high, associated with a curious wire enclosure which had a battery attached to it. This was pointed out to me and, when I investigated it, I found it to be exactly on the main line from the temple and the old barn, which was the main line of Southern France. It was a stupa. Curiously, one of the few books on sale there was called "Psycho-Cosmic Symbolism of the Buddhist Stupa," by Lama Anagarika Gounida, Emerville, California 1976. William Reich would have loved it all. Here was his orgone accumulator at work, with the difference that he constructed it and he assumed it became automatically charged, whereas the Tibetan Buddhists went to extreme lengths to charge their stupas by chanting. Of course, the intent of Reich may well have achieved the same objective. At Chataeu des Soleils, I believe, is a case of modern mystics using an ancient Templar site through which passes a main line. Through chanting and meditation and the use of crystals, they are charging up a single stupa with etheric energy, (or odic force or orgone energy,) into their Reichian accumulator.

Suffice it to say that alchemy does throw some light on the function of ley energy, odic force or whatever. It seems that paranormal depend on this energy:

- Spiritualist circles produce dowsable symbols.

- All functioning mediums have a line plugging into the system.

- Healers, when dowsed, exhibit the same phenomenon.

- Telepathy and hypnotism at work exhibit lines.

- All stories of "ghosts" walking show them to be on lines of energy.

- A visit to Professor John Hasrea's laboratory at Birbeck College in the University of London, where he conducts his post Geller metal-bending experiments, revealed it to have an 8-bar line running through it, the 8 circles around the desk, and one terminal of the 8-bar line was in an old churchyard, exactly on a white obelisk about 15ft high with no inscription. The other terminal was a modern church on an ancient site in Tottenham Court Road.

- Lectures by genuine folk on "esoteric" subjects produce a cross of 4,8 or 16 lines on the podium on which they speak.

- Long range healing experiments produce such lines.

If our observation is correct, then to call whatever it is the Universal Agent is perhaps not so wide off the mark. If we accept that form creates this energy or channels it in some way and that the pyramid experiments are correct, we would certainly confirm that charged stones can be used in specific layouts to charge water which assists or retards plant growth. Moreover, proportion is important, ergo, sacred architecture. Proper mental and spiritual attitudes can enhance the energy, as a well- said Mass appears to, and we also accepted that two-dimensional form appears to function as well as three dimensional. We are also left to grapple with the observation that forms, invisible to our eyes, such as dowsable seven circles, appear to function in the same way. What I feel we learned, or were shown, about invisible forms was that the seven-circle phenomenon, which resulted from intuitive or guided or accidental courses, was the form that either produced consecration or resulted from it. We had learned to recognise it within octagonal forms, under octagonal towers and domes. Thus, it appears around the high altar at St Peter's in Rome, and the cathedrals we investigated and, having decided that it was caused by the physical form, it was quite a surprise to discover it functioning in ones living room. But as Christine Hartley said, *"it matters not if the place be a tiny room or the most majestic cathedral, so long as it is consecrated"*. Thus, we felt that the production of the seven circles was dowsable evidence of consecration, and the act of visualisation and projection within these seven circles produces the same results as we achieved with stones and swords. Drawing the seven circles achieved the same effect as well, so long as it was placed within a larger circle.

And then a more important discovery took place in September 1977. I was staying at the hotel near Barcelona on the coast, one Sunday morning, and I was reading the "Vanguardia", the Barcelona daily newspaper. It was the 11th September. The newspaper was full of foreboding. The 11th September was the day of Catalonian

Independence and in the Plaza de Cataluna, in the centre of Barcelona, a huge demonstration was being planned to press the central government to grant some degree of autonomy to the old kingdom. I had dowsed the Square and found it to have seven circles in the centre and, in mosaic, a fairly esoteric layout of stars and circles, as if the designer had seen it quite specifically as an energy centre, perhaps for the whole of Catalonia, (which incidentally included quite a chunk of the south-eastern corner of France as well). Anyway, this was the place where one and a half million people were expected to meet. The Communist parties were highly involved in it all, and the Vanguardia. Everybody I talked to was very apprehensive that blood might flow that day in copious quantities, and I myself was only too well aware that radical movements need martyrs and are not above actually contriving the martyrdom of their own folk.

What could one do? Even had I the external paraphernalia, I could hardly arrange symbols in a Barcelona hotel. Suppose I visualised the seven circles and asked that it should work? I did so. It was a mixture of asking, projecting and visualising, plus invocation. I got up to dowse around, with the hand, as I was now able to do this. It was there. Good! I placed myself in the middle, as if wrapped in thought so as not to attract too much attention from holiday makers, and made further visualisations and invocations concerning the peaceful outcome of the demonstration. A line abruptly started in the direction of Barcelona. That afternoon we went to the Corrida in the Plaza de Torros Monumental. On the way in I felt the line at many points. It was huge and it incorporated symbols which I later established were the double square rectangle. We saw huge crowds breaking up, and I returned to the hotel. In the newspapers, the next morning a huge sigh of relief was expressed. No deaths, no wounded. The only arrests were late night hooligans, and everybody was congratulating themselves that such a huge affair had gone off so peacefully. Whatever the cause/effect relationship, I was satisfied about two things – the seven circles had appeared and had produced a huge line in the direction of the centre of the demonstration. We found subsequently that we were able to operate anywhere anytime, by "consecrating" the locality of the immediate vicinity in this way.

The cynical will say that the relationship between our activities and the outcome of events is non-existent. Therefore, it was with some interest that in August 1978, with Paul Dolphin, I conducted in Andorra a series of experiments with less grandiose but more measurable objectives. We repeated our earlier objectives with the drawn symbols producing single lines, and using the drawn prism, 64-bar lines, all of which was very satisfactory to us. I then drew to Paul's attention the phenomenon that Michael had first established, namely, that if you entered an energy form, which we had now come to call symbols, or crossed a line, a pendulum, held between finger and thumb, moved 5 degrees or so out of plumb and remained so until one moved out of the zone. (To observe this, hold the finger and thumb immediately under the eye, resting them upon the bridge of the nose.) This is, when you think about it, a pretty starling piece of observational evidence, undramatic, but starling. For what is being demonstrated is the fact that gravity is distorted by these fields and this energy! I have demonstrated this to quite a number of people to their satisfaction and mine. We have also shown that unless the pendulum is held by a person, a living organism, the phenomenon does not work.

I then moved on to a further experiment. Invoking a seven-circle configuration, and holding a brass dowsing rod in the centre and rotating it, as Michael had done over the electrostatic generator, I produced a sweeping beam of energy, and when it was directed by me at the pendulum in Paul's hand, it went 5 degrees out of true. Thus, its movement and anti-gravitational effect had been produced by an act of will by me. "We have just produced an empirical basis telekinesis," I said. He agreed. We went onto a further experiment to show that it was possible, by the usual visualisation techniques, to produce single and multiple lines from the invisible seven circles, duplicating the results obtained by drawing symbols, prisms, etc. Thus, we concluded that, four years after finding the Grail Stone and all that we had learned from it, we had also discovered that all aspects could be achieved by acts of proper visualisation, on any site, which could be consecrated at any time.

This may be a hugely significant discovery. On the other hand, one must try and explain how it is that, over the centuries, deeply mystical and learned men and women have insisted on the importance of material form and outward ritual in order to achieve results. The Church is a classic example on the one hand, and the Golden Dawn on the other. The answer, I believe, may lie in the evolution of human consciousness. I had often thought, having heard Trevor Ravenscroft talk and talked with him about the subject, that one of the great services he could perform for contemporary man was to write the history of the evolution of human consciousness, based on his own experience. He has hinted at how a new view might be taken in which man's evolution from a tribal being, living and thinking of a nation or a race, (and let us say, with several false starts). Then, from the Renaissance onwards there is a growing awareness in the West of Man's individual ego awareness. This is leading to an appreciation of his position in a world consciousness, from which he may, as a whole, develop into a totally liberated individual consciousness. In that state, Man's true destiny may have been reached. Of course, it doesn't all happen at once, and some start to achieve it ahead of the majority.

Religious and magical ritual have the stated objective of raising the participant's level of consciousness to the point at which they perceive the divine or the diabolic. Artefacts are prophetic devices in this process. It is very impressive, no doubt to some, to dress up as priests or magicians in expensive vestments, with their swords and crooks, censors and incense. The mandala of the East are visual forms which, if stared at, whilst the mantra is intoned, provoke the higher states of consciousness, rather as a deaf-aid helps the deaf, or glasses help the myopic. But what if all this can be achieved without all these artificial aids? And what if their function has only been to stimulate a mind into magico-mystical individual ego state, because it has been traditionally too deeply enmeshed in its particular group consciousness? Modern man is developing his own individual ego consciousness and, if he achieves it, his function may well depend less and less upon the outward form and ritual and more and more on his ability to summon up the particular brain rhythm and the proper visualisation. At least this explains our own experience in a more acceptable way.

I am not a physicist and cannot put forward a coherent framework for the phenomenon we have observed, I do feel most strongly, however, that we are not discovering anything new. Moses understood it, not to mention his dowsing ability or his familiarity with the Elohim-Jahweh phenomenon. Then there is the case of Joshua and the battle of Jericho! Dr Patrick Flanagan says that the Ark was a very large electric capacitor. Such a capacitor placed in the Earth's electrostatic field and charged, would have a charge of some $600 - 1,000$ volts, and would kill anything that touched it. The size of the Ark is exactly the same as the coffer in the King's Chamber of the Pyramid of Gizeh in Egypt, whence Moses, Joshua's mentor, had come, having been a priest in Egypt. The use of the Ark to part the waters of the Jordan is reminiscent of the parting of the waters of the Red Sea when the Israelites escaped from Egypt, when Moses took his staff and stretched out his right hand over the waters, not his hand. This version certainly conforms with our observations. At all events, waters were parted by the passage of an electrostatic accumulator, a circle of stones were built, seven marches were made around the walls with the Ark, seven trumpets were blown, and at the culmination a great shout sufficed to bring the walls down. Is this all biblical nonsense? Moses points his staff, and Joshua points his dagger, and all is well. What is all this about? Wilhelm Reich once made an orgone gun to disperse clouds, as we have seen. Is it not all the same thing? And has not positivist science of the last 300 years set itself up on a rigid basis of first premises, which permits no appreciation of past non-positivist technical knowledge? Moreover, it has little appreciation of the future possibilities of harnessing the undoubted gains of positivist sciences with energy realities which do not necessarily conform to their rules – I refer to the study of Pyschotronics.

I have been present in a private room of the House of Commons when an eminent professor of Electrical Engineering told a group of MPs that the Russians were 20 years ahead in this field. In Russia, and perhaps in other places as well, radio effects are causing localised changes in the electro-magnetic field. If this is so, then the ley system is involved. I think it works like this. As a preliminary hypothesis, ley energy appears to be a type of general plasma that pervades all the Earth's ecosphere and noosphere until a process of monument building began. Monument building occurs on two levels, the implantation of a stone or other artefact in a place to mark its sanctity, or the focus on a well which is marked with stones. The act draws the amphorous nature of the plasma into specific relationships with the focal point thus created. As more such sites are created, the amphorous nature of the plasma becomes specifically channelled between points and thus a network of "energy" is created. Just as electricity was always there, we have not invented the ley energy, merely harnessed it and channelled it. We have observed that this energy assumes reality in our dimension to the extent that some form of spiritual consciousness exists in a specific place. To the extent, the cosmic reality can concentrate itself in a place where two, three or four, or more people are gathered together in its name.

As an example of this, I cite the phenomenon I observed at the First National Congress of Radiesthesia at Barcelona in June 1978, when the podium on which addresses were given was the object of a cross 64-bar lines, until the moment the congress ended, when they disappeared. I have observed similar effects at conferences, séances and general discussions of topics that may be held to be spiritual. Where the point is ephemeral, as in a lecture theatre or a conference hall, it disappears when the participants disperse. If it is your own home or place where the experience is repeated several times, then the phenomenon persists. Thus, it may be held, a form of consecration takes place. As Christine Hartley says in "The Western Mystery Tradition," *"a place used for rites and ceremonies throughout the centuries will keep within itself the influence and the power poured into it through the work of those who have used it in the past, thus the "atmosphere" felt so very often by sensitive, and not sensitive, people in certain places. The men of knowledge consecrate with a force that is retained, more especially within four walls, and unless the contacts be broken, it will linger for an untold time, the time depending on the circumstances. These consecrations can be for good or evil."* For an example of this one can consider Albert Speer on Hitler's comments about consecrating his buildings for government. We have also observed elsewhere how the ley energy can be modified by acts of spiritual will and indeed by introducing an electrostatic field into it. The observed fact is that all the transmitter and repeater stations I have examined, whether the mast of the BBC TV at Brighton the RTVE Centre in Barcelona, the GPO Tower in London, gendarmerie communication centres in France or RTF in Paris, they are all within the system.

One may speculate as to why this is so, and which came first, the chicken or the egg. The fact appears to be that, apart from its apparent association with electrostatic fields, the electromagnetic field has some relationship with ley energy. Thus, we have a hypothetical relationship between ley energy, electrostatic fields and the bionic field. Professor John Taylor, in his book "Superminds," recounts a phenomenon which Andrija Puharich also observed, namely that Uri Geller could influence a Geiger counter to the point that it signalled a mortal level of radiation in the immediate vicinity by an apparent will. Of course, the radioactivity did not exist. However, the act of will produced parallel conditions to a dangerous radio-active field. Alternatively, it may have demonstrated that the radio-active field and the bionic field have something in common and it is not just a question of applying some telekinetic effect to a sensitive piece of apparatus but, conversely, that a human mind, in certain conditions, can modify the radio-active effect. My brother David dispersed an electrostatic field and absorbed what was left of a significant charge without any difficulty.

I suggest that the three major fields know to have established science, plus the gravitational field, have something in common with each other and the bionic field. Thus, one may tentatively conclude that the unified field concept has potential validity and that it includes the bionic field. Earlier I have recounted an experiment which again seems to show that the human mind, properly functioning, can to a limited extent overcome gravity. This being the case, modulations of any aspect of the field in any of its various manifestations would affect its other manifestations. Therefore, mind affects matter, matter affects mind, and radio transmissions at specific frequencies could have effects in any of these fields. It stands as a hypothesis. What Clarke, Maxwell and Einstein would have made of it, I don't know. I am only an Arts graduate attempting to grapple with certain phenomena and experiences which I have had the privilege of encountering,

Thus, I adopt as a working hypothesis that traditional magic and modern technology are capable of being related, and in a highly specific way. This is, for example, reason to believe that one of the modulative effects on the Russian transmissions is supplied by trained psychics, their visualisation being carried on the transmitting beam. This is not so fanciful as it might first appear, when one considers the following: ferric tape can carry ley energy effects. We observed this phenomenon thus. Casual attempts to duplicate the Raudive experiments, in which a tape recorder left playing in vacuo produces, on replay, voices of an unexplained origin. David and I did this. We received no voices, but dowsing of the surrounding area revealed that, if the tape recorder had been live in situations where ley energy was active or geometrical form fields were present, these were reproduced when the tape was replayed. This was also provoked as an experiment by two observations concerning Uri Geller programmes. One, that similar paranormal effects to the ones he was demonstrating occurred amongst receivers and listeners to his programmes. Geller is not an isolated phenomenon. He has stimulated and provoked many more to develop these abilities. Two, that similar effects were witnessed by the audience when the programme was recorded, as in Sweden. As a hypothesis we felt that, in some way or other, Geller in his live programme was projecting some energy which was capable of transmission over TV and radio channels. We could not necessarily explain, but we did feel that it happened. Of course, if it happened when the TV programme was recorded, then it was another reasonable hypothesis that somehow or other the ferric tape not only had the capacity to record changes of input in the electro-magnetic spectrum but also localised effects of the energy associated with leys, metal bending and geometrical force fields.

In any event, David showed to my satisfaction on numerous occasions that the tape recorder was capable of recording and reproducing these strange energies, to the extent that he was able to boost a single 64-line up to three 64 lines. What was interesting was that in this case, as in the atomic arsenal at Torrejon, each line had a single parallel on either side. This observation caused us to speculate that a Noddy programme transmitted on Children's TV could carry such additional data and influences. Thus, I eventually went with Michael to dowse the BBC TV Shepherd's Bush Centre and found the confluence of lines had its output directly through the presentation suite, that's to say, the control studio through which every BBC TV programme must pass in its transmission phase. I hasten to record that I haven't observed any use or abuse of this system by TV systems. One deliberate use which made me feel this to be possible was the witnessing live on RTVE in Madrid of the Pope's Christmas blessing in 1975. It activated the lines that passed through the Madrid flat, causing it to produce symbols. Therefore, I think I need to dwell further in my own particular unscientific way on the apparent possibilities of adapting radio transmissions to create localised changes in aspects of electromagnetic, electrostatic and gravitational fields which could affect the nervous and psychic aspects of organic life, and shift weather and seismic patterns.

Having said all that, however, one crucial factor emerges which accounts for the often-observed fact whereby so-called psychic phenomena, do not take place according to order. Indeed, it is usually quite the reverse, the more one makes an effort the less likely they are to take place. One might deduce from this that one of the key factors in all this is a state of mind which is not concentrated, expecting and demanding, but relaxed open and submissive. It will be interesting to see the EEG results on such distinctive states of mind. I hasten to add that this is not in any way contradicting what I have tried to say about the magical consequences of the act of visualisation. That act does not appear to require beads of sweat to stand out on the brow, but rather depends on the contemplative, quiescent but consciously open state of mind, in which the ego is eliminated. However, these phenomena depend on the human being as the essential link and his adoption of the proper state of mind. To quote Christine Hartley again, *"Magic, which is the work of the magus or wise man, might best be defined as the knowledge of how to use powers that are not fully comprehended by others, the ability to control natural forces, to work with a superconscious mind deliberately and not with the conscious one."*

Herein lies the distinction. What appears to happen is that the type of energy with which we are trying to grapple does not exist in a wholly objective form in our continuum. The American new scientists call it "zero point" energy. That is to say, its source is not identifiable in terms of conventional physics. A lightning bolt is undeniably energy, produced in a wholly objective way, independent of human intervention, mechanical or psionic. Nobody will argue with that. However, we note that we cannot disturb the line of a pendulum unless it is held by a co-operative person, it will not work if suspended from an inanimate physical point. The whole tendency of our work has been to show that these energies have little or no reality in our dimension unless activated by human beings and those human beings adopting a proper state of mind, which permits the energies to manifest. Thus, the human being is essential in the process. The de la Warr Black Box or the Hieronymous Machine does not produce energy effects without a human operator.

Actually, as we have observed earlier, it does produce energy, but for it to be effective the human is necessary. We have also observed that the electrostatic field seems to be capable of manifesting different phenomena if the human is present as is introducing ley energy as a deliberate act or modifying the field by a deliberate act of will.

Consequently, it appears that we have to take into account the fact that man has a specific relationship to these energies, which do not appear wholly to conform to the requirements of our continuum, as presently defined by established science. *"If you believe in magic, you'll have the universe at your command,"* went a song by Crystal Gale, in 1978. Of course, it isn't that simple, but it is true in a certain *and* highly specific context. States of consciousness can modify the energy fields around us, energy fields that do not yet occupy a place of honour in the pantheon thus far created by the establish scientists, and which are less dramatic in some of their manifestations, but perhaps more far-reaching. They function in this dimension because of human intervention at a conscious or subconscious level. We are a link in the chain and the potential manipulators. It may answer some aeonal questions, at least at our level. The divine, (and I use that word in the sense of non-material,) energy functions through man. Thus, the question of God's responsibility for our world, as we know it, does not arise. Man, as we can now see, has the whole matter in his own hands. By proper application of spiritual alchemy on a grand scale, we could, (but don't) organise the necessary energies to create the millennium. Many factors so far have prevented it. Jesus endeavoured to show us the way. Unfortunately, his followers misused his teaching, for the imposition on the Western World's consciousness of an institution weighed down by treasure, pomp and circumstance, as I have observed elsewhere, and which puts its own survival higher than truth.

The early Christians and the Gnostics attempted it, but the Gnostics were subjugated in the end. The latter, it may be fairly said, were within the Pythagorean tradition, (a tradition claimed by the Druids). The Gnostics books, such as "Pistis Sophia," and other works attributed in their tradition or knowledge, involving gematria, that is, the relationship between number and letter. Thus, the Gospels in Greek may be seen to have a hidden significance, expressed in number, the "Revelation of St John", a visionary tale expressed in terms of number and measurement, is the same. St John had a reason for writing "Revelations" in this manner. Those who wish to pursue this mystery further should read "Gemtria" by Bligh Bond and Thomas Simcox Lea. However, I limit my comment on this profound book to one aspect, which is relevant to the thesis I am trying to develop here. *"Thou art Peter. Upon this stone, I will build my church,"* said Jesus. (A statement which the Roman Catholic Church has taken as a justification for its existence from then on.) Yet Peter was crucified on Vatican Hill. I find Bond and Simcox's interpretation of this relevant, for it brings us full circle, back to the drawing of the sword from the stone.

We have noted earlier how the double square (or in three-dimensional form, the double cube), seemed crucial in the initial communications, and how the progression was significant, the final two symbols being displayed in the Church of the Holy Sepulchre in Jerusalem. Here one must stress that, whatever low level Masons may say, Wilmshurst in "The Masonic Initiation" was quite clear as to the magico-religious nature of Masonry. Thus, when Masons talk of the Ashlav, the cubic stone and the double cube altar, whatever their current beliefs, they are referring to a tradition which had reality, and has reality today if the practitioners are believers. We have also noted how, before Glastonbury, the seven circles were an important symbol and how we came to understand the way to use it. We have noted also how the Trionis symbol, the three consecutive circles, and the reference to the Great and Little Bear emerged from Trionis, which we also equate with the Tri-une God, the God of the Masons and the Gnostics and their link with Egypt and a man called Jesus Christ, (whose name has been taken in vain so many times both doctrinally and blasphemously). Bearing in mind also the significance of the 3, the 7 and the 8, the whole exposition of the significance of the Cube by Bligh and Lea takes on a disturbing significance.

I do not propose to go into the detail of this. It is difficult and precise. Those who have followed so far will perhaps be prepared to consult this extraordinary book for themselves. Then they will comprehend how Druids, the Christ, the Gnostics, Arthur and the Round Table, Robin Hood, Joseph of Arimathea and his settlement in Glastonbury and Pythagorus are all evidence of a common phenomenon. All is form. Measurement and number. Thus, Platonic solids emerge from zero-point energy, converting that energy into specific channels as they manifest in more planes. These give rise, as they take an additional numerical function, to all the intricate and apparently amorphous nature of life. The cube is the first three dimensional solid and thus is the first manifestation of energy in our continuum, if we accept that form produces energy. The pyramid is a solid after the cube. As Bligh and Lea explain, its functioning with a 7 and an 8 seems particularly relevant to our story. The double cube was essential to the building of the Temple of Solomon, another relevant factor. What we are faced with ultimately is alchemy, not in the popular sense of the word, but in a sense alluded to earlier, namely, that the periodic table my well be capable of a further reduction into four, earth, air, fire, water, as an intermediate aspect of the unified field, ie God, before it manifests in the elements in which organic life is based. For, although we are a carbon-based phenomenon, the trace elements are essential. Thus, he who can draw the sword is the channel for a mighty power. Assuming that he can go through the necessary visualisations and identifications with the Christ, who built his real church, the church of the Holy Grail, on the perfect stone, and that he can place himself at the total disposal of the Holy Spirit, he or she may be the channel whereby the directions of organic life are changed for the better. Of course, he who chooses the Faustian pact with the devil, and has the knowledge, may do the exact reverse.

By dint of knowledge and adaption of consciousness, he who wishes may offer himself as a catalyst in this process, but it is not easy. Some may reach it by meditation and deduction, others by placing themselves in a state of mind in which dowsing is possible. The brain rhythms are identical, but they require dedication and training to achieve the complete process. Such is the function of the Knight of the Grail, who wields the sword against the dragon, identifying himself with the appropriate zodiacal archetype, and acts as the means whereby that function manifests. He brings the spiral energy under control, so that it may play its part in the creation of a New Jerusalem. In this way, the chaotic energy is placed in a precise mathematical relationship with the macrocosm in its divine aspect, and the millennium may be achieved on Earth.

Research and Knowledge into Action

The idea of applying healing to communities was something that evolved over several years, particularly as a result of observations through dowsing of the nature and function of what are loosely called "ley lines."

By 1st May 1981, the subconscious mind had done its work, and suddenly the idea was on the table. Eric Bosshard of Washington DC and myself were reviewing the dowsing work we had done together in various countries and we had reflected on a number of apparently significant observations, and it all came together in a "Let's see if it works" conclusion.

The idea of dowsing to see if ley lines carried energy, we had started some eight years before. What we had determined was that the

Watkins type alignment was perfectly valid, in the sense that they combined the sacred sites of megalithic man and medieval churches, for they were built, in the main, on sites of pre-Christian religion. But as energy lines, many of the old alignments no longer functioned – indeed, the dowsing showed that the old node points had, in many cases, been replaced by modern ones – town halls, political party HQ, TV and radio transmitters, contemporary war memorials, modern fountains, football stadiums, and even nuclear power stations and, one day, as his father was chief engineer of the Great Lakes chain of reactors, Eric dowsed inside the heart of a closed reactor – it was really in the system.

Not only were there new permanent points in the system, which caused the energy lines to flow in new directions, but as a result of some experiments in a 12th century church in Andorra, we had come to realise that these energy channels were related to consciousness and that spiritual activity changed them for certain periods and by spiritual activity, I mean input from higher states of consciousness – states associated with meditation.

The "pathways of consciousness," as we now call them, function in terms of form and number – the number of parallels in the line, and the geometrical form that may be dowsed when it hits a node point and goes into function. Indeed, we eventually came to realise that the ley system was, in fact, the basis of the collective consciousness of humanity, the pathways were the meridians and the node points, in the Tom Graves sense, were the acupuncture points – and in a very real sense the collective consciousness was an objective field in the collection of fields that surround the physical globe and all of which go to make up the being – Earth.

What was even more important was the observation, through dowsing, that someone who momentarily puts himself in the higher states of consciousness, plugs into the nearest node points and the nearest available form of a cross of energy lines forms him – and if he is, in particular, placing himself in the healing mode, then a vertical line, seen by sensitives as a column of light, descends upon the healer. It has been photographed and in Christian culture may be seen to be the Holy Spirit. It is an energy which corresponds to Mana, Prana, the Primum Mobile, the Odic Force of Von-Reichenbach, the orgone energy of Reich, the etheric energy of Oliver Lodge, etc. Whereas many of its characteristics conform to the electromagnetic spectrum, to the behaviour of light, the gravitic field, weak radio-activity, none of these are adequate to properly define it, and it defies positivist scientific attitudes because one of its more critical aspects is its relationship of the higher states of consciousness – fields which do not yield to positivist analysis. The alchemy of the spirit is intelligible in the context of the results of the proper use of this energy; Rudolf Steiner's "Spiritual Science" takes account of it.

Nikola Tesla observed that the frequency of the physical globe was around about 8Hz: Schumann observed a similar frequency in what is now known as the Schumann Resonance Cavity, between the earth's surface and the ionosphere: 8Hz is the onset in EEG terms of the well-known Alpha state, when the brain exhibits a shift in frequency due to dowsing, meditation or healing.

Dowsing reveals that a healer apart, from plugging in vertically and laterally, forms a common etheric field with the person receiving the healing. All the charkas and vital energies disappear from behind each to combine in one field – common consciousness, and the subject takes on the healer's brain rhythm – thus successful healing takes place – in proximity or at a distance when an energy pathway is created between the two even if they are in separate countries. Map dowsing shows that consciousness can expand around the world – for consciousness does not reside in the brain – it is holistic and resides in being – and we in the highest states can be everything. When the motive is correct, that is the higher expression of LOVE, that much abused and misunderstood word. To heal spiritually, you must love, and embrace the subject with your total being.

Healing by groups works – absent healing works. This it occurred to us that collective healing might also work. The Maharishi has spoken at length about the gains for communities that accrue when more than 2% meditate and has set up brigades of spiritual commandoes to go into communities to do it. Once done, they leave.

We felt that this was a step forward in spiritual science, but that it should be possible to go even further. In the first instance, we had come to realise that for non-intuitive healers, the "visualisation" was the key to the exercise in the higher states of consciousness – in the second, passive meditation was one thing, active another, thirdly by dowsing you could actually measure the input and monitor the results – fourthly, that if the collective consciousness were a reality and expressed through the ley lines, then communities were also beings, and fifthly, that individual diseases might well have their counterparts in collective diseases such as violence, stress and unloving attitudes. Collective healing should yield results just as one to one healing.

In that May of 1981, we decided to put it to the test, and sent out a call to the healers of Brighton to join in. They did. Within a few weeks, more than 100 people were ready to take part. It was suggested by Father James Holdroyd, that the 29th September, St Michael's Day, (St Michael the dragon saint,) was an auspicious date to start, at St Bartholomew's, Brighton. The Dragon is held to be the murky subconscious from which the dark thoughts come, and so far as I am concerned, it is also the "Woivre" of the Celts, the spiral earth energy that comes out of springs, valleys, stone circles, earthworks and so on, and which, when with the Spear or Sword of evolved consciousness, it is channelled into the community in straight lines, creates harmony between man and earth. After all, there are no dragon bones in the museums and the Chinese dragon-men are in total agreement.

Every individual has a "hara" in oriental terms, round the Solar Plexus, the portal through which a healer puts basic life energy. We had to look for the "hara" of Brighton, which we found to be the fountain in the Old Steine, the physical hub of Brighton, and on the main energy line. The stones of the old stone circle are still in the base of the fountain.

What was curious was that the line had been a triple 64 and about 20 yards wide – but the moment more than a few people had taken the idea into their consciousness, the line began to expand, indeed to an extent outside our experience – even before any operation was undertaken.

The Archdruid of France stated that there was a macro-system in Europe, combining earth faults, cathedrals, ancient sites and so on. We checked – he's right, and it conforms to the great pilgrim routes. Thus, a pilgrimage can alter your consciousness.

On 29th September, we performed, in group terms, as one individual healer, but towards the collective being of Brighton and Hove. Meditation, prayer and visualisation. That through the Fountain, the "hara", came the healing energies from above, revitalising the veins and arteries of the community. The visualisation was involved in various matters – the disease of weekend violence, of which Brighton was a notorious victim, a reduction in stress which would have potential consequences in public health, road accidents and civic awareness – and we would monitor the results.

First consequence: the main line of Brighton multiples by 2,400 times. This staggered me, for we had no idea what to expect. We eventually concluded that the "patient", and indeed the world system had been on its last legs, and what we had thought to be a vital main line, was but a vestigial memory. More important was that a series of squares about 2 yards each side appeared and eventually formed into a chequerboard pattern, (1.8 metres each side of the squares), just as appears around individuals when healers have given them initial healing.

(Knights Templar were known to be guardians of energy lines, and it is interesting to note the link between the chequerboard effect that appeared in Brighton after the meditation, and the Templars flag, which is a chequerboard. To me it talks of balanced energy, a western yin/yang. At this point I would like to include an article by Jenni Lansdowne for the Fountain Magazine, as it is an insight on the chequerboard and why the Templars valued it. -Suzanne)

The Game of Life Knights Templar Style

Whilst the King trembles in his ivory tower, unable to stop the power game unfolding before him, the Queens of Light and Darkness are locked in battle. Not a head on confrontation you understand, but by strategy and manipulation.

Pawns are rushing off the board like lemmings, no longer of any tangible use, and pleased to be out of the struggle.

The bishops' manoeuvre first one way then the next, causing surprise and confusion at their insistent moves.

The castles remain quietly aloof from the battle, moving slowly and ponderously, although knowing that their time of reckoning is coming.

The knights weave their strange pattern of movements around the board. At the end they might survive, but in the meantime, they move to their own mysterious vibrations.

This might be how somebody who did not know the rules might view the game of chess. To those who understand the point, it is, of course, a logical sequence of events.

If one were to parallel the game of chess with the game of life, how many people could say they really understood the moves and events, much less the point of it all? There are a number, of course, who do, as there are those who understand chess. Just as well, or there would be no one to write or teach about either game.

The Knights Templar placed great emphasis on the game of chess, although forbidden to play it. This would seem a little puzzling, given that under normal circumstances to play a game of chess would be a rather innocuous pastime. Might it be possible that the Templars understood a certain symbology in the pieces and the format of the game itself.

Why would we leave messages that could only be decoded by moving letters in the same way as pieces on a chessboard, (as Henry Lincoln recounts in "Holy Blood, Holy Grail.")

The word "Knight" has been used many times in history and is associated with guardianship, quests, discoveries and purity. Was it purely coincidence that this name was adopted by the Templars? And that it also happens to be a chess piece?

And what of those people who can dowse and "see" quite distinct. It seems unlikely. Chequerboard patterns around Templar sites? So many cannot all be imagining it. Why the Chequerboard?

The pattern has also been dowsed by Fountain members in and around their towns and focal points, among other places. Is there a link here and if so, what is it???

Look down from above upon a giant chess board, as though you know nothing about the game – confusion and power struggles seem to be the order of things, don't they? Now if you were to look down from above upon the planet Earth, how would that appear at the moment.

Perhaps if we all understood the true symbolism of the game of chess, we might understand the game of life.

(This struck me as pertinent to the symbology of the Chequerboard, and a worthy explanation. Suzanne)

Consequences in behavioural terms; first, with one notable exception, weekend violence has disappeared, and Brighton is no longer prey to this sort of group aberration. The fact of the greater civic awareness is far less easy to quantify, but there is general agreement that it is so, general crimes of violence present a serious difficulty. First, they are classified on an East Sussex basis and secondly, the police computer programme classifies them in a way that does not limit them to crimes where violence was committed, but includes crimes where violence could have been committed, all of which could be misleading. More time is necessary, but what is important is that elsewhere where Fountain Groups have come into being, weekend violence has virtually disappeared – viz; Isle of Thanet.

But whereas we had no idea what to expect either in terms of results or dowsing effects, some important new dimensions have been appreciated. It was curious that whereas the chequerboard field extended over Brighton, Hove and their environs, and stopped for a period of three months, a sort of finger of energy went up the main road, and railway line to London. It took some time for the penny to drop as to what that was all about.

Just as in one to one healing, the healer cannot know exactly what to do in all cases, yet the energy gets on with it, thus in the case of Brighton, the energy decided for itself to extend itself to London to achieve the major objective.

This chequerboard field, it now appears has the effect of shifting the brain rhythm of those who enter into it. As the vast proportion of the contributors of violence come from London, what more logical than to start the consciousness shift the moment they left on their way to Brighton, either road or rail, so that on arrival the Base chakra desire of violence would be mitigated.

I said earlier that consciousness is holistic when someone is in a state of violence, all their energies congregate in the base chakra, just as in a saint, they congregate in the crown chakra. There is an associated brain rhythm. Just as the healer shifts the brain rhythm of the sick person, so a community healing has a tendency to shift the collective consciousness, or so it would appear, a little bit upwards, thus rendering gut-based violence less satisfying.

The police, when asked whether the Fountain Group activity had been the source of the improvement, attributed it to better policing methods, and, of course, they are right, but any spiritual work has a subtle first cause, and quite a lengthy chain of subsequent effects in order to achieve the desired objective. I feel that more understanding and less provocative police methods may also be involved in a

214

general raising of consciousness. I also feel for the young policeman who knows a punch up is likely, but he, too, can get his base chakra going and over-react.

The affair of the Brighton bomb was revealing. I live about 100yards away and was a sad witness to that terrible morning. Whereas in Madrid, where a similar grid pattern exists, the terrible accident on the runway, and the affair of the discotheque had ripped a huge hole in the grid, which had to be gently put back by the Madrid Fountain Group, the bomb in Brighton had no such effect, to my great surprise, but then I reasoned that, in a consciousness sense, unlike the events in Madrid, it had nothing to do with Brighton. It was perpetrated by outsiders. I hope that is a proper explanation, the being of Brighton is about people rather than locations.

It's all still very naïve and neophyte, but many encouraging signs have emerged. It's great to fly over Europe or the States and dowse a Fountain chequer board below the plane. What if every community in the world eventually has a group working?

The problem of institutionalised violence and unloving attitudes is a higher citadel to crumble, but just as individual consciousness rises through the charkas to the Crown, perhaps the collective one can do the same. Human beings make institutions, and in the main they are based in fear and desire for power. Those who live in the Crown Chakra have neither. There is, therefore, hope but only if those who know do.

Whereas violence may be held to be a principle disease of humanity, be it physical or emotional, just as in individual disease, states of consciousness are still a major contributory factor for good or ill, and the raising of planetary consciousness may be held to have a direct bearing on our survival as a race.

The key of course is love, which unconditional, seeks no reward, knows no fatigue and is boundless. Strange it is dowseable and affects the ley lines. They truly are Pathways of Consciousness and therefore Healing.

(Wrote Colin in a 1985 article for Matthew Manning's magazine "Attitudes")

Before we move onto what happened after the Brighton experiment, I would like to share my background, and what lead me to work with Fountain from 1985 and beyond.

Part 2

Suzanne's (My) Spiritual Early Years

My spiritual journey started by reading science fiction as a child. I loved Isaac Asimov and Edgar Rice Burroughs etc, and I will also admit that I loved Star Trek, but never became a "Trekkie". Tales of the unusual, other worlds and realities really fascinated me, but perhaps that is my Aquarian nature. As I got into my teens, fiction began to wane, and I became interested in "non-fiction", for example unexplained mysteries, UFO's, ancient civilizations etc. I have always felt the pull of ground-breaking knowledge, rather than the mundane everyday life.

There was also a part of me, that felt a need of care towards humankind and wanting to be of service. As a child, on those long walks to school, my imagination saw me as coming from another planet, called Astron, where the vegetation was pink, and the waters electric blue, precious metals and gems were commonplace. I left my planet to serve humankind, and far from wanting to go home, I always thought that I would be here until the "ship went down", and be the last one to leave, and turn out the lights. Perhaps I did read and watch too much science fiction...

Later, I developed an interest in complementary medicine. Over many years, I have qualified in many disciplines including; healing, aromatherapy, vibrational medicine, aroma-cosmetology, but have not used them on a professional basis, except perhaps healing. My main interest in these therapies, was more to do with the knowledge of energetics, the energy systems of the human body, and how they worked.

My main weakness is collecting knowledge, with archivist tendencies, which is fortunate for Fountain. I enjoy collating information and being a signpost for people. I also love being on the forefront of discovery, and certainly would be bored by being in the middle of the stream. If I attend a lecture or workshop, I prefer it to be a leading person in that field, or someone with great insight. Chinese whispers are not always helpful, as information is invariably changed as it goes through various people.

My family was/is speckled with people who have mediumship abilities, mainly coming through my mother's family on the female side, in fact my great aunt Min Morris, was a spiritualist minister, who did trance work in Lowestoft. Min would never know what she said to people in trance, which was probably a blessing, but when she walked her dog along the promenade seafront, people would come up and compliment her for what she had told them, she would just smile back at them and have no idea what had gone on.

As a result of my family's history, and my own interest, I decided to visit a well-known gypsy clairvoyant in Plymouth called Acora who works on Plymouth Barbican, (and at the point of writing still does), to ask if I had any spiritual skills. At that time in my life I had no wish to become a medium, and thereby hangs a ghost story, (retold later in this book). I walked into Acora's shop, and he took me into the back room. There was a crystal ball on the table, but he took my hands, and looked closely at them, and with sparkling eyes of a purple hue he told me that I would make a very good healer, and was given the details of a local healer that he knew.

That local healer turned out to be Barney Camfield, (one of the best.) In his past, he had been a commando during WWII, had worked in films, and for the old south west television company, Westward TV. He was a larger than life character, with a big sense of humour. (On this path, a sense of humour always attracts me.) Barney, at the time I met him was a Unitarian minister, taking services in Plymouth and Moretonhampstead once a week. The "healings" took place after each service, led by himself and a few other healers, which attracted quite of few people. As well as the church healings, Barney also ran a clinic from his living room, on weekdays, in which other healers also attended to give healing, and founded the Westcountry Natural Healing Fellowship. All healings were given on a donation basis.

Now I am not really a church person, although I do believe in God. For me God is all around, and not just in the places of worship. Anyway, there was I having just sat through a service, a little uncomfortable, when one of the "helpers," came up to try and convert me to Unitarianism. As my "flight mode," was beginning to be engaged, I stood up to leave. Barney had spotted what was going on from the stage, and suddenly appeared beside me from nowhere, blocking my exit. I spluttered that I was interested in becoming a healer. He smiled and took me by the hand back to the person that he was giving healing to, sat me beside him, and talked me through the process.   Barney was a strong healer, and I could feel the energies being transferred to the client. Wow I thought, this is interesting and that started me on my next period of growth. After work in my normal job as a civil servant I would often take the 70mile round trip to Barney's clinic and the two churches, three to four times a week to train as a healer. The main road down to Plymouth from where I lived was the A38. I knew the roads between my home and Barney's like the back of my hand, and when the thick fog came down and I could only see the "cat's-eyes" I still knew exactly where I was. Another joy of that drive home was when it was full moon, I was entranced, and glimpsed it anytime that I could on such journeys. At one special spot having left the A38, along a country road was a big mound of earth, which had a single tree at the top, and when it was full moon the moon would show just to the side of it. Bliss. (Since that time the farmer has pulled down the tree, it's not quite the same now, but still has a beauty.)

Barney was an all-rounder. One of his favourite sayings was, "Never believe a word I say," and that's not to mean that he was telling lies, but to test everything for its validity, and what felt right for us. Also, he felt if you had a total belief in something, you were closing your mind to other possibilities.   He gave me a very good spiritual grounding and brought me into contact with other good spiritual speakers, so that I had discernment for the future.   Without Barney's attention in church that day, I might have missed the first real step on the path, or was it "higher management," giving him a nudge, or did he just see that I was in distress and needed saving from the "helper"?

Healing for me started, way before Reiki and Mindfulness came to these shores, in the 1970's. At that point in time healing involved three types, Faith Healing, Spiritualist Healing or just plain Healing.

What you called it depended on how you explained the interaction between healer and client. In Faith Healing you both had to have a religious faith that the client was going to be cured. With Spiritualist Healing it depended on a spirit working through a healer to evoke the healing. The one that I preferred was just plain Healing. Barney Camfield's book "Healing, Harmony and Health," published in 1985, gives a little of his background and how he explained healing. Here is an extract.

"How are you? I'm fine thanks!"

Apart from crushing my left foot between two ships, and having a hole put through my chest by the Waffen SS. Plus a fractured skull, broken neck, broken ribs, and crushed right leg. Oh yes, and depression, shingles, diverticulosis/itis, pancreatitis, angina and a few little things like jaundice, bronchitis and the usual plethora of childhood ailments. Apart from the aforementioned, I've kept remarkably fit.

And I've spent, mostly during wartime, about 2 years hospitalised in 24 different hospitals. In over 60 years I've been treated by physicians, consultants, surgeons, osteopaths, chiropractors, healers and physiotherapists, etc.

All of the above therapists can be described quite correctly as "healers". But the term "healer" is commonly used to describe those who heal by the "laying on of hands."

Not that it is strictly accurate as the healing practitioner will only too readily admit. They say that a healer is but a channel of healing energy. And they feel, too, that the healing energy does not just come from them but through them. That's not necessarily simply a theory; it feels that way. The patient appears to draw through the healer a collection or blend of energies, some of which can be measured, which assists the body of the sufferer in some way or other to correct the physical or mental problems.

I can't remember when or who, but I recall hearing of a surgeon who said that a surgeon can cut and sew, medicinal treatment nursing can be given, but the body has then to heal itself. Our own "life force" takes over and completes the job.

But what is that "life force"? Some healers speak of etheric energies and, while science may well be on the verge of discovering the nature of some of them, they haven't done so yet. Infra-red and ultra-violet can be measured emanating from the hands of a healer and increasing up to a thousand times more than the usual minimal amount present.

That doesn't happen, though, when it is not needed. Often, I have been asked by someone, including reporters, to put my hands on them because they have been told that my hands have been "red hot" or someone has felt tingling or a pulling sensation. I ask them if they have anything wrong and if they say that they have not then I tell them they are not liable to feel anything. Only when there is a need, it seems, are the healing energies drawn through. And it's not my hands which are hot. The energies involved heat the patient's body.

It seems too, that there are many and various sensations and reactions experienced by patients, some of which just cannot be described. Time also plays a part; For example, I try to make sure that anyone suffering from a blocked sinus does not leave until half an hour after the treatment has finished. I have often found that if patients drive off directly after treatment, they often have to stop their cars to deal with a flood of mucus. This tends to start 20 mins after treatment.

Those with a hearing problem may experience heat inside the ear during treatment, but very little increase in hearing. Later, they comment: "I left you in Plymouth and while driving through Truro realised that I was hearing more clearly." There appears to be about an hour's delay in effect when treating those with hearing problems.

That's the rule but there are exceptions which test this rule; probably depending upon what is exactly wrong. It must be made clear, too, in a vast majority of cases the benefits are temporary. That is, they do not last after just one treatment but that several, or even many treatments are necessary before there is a sustained improvement. I have experienced, however, a number of "one off" cases where the benefit has lasted after just one treatment but that several, or even many treatments are necessary before there is a sustained improvement. I have experienced, however, a number of "one off" cases where the benefit has lasted after just one treatment.

In a number of cases where there is a displacement of some kind, say in the spine or a joint, the correction time can vary. I have been told by patients, for example, "Two hours after I left you, I felt a movement in my back, there was a click and it went back into place!" Sometimes the move can take place the next day, within half an hour or perhaps even minutes after treatment,

I remember one 16yr old girl, over 6ft tall, who had been brought to me by her mother. I was told that she had had repeated treatments from an osteopath or chiropractor, who succeeded each time putting her spine back in place, but that it was painful, and she had come to dread these sessions. They had been told of me by someone who had benefited by my "laying on of hands" – I do not manipulate at all – and felt that perhaps there would be a gentler and more lasting effect.

223

I gave her treatment; she could feel a "pulling" in her spine and a certain amount of heat. She changed places with her mother who was also in need of help for a physical condition, and I had been working for about 10 minutes when the girl gave a yelp and said that her back was alright now and that the ache had gone. But the pain when the back righted itself was a bad as when she had been manipulated by the osteopath.

Where there is a displacement with resulting pain or ache, there is usually an intensification of the pain during treatment, but the area lessens, and the pain seems to come to a definable point. It appears that energy healing continues to work for some time, even after treatment has ceased. Again, it may take a number of treatments to correct the problem. The character of the patient has a part to play too.

Arthritis in its various forms is something which is crippling and exceedingly painful. Many and varied, too, are the treatments but so many of those suffering from arthritis, who come to our clinics for treatment, have been previously helped primarily by painkillers of one sort or another. I make sure that these patients are told, and given written material, explaining that, while they usually experience great relief during the treatment, within 12 or 24 hours the pain is back with a vengeance with perhaps a slight improvement after that. They may say while having the treatment that it is "wonderfully soothing" or "comforting" but there is an inclination next day to say that they wished they had never met me.

Barney Camfield's book was written at a time when physical claims with regard to healing were possible. This is now not the case, and it is more likely that any advertising claims where healing may help, relate to mental issues such as stress.

As previously noted, Barney used to work for the local Plymouth TV station, and he kept in touch with them after he had left. They asked if he was interested in doing a healing experiment on TV, and Barney agreed.

Dr Alec Forbes, (founder of the Bristol Cancer Clinic,) asked Barney to give healing to a patient whilst linked to a battery powered electro-encephalograph. The patient would be connected to a separate machine, both of which would show the individuals brainwaves. Healers are supposed to have a strong "alpha" wave, and healing experiments have shown that when healing is given the patient's brainwaves tend to change and match the healer's pattern of waves.

Barney giving healing for dental surgery at Moretonhampstead
Church, at Harvest Festival
(old pre-digital)

For the TV experiment Barney asked them to supply people he didn't know, and hadn't had healing before, so that there was not any influence. Taking him at his word they gained "guinea pigs" from the Arthritis and Rheumatism Council. Also, one volunteer turned up at the stage door, shortly before the programme was about to be taped. The electro-encephalograph machines also arrived late from London and were still being set up after the programme started, whilst a film was being shown. Barney's brainwaves were checked, and yes, he did have a strong Alpha wave, and the volunteer from the stage door did have quite a different brain wave. As healing was given the "patient's," brainwaves matched Barney's. The lady suffered from arthritis and commented that during the healing she felt a comfortable glow, but due to the filming process, Barney gave the lady a longer healing treatment than was normal for the condition. When the volunteer reported back to Barney a few weeks later, she said that the pain had been so bad following the healing, that she stayed in bed all day, but after 24 hours she was fine, (and the pain did not return for at least 6 years after treatment.)

In the late 70's – 80's Barney's clinics were often seen as the last port of call, after trying all else. With certain types of condition, we would always advise people to use healing in conjunction with orthodox medicine and make their doctors aware that they were having healing, and in some cases to direct people to their doctor if they had not already been. At the end of the day, a doctor is legally responsible for their patient's health, and it wasn't for us to say that a client should stop their medication, or to make a diagnosis. In my view, it was always about complementary medicine, not alternate. For example, I have known in some cases that healing can alleviate some of the side effects of certain drugs, or to boost energy levels, so why not use the two in conjunction. Orthodox medicine is best at certain things, and complementary medicine at others, and sometimes a blend of both can be beneficial for the patient. When I started healing, complementary medicine in general was frowned upon by most doctors. But over the years, certain therapies have become more acceptable, and even advertised in the doctors waiting room!

It depended on the client, but Barney's front room was where most of the healing happened, and four or five healers awaited. Normally the room was filled with chatter and laughter, which was a healing therapy in itself. For new or difficult cases, Barney would take them off to his study or "insulting", room as he liked to call it. Sometimes with new people, you would only get the one chance. With Barney's training in psychology, he would go in hard and get straight down to the nitty gritty.

At the time, Barney was one of the first people to start talking about the mind relating to the body. Many illnesses can start in the mind, later to manifest in the body, and since then many great books have been written on the subject. One such book that I can recommend is, "Your Body Speaks Your Mind", by Debbie Shapiro. Barney also used dreams, and graphology as aids to healing. Any healer worth their salt tends to use more than one discipline in complementary medicine, to aid healing. Everyone is different and drawn to different things, even within one discipline. For example, with Flower Essences, some people are drawn to the Bach Flower Remedy range, others to the Australian Bush Essences, or many other ranges and combinations. Usually, what people feel drawn to is what they need.

So, it is within this type of environment that I learned healing and qualified in 1981. The skill of healing is not a special thing. What is more special is the desire to want to do it. Most people have done healing in some form in their lives, for example when a child scratches it's knee and runs to its mother crying, the mother will say, "Lets kiss it better," cuddling the child lovingly The tears of the child will subside, and they do feel a little better. Or similarly, holding a person's hand, if either they are ill or in great distress, helps that person. Like any skill, virtually anyone can do it, to some degree. If I can equate healing, to the playing of a piano. For a few people, it is innate within them, it is a gifted talent, like the Matthew Manning's of this world, (Matthew is the most tested healer.) The vast majority of us, which includes me, have to practice/work at it to get a level of skill. And finally, the few of us that are tone deaf or just don't want to do it.

It was good to work at Barney's clinics because with the number of people attending, and frequency of the sessions, it was a more intensive training, with each person being unique in their personality, experiences and "dis-ease".

The general format for healing, was to have the person receiving healing to sit on an up-right kitchen chair. My own personal quirk was to have the person sit with their back against my legs, because I could also transfer healing from my legs as well as my hands, and felt that it was working from a central basis, and you will not be surprised that backs seemed to be my specialty.

Next was to place both hands on the top or just above the head, and try to key into that person, working to their highest potential. (Sometimes I would receive psychic impressions from the person, sometimes not, it was just a possible added tool, not a requirement. Even if you just stayed on the head channelling the energies, generally the energies would go to the place which most needed them). I would visualise their energy centres opening up.

Then from the head, my hands would then be placed on either shoulder, for a few minutes, then down through the arms to the hands. I then worked down through the chakra system at the front of the body, and then placing the hands on the spine then hips, working down through the legs to the feet, via the joints, ie knees and ankles.

If the client told me what their health issue was, or I sensed a problem in a certain part, then I would give it more time channelling energies.

Towards the end of the healing I would place my hands back on their shoulders, visualising all their energy centres closing like a flower, so they would be protected, from their outer environment. Some healers would shake any "dis-eased" energy gained from their hands, which is not particularly advisable. A better way is to physically or mentally wash the hands, so that the "diseased" energy is not passed on to other people or stays with the healer.

The biggest mistake that I ever made was at the beginning of my training, whilst healing I acted as a battery and not a channel. Not a wise move as I nearly passed out. Very few of us have a great surplus of energy, so it's best not to act as a battery.

If you want to train as a healer, or looking for a healer in the UK, then I can recommend going to the websites – www.westcountry-natural-healing-fellowship.co.uk *,* www.thehealingtrust.org *or the* www.britishalliancehealingassociation.co.uk

As well as being a healer for people, Barney also performed healings on animals, and did exorcisms of houses. I was wary of the last one for a long time, as I didn't want anything to do with ghosts, although I do have a couple of interesting experiences. When I was a young teenager, my mother went to visit my grandmother in Birmingham with my sister and I, staying over. My grandfather had died quite a few years before, but I always remember my grandmother making paper spills for him to light his cigarettes. I must admit that I was a bit worried about staying over, and him appearing to me. In my mind I kept mentally saying, "please don't show yourself to me, or do it in a way that won't frighten me". The following morning, I was the first one in the household to get up. So, I went downstairs and sat by the embers in the fireplace for a bit of warmth. (This is pre-houses generally having central heating.) Not thinking of anything in particular,

I suddenly had this great urge to smoke, and it wasn't going to go away until I had had one. Fortunately, my grandmother also smoked, so I stole one of her cigarettes and lit up and sat there smoking right to the end feeling satisfied. It wasn't until I thought about it afterwards that I realised what had happened. I had not smoked before or since, but my grandfather had been a strong smoker, and he died of lung cancer. Therefore, he did find a way of getting in touch with me without scaring me!

So why was I originally scared of ghosts? This is mainly to do with the house of my other grandmother. That house always felt very spooky. I was told by my mother, that when she took me to the house for the first time as a baby in a pram, I cried my eyes out, as soon as I crossed the threshold. Each weekend my sister and I were taken to this grandmother to stay overnight, and my parents would pick us up on Sunday. This was an old Victorian house, which had servant quarters. To cut a long story short, both my sister and I had a great fear of the hall and stairs in this house, and unfortunately for us the bathroom was at the top of those stairs. My grandmother lived with my great aunt, Ida, and for some reason would only put the hall light on, but not the stair light so we had to run the gauntlet up these very bad feeling stairs to the bathroom alone, and of course we tried to do this as little as possible. On the whole, I would say that the house did not have a good feel, and both my sister and I were always grateful when my parents came to take us home. Many years later when my sister and I told our Mother about our feelings with regard to the house, she apologised and said that she would not have left us there if she had known, but she had also had her own nasty experience in the house. Not long after my grandmother had died, my parents who were now living in Devon stayed overnight at the house to clear it and slept in the grandmother's bed. My grandmother had never really liked my mother, and she was woken up in the middle of the night, feeling hands around her throat trying to strangle her. (I would have definitely freaked out at that one.) But the house was finally cleared, no mean job, as my grandmother and great aunt never threw anything out, even sweet wrappers. The place was sold to a developer, and as the way with a lot of large houses in Birmingham they were going to turn it into two flats. Having knocked off for one day, and locking up behind themselves, the builders were surprised when they returned the next day to see white paint and feathers splattered all over the hall and stairway. I often felt that there was an evil presence in that house, and I often wondered what has happened to it since then.

In the past, whenever I had a nightmare, it was always about that house, and I would wake up in a cold sweat. Many, many years later, when I was talking to a hypnotist friend about it, he suggested that it might be interesting to get to the bottom of this problem. I had never tried hypnosis before, and probably like yourself had only seen programmes on TV where hypnotists get people to make fools of themselves, which didn't greatly impress me. But I trusted him so gave it a go.

Now this took a few sessions, and not everything came out in one go. He relaxed me down and took me back to the time when I was a baby and had crossed the threshold of that house for the first time. I saw myself crying from outside of my body, and as we went in and I looked up the stairs I could see a Victorian lady, with a dead baby in her arms. She was looking straight at me as a baby, wanting to exchange me for her own child. (Oh shit, I thought. What am I going to do now?) The only way around this was going to be exorcism, and to try and get the lady to pass on. Taking all the courage that I had, I spiritually went up those stairs, to talk to the lady. I bought down the column of white light and talked to her. She offered her dead baby to me. I had to decline her. It was not right that she wanted to swap babies so to speak, and that her own baby was waiting for her on the "other side," so giving her back her baby, I brought the spirit of her child into view. As she saw the child, tears fell down her cheeks, she opened her arms wide and embraced her child for a few moments. As the lady stood up, the child took her hand and they both walked into the "light", very happy to be back together. Afterwards, it was like a big weight had been taken off my shoulders, and since then I have not had nightmares about that house.

Years later, at a workshop at Chalice Well, Glastonbury I did a meditation to find out more about the spirit lady. Her name was Kathleen May, and she was an intelligent schoolteacher in service, who became pregnant but was unmarried. She almost went full term with the baby but was thrown out of service. Her career was ended. She could not support herself and the child. Therefore she "murdered the unborn", just before it was due. Although this was not one of my past lives, I did feel as if I was inside her. Kathleen felt as if the abdomen was burning internally and had used her education to get rid of the baby, pushing the baby out. It was fully formed. She was overcome with remorse and grief and had a mental breakdown. Kathleen was shunned by all in the village, and scorned. She said that she had failed her charges, ill-used her knowledge and was totally alone and reviled, but most of all she had failed her child. I asked why she had offered her baby to me? "When you first came to the house as a baby, you cried, because you felt what I had done, and was fearful, so you protected yourself and closed down any mediumistic ability. That fear continued as you grew up, to the extent that you feared the house. When you came, through hypnotherapy, I saw that you were a healer. I tried to give you my baby to heal. You sent me to the Light, and I found the living spirit of my baby on the other side".

When we are talking general house exorcism, Barney always taught me the way to do it was to go into each room of the house and fill it with love. I did have one occasion when someone asked me to do a house exorcism, but I don't think that she will ask me back again. It was a little house tucked away up on Dartmoor in Devon. The lady had a lodger in the house, and a lot of strange unexplained happenings had been going on. The house itself felt quite heavy and dark, and I must say that I was a little bit perturbed by it. However, I thought that I would put Barney's training into action and went into each room filling it with love. By the end of the session, the house felt a lot better, cleansed and not so dark. A few days later I received a call from the lady, saying that a pipe had burst in the loft, and the house had been flooded, so it cleansed physically as well as spiritually.

The final exorcism I want to relate to you happened at Compton Dundon a few years ago, not far from Glastonbury. I had spent the day with my friend Jan in Glastonbury, and before I made my way home she wanted to go to Compton Dundon Church, as it had a very old yew tree in its grounds from which she wanted to make a tree essence. Yew trees are often planted in church graveyards as they are supposed to ward off evil. The yew tree is amongst the longest living of trees, so they also have a reputation of being the storyteller, probably because they stand as sentinels in time, and have seen it all.

Anyway, back to the experience, this yew tree is huge. We walked around this tree looking for a spot where Jan could secure her small bowl of water, in which she was going to collect the energies of the tree. Having found a spot, where it would be tucked away out of sight of passers-by, we aimed for the church itself. Jan had been told by another friend that the energies in the church were not all that they could be. As we walked into the church it was a little oppressive. Fortunately, there was no one else around, so Jan and I sat on either side of the church, trying to key into the energies to see what was going on. Sitting quietly with my eyes closed, filling the church with loving energies, I had an impression of an old man dressed in 18th century clothing. He had a rather sour disposition, and a very god- fearing nature. Certainly, didn't want any "mumbo jumbo" going on in "his" church, and was very proper in what he thought was right and wrong. Although I do believe when we got his story from him, his wife had run off with the vicar of the time. My friend was wearing a hippie style of dress, with the long flowing skirt, and I was dressed very much in a non-hippie style. So, I thought that it would have to be me that took him on. He wasn't going to listen to Jan and was very stuck in his thinking that he was the guardian of the church, and the judge of the morals of the people who used it. His spirit was very difficult to dislodge. Having already brought down the column of light, I reasoned with him for quite some time, that he was only hurting himself, and that he needed to move on. A "being" was standing in the light with their arms outstretched to him all this time, finally he relented and decided that he would leave. Since his departure the energies in the church have been a lot lighter.

The essence from the Yew tree outside, when it was ready was used for past life recall, and according to Jan it is quite effective. If you want to take an essence for a specific condition, it is always best to contact a qualified, registered practitioner. In the UK, a good website to use is www.bfvea.com

Returning to Barney, he developed something called Psycho Expansion, which is basically a relaxation technique (not hypnosis,) that apparently allowed people to visit their own childhood, past and future lives, remotely view other places around the globe, planetary travel, micro and macrocosm, into animals, into trees etc.

Barney would continually ask me to join in with these sessions. It was something that I really didn't want to do, but one night he caught me off guard with no excuses, so I weakened and joined in.

For newcomers, the first exercise would be to go to, say your 5th Birthday in this lifetime, and you would be watching it outside of yourself. As with any of the exercises, if you could change anything that you were seeing, it was your imagination that was talking. If you couldn't change anything, then it wasn't your imagination. Normally we would do three different types of exercise a session, and after each exercise we would write down our experiences. After many years of doing it, I have yet another ring binder full!

All walks of life and ages attended these groups, and it was interesting after each exercise, to relate what we received. From those who felt nothing, only sensations, only colours, colours with shapes, what I call black and white TV, to those who had virtual reality.

Generally, incarnations are either male or female, and could be anywhere on the planet. From my experience, I have been both male and female, and had lives all over the world, including England, Australia, North and South America, China, France, Africa, and the list goes on.

It was very amusing to one gay young gentleman that any time he went into a past life, he was always a male in the haybarn with a milkmaid. It became a good-natured standing joke.

One golden rule that we never broke was viewing our own death in this lifetime. Life is for living, not for the manner of our death to hang over us. Death for all of us is a certainty. All things reduce down to vibration and energy, and energy cannot be destroyed, only transmuted. Psycho Expansion taught me that death is just change, and part of the journey.

There was always an added safeguard during the relaxation. If there was something we didn't want to experience, we could always safely and quickly come back to the room. For example, sometimes people did not want to experience a death in a particular lifetime, because it was too traumatic, then they had the option not to.

When looking at your past lives, quite often a theme will keep emerging, ie herbs, health, music, art, clergy, soldiers etc.

Quite often people reincarnate in groups, but change roles within that group, in various lifetimes. Many years ago, Arthur Guirdham a physician and psychiatrist, wrote books on reincarnation "We Are One Another" and, "The Cathars and Reincarnation", and through his work, and using hypnotherapy he had found a group in his area that had been Cathars in previous lives at Montsegur.

Although using a different method Barney also found evidence of group reincarnation, and that the group recurred at many times in history, depending on the learning or "job" required. We did not have many Cathars in the group, apart from perhaps one, but Barney often said that he had found twenty- six members of the Arthurian set. Even finding Arthur himself, who at that point was a woman in her fifties, (and probably now passed onto her next incarnation.)

Having said this, I did have had a strange "light bulb going on" moment within the last year, when I was reading Paul Broadhurst's book "The Axis of Heaven", in which he mentions an energy line that runs down from Tintagel on the north coast of Cornwall to Plymouth on the south coast of Devon. Perhaps this is why Barney found the twenty-six members of the Arthurian set. It was like moths being called to the light.

During my time in Psycho Expansion was when I first found out about my life as a Knights Templar, which later had a connection to Fountain. I do feel that in a previous life that Colin Bloy was also a Templar, as the Knights were guardians of the energy lines, and he was also very interested in them.

Here is a very short excerpt, from my notes of when I first met my Templar life, way back in 1982, although it starts before I became a full-blown Templar in that lifetime.

1150AD? Looking at a stain glass window of Edward the Confessor, he has an orb in one hand and a mitre in the other. I know myself to be male, with dark short hair, in the prime of life, and as I look down at myself, I am wearing a brown habit and sandals, so I must be a monk. My hand is holding something aloft, and as I gaze at it, it is a cross. When Barney asks me what my name is, Harold comes out of my mouth.

My view drifts, and I see myself praying in the Cathedral, feeling frightened. I see an image of a devil gargoyle, with its eyes lit up and breathing fire. (Perhaps I should have come out at that point!) *Something is drastically wrong, feel evil, demonology? I am trying to exorcise it from the cathedral.* (Some things don't change - sigh.)

Again, the scene changes, and I see the death reaper, but jump back to the altar of the cathedral, where I notice that the energies have now been returned to balance. As I stand there, I notice the sword now hanging at my side.

Seeing the reaper was a precursor that I would see my death in that life. I view a distant battlefield far from home, with a sword in my chest. I am wearing a Crusader tunic with a red cross. As I die, I have a feeling of getting lighter and lighter, and being guided up. There is a feeling of peace and warmth.

Then I go to my next linear incarnation as a woman in 1300AD...

When you view a past life, you rarely get the whole thing in one go. Quite often you only get shown a highlight or highlights, and each time you go back you find out something new about that life.

Psycho Expansion is very good at letting you feel what it is like to walk in another person's shoes. Barney would always say, that if you are happy in your present life, don't do Psycho Expansion as it will change you, or give you a different perspective on life.

My next big growth period was with Fountain International, which seemed to be a natural progression from being a healer of people, to a healer of places. It was a little bit like preventative medicine. If you could heal a place, then fewer people would come to you for healing, but more of this later. Over the years I have been to many workshops, lectures, conferences, and met many great people with wonderful knowledge. I suppose I would describe myself as a "spiritual mongrel." I know a little about a lot of things, but this learning has enabled me to make connections between different subjects, rather than be immersed in just one subject.

Now I am beginning to get ahead of myself, and in Part 3 we will return to 1981, and what happened after the Brighton Experiment, which both Colin and I would say is the most important part of this book.

At present, we are globally going through troubled times, and using Colin's research, YOU can do something, to help your community, which will then ripple out around the world.

So here it is for your serious consideration.

The World needs your input

Part 3

Fountain, 1981 And Beyond

After September 1981, as a result of the experiment in Brighton, and the promotion of the "idea", more people became drawn to the Fountain concept, and wanted to try it in their own communities.

Fountain, later to become Fountain International, became a world-wide healing project, based on the concept that communities like people suffer from dis-ease, and may be healed. Advocating that by tuning in one's healing/white light/Pure Love thoughts to an agreed point of focus in one's own community for just a few moments each day, (from whence it goes out into the locality), it is possible to improve the health of the community, and ultimately the health of the world. Changes in the earth's energy field can be detected after meditational work, as shown in the Brighton Experiment.

The "idea" has immense power. When people meditate together the energy they generate multiplies and expands. The mind is a very powerful tool. By learning to use it constructively we begin to glimpse the boundless possibilities that are available to us.

On an individual level, people who regularly practice this "work", experience an expansion of awareness and sensitivities. In a world where the majority feel disempowered, and despairing, there is something that you can do, which has an effect. Fountain and other similarly like-minded groups can provide light in the darkness, for healing has the effect of raising the level of both individual and group consciousness.

Fountain International has always been open to EVERYONE, of whatever faith, colour, nationality or political persuasion, etc, and gives the POWER TO HEAL THE WORLD, back to the people. We have no rules, creed or dogma, acting more like a network of like-minded people whose desire is to help and uplift humanity, and thereby help it fulfil its true potential and destiny.

What constitutes membership? Fountain International claims to be an idea rather than an organisation and has studiously avoided hierarchy and structure. Too many well-meaning spiritual groups have become so structured, that the preservation of the structure of the organisation becomes more important than the work itself. As we are without structure, each member or group works independently of the others. However, people working with the concept may also come together on a spiritual daily basis for global purposes, e.g using Glastonbury Tor, England as the focal point, or with events like World Healing Day, and times of crises whether manmade or natural etc.

There has never been membership fee. (Although donations are gratefully received.) Fountain is not competitive with other groups, nor does it seek to be authoritarian. It is about doing the work and nothing else. It is not a refuge, nor a club, it offers nothing, save the sharing of ideas, and networking via the Fountain International Magazine http://www.fountaininternationalmagazine.com quarterly, monthly Newsletter, which are both free, and our Facebook page. If a person is ready to become a member, they know and do. If someone understands the spiritual truths and the notion of love, then they are already a member, and for no other reason.

So, stripped back to its barest form, we are about, sending out Pure Love energy, to a community focal point, and then through the energy system, to balance, to heal, and inspire communities to reach their highest potential. It's about cleaning up our own backyards, and self-empowerment. Everyone can help to heal the ills of their community no matter what their circumstances, if they so desire, even the bedridden.

There is no need to be a dowser, to do this work. If you want to track the results of your personal or groups efforts, you can keep an eye on the local papers, the police reports. Or just by looking around your community and sensing the general feeling. I remember some years back, when I was putting on a Fountain Conference in Torquay. The focal point for the Torquay Fountain Group is a clock tower on the harbour side. One road led between the clock tower and the venue for the conference. At the time, the tower had been ignored for many, many years, and as a part of the conference we performed a Fountain meditation using the clock tower as the focal point, through which we were going to send energy, before sending it out into the community. Civic awareness is often triggered by such action, and within weeks of the meditation, Torbay Council decided that it was time to renovate the old clock tower. It's now been loving restored, even to the point of renewing its bells, to strike the hour. Not many people in the town even knew that it had bells.

Starting a Fountain Group

Anyone can start a Fountain Group. It is not necessary to have a large number of interested people, just two or three "regulars" to start with is fine. Meet together and decide what should be your focal point. This may be a fountain, clock tower, sacred site or whatever seems appropriate for your community. You may also like to discuss various local problems, which you feel may need healing, but it is vital that no judgements are made, because we work with Divine Will, and not our will. Then you are ready to start. You may like to begin by asking for the help of higher consciousness, and then strongly visualize a column of white light descending onto your chosen focal point. Once you have sent the white light to the focal point, visualised in your mind's eye, the energy flowing out into the whole area.

Each person or group involved with the work is unique, no two are the same. The only thing that they have in common is that they put the concept into action, which is great. In fact, they don't even need to call themselves a Fountain group, because the concept can easily be tagged on to a variety of meetings, and gatherings, the options are endless. I'll talk more about the magazine later, but in the old-style Fountain magazine a prominent place was always given to explaining what Fountain was, and a technique that could be used in doing the work. What follows is an example of such a page.

A FEW MOMENTS OF YOUR TIME EACH DAY

The technique is beautifully simple. All it needs is an individual or group to relax into a peaceful frame of mind (a meditative state) and send healing/white light/pure love thoughts to the focal point within the community, recognising its problems. This may give a positive reaction in the Earth's fields to this movement of energy. The extension of this on a world scale will produce a network of Light around the Planet.

Now I can hear a few groans. I don't meditate. I don't have the time. So, I can make it simpler than that. Thought is our strongest power. If you are working alone, and you are doing the washing up, walking the dog, etc, just send a thought of Pure Love to your focal point, on a daily basis. (If you have a problem with focussing on your focal point, use a photo.) For groups, it's slightly different, only in as much as the energy from each group member should go out from the

242

focal point at the same time each day, to increase its power. Now obviously if you are meeting as a group, you are doing it together, but on days when you are not meeting, it is best to agree a time on when the energy should be released from your focal point. So that when you send your thought to the focal point, you put a proviso on it, that the energy goes out from the focal point at the agreed time. A number of people in the same locality performing this action each day will gradually build up a reservoir of loving energies at the focal point, which is kept "topped up" by daily continuation of the concept, to daily go out into the community.

A point to remember about the individual and the non-dowsing point of view, the great attraction of Fountain work is that everyone is valued, nothing is ever wasted. Caring people who formerly felt powerless to transform the problems and suffering around them knew for the first time that a few minutes a day of dedicated and focused thought makes a difference to the community, and to the world.

So how do you pick a focal point for your community? How will you know that it is linked into the energy system? Picking a focal point for your own community is simple. As I have shown for the Torquay group, it doesn't have to be a fountain. But it does need to be something that you and/or others can strongly visualise, and from past experiences I know that it doesn't need to be on an energy line before you start, because once you start practising the concept, it will plug itself into the grid.

If you would like to work using a guided meditation, here is an example below. Again, if working alone, record it and play it back to yourself:

Fountain Type Meditation

Visualise yourself under a dome of golden energy…

Feel yourself drawing up silver energy from the Earth, through your feet,

Up your legs and into your chest, and place this energy in your own heart centre…

Feel the bond of love between the Earth and yourself…

Then begin to draw down the white light of Cosmic Love from the spiritual realms, through the top of

Your head, down your neck, into your chest and place it, too, in your heart centre…

Allow these two energies to mix and blend…

Slowly the combined energies expand and fill the whole of your being…

It fills you with pure love, light, harmony and joy…

Accept any of this energy which you may need to make yourself whole…

Then visualise this field of love expanding out into the room, filling the building

And spilling out onto the street…

When you feel that the time is right, visualise yourself sending this energy to

Your focal point, cleansing it and filling it with unconditional love...

See the focal point sparkling and buzzing with energy...

See this energy then pouring from your focal point, flowing into the earth around it

And flowing throughout the community...

See it radiating Pure Love and Light to all, uplifting everyone within this energy field...

When you have finished, retain part of this pure energy, so that you can share it with others...

Sense the room again, feel yourself back in your chair, wiggle your toes, and then open your eyes.

A physical fact about our brain rhythms is that they are active, to some degree throughout every moment of our lives. They are measured in cycles per second. In a relaxed meditative state (alpha) the frequency is from 7 to 14 cycles. This is the level of tranquillity and well-being. Our normal active, waking state (beta) is 14 – 30 cycles. On the borders of sleep, we function at between 4 – 7 cycles (theta). This is the creative, and problem-solving level. Below 4 cycles is delta, the level of deep sleep. In beta we seem to separate from each other, but in alpha, delta and theta we are subconsciously communicating all the time.)

You now know what Fountain/Fountain International is, and how you can work with it, the rest is up to you there is no right or wrong way. So, if you feel drawn to put it into action, WELCOME.

The Fountain Logo

As the number of people becoming involved increased it was felt that there should be some sort of linking logo, for "Fountaineers", or people working with the concept.

Now this is not quite the original symbol. The original was a black and white drawing of the above, with the dove facing downwards. In my stay as Fountain Co-ordinator I, with the backing of the conference changed the direction of the dove, but with many years of hindsight I do regret doing this, although I did have my own thought processes at the time. The downward dove is the descending Holy Spirit, talked about by Colin at the Glastonbury gathering. My mind at the time latched onto spirit, and I thought that it should be rising.

However, I have always cherished this logo and since the re-entering back into Fountain in 2011, though a few people have said to me that I should change it. Not that it hasn't been different in the past. When the energy fields moved from 8 up to a 12, as did an increase in known chakras, the logo changed to a banded circle with a twelve-pointed star within, and a downward dove at the top to reflect this. It's also been a stylised fountain, radiating out, within a banded circle. But to me this symbol is the best spiritual representation of Fountain.

The colour blue relates to the colour of healing, the gold the divine, and the white dove purity. The two circles represent the microcosm and the macrocosm. The microcosm is you/ your community/your country, with the dove coming out of the microcosm which is pure love and spirit reaching out towards the world and earth, the macrocosm. The dove itself is springing up from a fountain, the fountain of knowledge and wisdom, gained over the years by Colin Bloy and his many band of people.

Another way of looking at the symbolism of the Fountain logo, was kindly submitted by Alan Peskett in the following Fountain Magazine article:

"The Logo comprises of an Inner Circle and an Outer Circle, a Six-Pointed Star, a Fountain and a Dove representing the Holy Spirit.

The Outer Circle is representative of the Macrocosm, the greater expansive beyond contemplation or beyond limited thinking this is expressed as the white squares of the Templar, (temple floor grid) Black and White Checkerboard Grid (the universal healing grid). The white squares are empty beyond belief because it represents beyond the limit of our thinking it is the pure space of the that not yet formed the space in which existence can.

The Inner Circle is representative of going within to the Microcosm the greater definition of the inner universe of all that is beyond expression of fineness beyond the smallest particle we could possibly express. This is represented as the Black Squares on the Templar Grid (the temple floor of healing) that forms when we commence healing in our own way. The darkness here is merely the closeness of all energies of sophistication and saturation formed from that which has been created and defined it is the pool of Knowledge and viability of potentiality. It is the myriad of formed expression. The black squares are black squares full of black squares and so on ad infinitum = the microcosm. The Harmonic and its harmonics repeated into the infinite (that which produces the Harmonious and Harmony).

Healing occurs at the balance point of the Macrocosm meeting the Microcosm, it is the floor of understanding where we are when the Holy Spirit meets us in healing, the perfect balance point, the meeting of where the inner meets the outer meets the universal, the perfect place of uniting balance, this is why it's the best place to be for healing, start here and heal the within and the outer, this is why there is no separation, the temple floor is the planet earth, the grid of light forming is the healing grid developed from our thoughts our vibrations of interaction with the holy spirit and our balanced pivotal point. The temple is the perfect dome of above combining the inverted dome below (a bowl), forming a circle of healing around which is in fact a sphere (a three-dimensional circle), it is a perfect balanced energy field and equal yin and yang, feminine and masculine, above and below, earth and cosmic, inner/outer, physical/spiritual, combined oneness with the holy spirit. We create this bubble of light, The Temple with our altered state of good intent, natural healing capability available to all, we do this by transferring our lower ego state to our higher ego state by invoking the greater good and the divine plan (not our own personal will, but ego less), in all our healing. This is healing, self-less healing.

The Six Pointed Star, (Star of David or Solomon's Seal), is representative of mother earth's natural energies, being a reflection of the mineral kingdom hence the six fold crystal lattice, The Earth Star, it is representative of drawing and uniting it with the divine Kingdoms of inspiration and the love from above (the Dove of peace) the energies of no limitation, and then spreading the resultant energies of highest good towards wherever, with these unlimiting thoughts the divine angels can back and support us in what we can achieve for the earth, from the greater good, of the unfoldment of the divine plan on earth. The reformation of Temple Earth.

The Fountain being the symbol of the fountain head of all knowledge and wisdom that springs forth from within each of us the natural inspiration of that which arises within, sometimes referred to as the source within us all who gather together to heal beyond our own limited thinking. Remember One with God is a majority. The Fountain is that which naturally springs forth from within towards any and all healing. The Dove, which is the symbol of the Holy Spirit, is the symbol of uniting all, and is the representative of the divine in all kingdoms in all healing.

The Dove never flies until it has somewhere else to land where it can be received, it naturally flies up to heaven and down to earth and repeats this where required. It is the symbol of purity and peace, and sometimes reaches down to where we are and then lifts us up beyond our limit thinking towards where we are going in our thoughts, inspiration and motivation, towards uniting with and within a greater whole, the microcosm and the macrocosm joined as one (The creator of the universe really knew what was to be done). We can now join in as co-creators by giving ourselves the opportunity of joining in with the Holy Spirit and enabling our other co-creators to join in and enjoy the same opportunities of healing. Healing is simple, it is a matter of combining self with selfless spirit and in that uniting, spreading the greater universal good available to all".

Spreading the Fountain Concept

Moving on to the "being" of Fountain, as stated before there was very little structure, apart from what was essential. Within a few years of inception, it was felt that it would be good to have a conference, where "Fountaineers" could meet each other, to share and swap information. The conferences over the years were very popular, it was a good way to inspire and re charge your batteries for another year.

The daily enquiries from people wanting to learn more about Fountain, and how to do it and the putting together of the conferences necessitated that there be a Fountain office. The office for Fountain/Fountain International has generally been in south of England, Sussex with Jenni Lansdowne, then Lelant, Cornwall under the auspices of Sheila and Trevor Nevins, back to Seaford, East Sussex under the care of Peggy Bunt, to come to Torquay, Devon and myself, then on to Chandlers Ford, Hampshire and Rosemary Barry plus a committee, Peter Barker in Evesham Worcestershire, and back to Brighton with Joy Byner. Here I have to also mention Giles Bryant, who promoted the Fountain Concept, at festivals to a younger generation. At present, there is no office as such or committee.

But returning to when the office first went to Cornwall. Here they set about producing 6 booklets, and leaflets which gave a basic background to Fountain and related subjects. The titles were 1) Introduction to Fountain International, 2) Leylines – Pathways of the Collective Consciousness, 3) The Gentle Art of Dowsing, 3) Meditation and Spiritual Science, 4) Living Leylines, 5) Community Healing, 6) Dowsing Ley Energies and the Search for the Grail. They also produced an A5 magazine with interesting articles on the further research going on within Fountain and other related subjects, which came out four times a year. When grabbing one of those early magazines, which so happened to be Spring 1988, the articles included A Geomantic History of Gaia, Moon Magic, Revere the Old Places, the Magical Principles Behind Fountain, Songlines, The Change of an Archetype, How to Move Mountains, Networking, and Conference details. It was all on the leading edge of research and knowledge. Hamish Miller was part of the "team" in Cornwall, and being a blacksmith, he produced dowsing rods for people who required them. The leaflets, booklets, Colin's past two books, and the hardcopy magazines are all out of print, and I have no back issues, apart from my own personal copies, but some of the writings have appeared in this book, and crop up in the current e-zine.

Each group or person was a power unto themselves, and the office just an information post, which also arranged conferences and visits to places of interest; ie Malta, Majorca, Rhodes, and Russia. In general, any profits from the conferences or the holidays went towards the running of the office, the production of the booklets and magazine. No one who worked in the office or did anything else was paid. We were all just willing volunteers. (More of the e-Magazine later).

As a result of each person or group working under their own power and auspices, without a formal structure, a strong, self-reliant network developed, whose heart was everywhere and nowhere. But one also needed to take into account the charisma of Colin Bloy. He was not just a leader, but the glue that kept us together. He attended all Conferences, did workshops, promoted Fountain whenever he could, and his continuing research kept us all enthralled. As I have said before, Colin did not have ego, he was always there to encourage other researchers, and always ready to give healing to anyone who wanted it.

The instalment of an office at Lelant in Cornwall, through the kindness of Paul Hawkins who lent us office space, and under the full-time care of Sheila and Trevor Nevins, communication within the network became possible and fruitful, leading to more dedicated Fountaineers.

Over the years, at times, Fountain has identified itself with world-wide campaigns, leading to link ups with various groups, which are not Fountain, but have a common aim. Some of these qualify as high spots in my memory, not only because of the sense of unity, but even more because of the obvious beneficial effects. I particularly recall the Harmonic Convergence in 1987. Inspired by the Mayan prophecies, the World Federation of Peace sent out a call for 144,000 people to link at sunrise on August 16th at sacred sites around the world. The purpose was to unite at the Earth's acupuncture points to create a resonating link between Universal Energies and the Earth. It proved to have far reaching results, and intuitively felt that it sparked off a huge change in collective consciousness.

My memory of the event, takes me back to a group of us, going to the wilds of Dartmoor, in England, to a Tor that is the home to the Ten Commandments Stone. At a very ungodly hour before sunrise, we trudged up to the Tor, carrying blankets, a waterproof sheet, candles etc in the dark. Sitting on that granite outcrop, waiting for the allotted time, wasn't at first too chilling, apart from sitting on granite stone, but just before the sun came up over the horizon, it became very cold and damp. There was a stillness in the air and from our vantage point we could see 360 degrees over the land that is Devon. Then I saw the faint glimmer of the sun, and as it rose, it was a beautiful sight, warming, lighting and caressing the land. At the allotted time, we did the linked in meditation, as set out by the World Federation of Peace. When we finally walked back to the car we felt that we had united with the other 144,00 people, and were uplifted by the energies generated.

Early morning sunrise – Harmonic Convergence - Dartmoor

Following on from Colin's work, others have been inspired to do their own research projects to extend the knowledge and understanding of subtle energies. The first major study came from Paul Broadhurst and Hamish Miller. While working on the famous St Michael Line, which runs from Cornwall up to the Norfolk coast, they discovered a hitherto unsuspected anomaly, which they subsequently described in their fascinating book, "The Sun and the Serpent", a must for ley hunters. They discovered by painstaking and meticulous dowsing over several years, that the alignment meets with and is entwined by two serpentine energy flows (caduceus, symbol of healing), which are the feminine and masculine energies.

Chris Street followed on from this with his book "Earth Stars". Which is a geometric ground plan underlying London's ancient sacred sites and its significance for the New Age. He states that, *"London's most ancient sacred sites are not scattered about the capital at random. On the contrary, they are laid out to a very definite pattern of perfect pentagrams, hexagrams, circles and stars. By no stretch of the imagination is this a chance formation. Every single individual pattern interconnect with the rest to form a vast and beautiful network linking sacred sites around the whole of Greater London."*

Gary Biltcliffe with Caroline Hoare also researched and wrote the book "The Spine of Albion", in a similar vein to "The Sun and the Serpent", taking him 15 years. The Belinus line, is Britain's longest north – south energy line. Starting from the Isle of Wight up to Durness in Scotland. Whilst researching this less known alignment, the authors discovered accompanying hidden pathways channelling a mysterious force that the ancient indigenous tribes around the world associated with a mythical creature called a dragon.

In 2016 Paul Broadhurst unveiled his latest discoveries in "Axis of Heaven". Which through research uncovers the energy line of preference, for royalty and power.

You can see, that the empowerment has worked, and there have been many wonderful researchers in Fountain, which unfortunately this book does not give me time to mention, as I am concentrating on

Colin Bloy's work, but perhaps sometime in the future.... However, there is no doubt that Fountain was a boiling pot of thoughts, theories, insights, experiences, and research, which was pure nectar to me.

In 1996, Fountain International decided to go online, and have its own website, (www.fountaininternational.org) instigated and first run by Ben Lovegrove, and latterly by Terry Monnery. This was an added voice in the world and moving with the way in which the world was going. At the time, it served the purpose of promoting the Fountain Concept, who we were, and how it all began etc. It was a static site, so as the years rolled by it did not encourage people to return to it. This website was taken down approximately in 2012, after being superseded by the website, www.fountaininternationalmagazine.com But more of this later.

My Early Days with Fountain

As you now know my first knowledge of Fountain goes back to late 1986, when I saw an advert in a local newspaper for the Fountain Conference. at Exeter University, and as I said earlier, it was the draw of listening to a talk by Michael Bentine, which stirred me to action. Exeter, which was my local University, so I wouldn't have far to go, and as I booked it was arranged that I would car share with another lady coming from Torquay, this was Anna Scott. (In the purple cardigan in the following picture, and myself in front of her).

In those times, the conferences were aimed at St Michael's Day 29th September. Once we had arrived, managed to find our way around the campus, and put our bags in our rooms, we went straight to the lecture room. You could feel the energy and happiness in the air. Whenever I went to a Fountain Conference, it was always welcoming, no cliques, just "down to earth people," with no flights of fancy. We did a daily Fountain type meditation, which lifted the energies of the venue even more, as well as ourselves. My disappointment of not being able to see Michael Bentine, soon evaporated. The speakers were all enthusiastic about their subjects, and lured you in. Leaving you not wanting it to stop.

What did I first think of Colin? Well I was a different person then, as I was chronically shy. He had the type of voice that I adored, which was a mellow, smooth, executive voice, very relaxed. Colin always spoke off the cuff and was very knowledgeable in his subject. It is not an understatement to say I was awe struck. I certainly couldn't go to speak to him, for fear of looking stupid.

By the end of the weekend Anna and I were totally sold and enthusiastic on the idea of getting a few people together and starting a Fountain Group, which we did. We found a room to rent for the meetings at the local Quaker House and advertised it. We felt that rather than people just coming for a short meditation, we would get speakers to give talks, and make an evening of it, on a fortnightly basis.

Early days of Torquay Fountain Group - Back Line: Ray Reynolds,
Anna Scott, Morwenna Lloyd
Middle Line: Von Reynolds, Me, Suzann Miller
Front: Nita Brass and Christopher Miller

At our first meeting, we had to decide what was going to be the focal point of the group, and in our case, it was the clock tower on the harbour side which was easy to visualize and known to all. It also stood in the middle of the main Torquay clubland. With all the problems such activities can cause, especially in a seaside resort. As in Brighton we dowsed around the clock tower to see what the energies, were. Now considering that the tower was on the busy holiday harbour side, on a roundabout, this was no mean feat, and much amused people watching from their hotel rooms, and those walking by, and making sure that we did not get knocked down by passing traffic. On this first trip, we found that the clock tower was not linked into the energy system, but as soon as we started to use the tower as a focal point, it clicked into the local system.

One of the first confirmations that something was happening, was to be found in our local "Herald Express" newspaper, from a police report. The title of the article was "Harbourside Clean-up Has Worked. The head of South Devon's police division, Chief Supt Colin Moore, highlighted the drop in on street disturbance to an all-time low. The Torquay group has run for many years, but has latterly been continued as a closed group, which meets at a member's house.

During its early years the Torquay group, saw many interesting speakers, talking on all subjects from spiritual to complementary medicine. As previously mentioned, we also took part in some sun rise meditations, and we went to Fountain workshops with Colin Bloy, Hamish Miller and others.

In those day's we were inspired by the closeness of the Fountain office, and the happenings in Cornwall. Every year we would attend the Fountain Conferences for our energy "fix" and recharge. The venues were normally in a different place each year on campus's, and generally in the south, although I did attend one in York.

It's funny what the mind remembers. About the conferences for example, I have a vivid memory at Exeter University of my first bear hug from Hamish Miller, of a well-known member being lost and unable to find a party going on and advising him to dowse for it. In Spain watching a flock of golden eagles fly over a canyon and standing on a table singing an English song to our Spanish hosts in a monastery where President Franco was buried, and an electric storm running around the rim of the cliffs.

Prisoners of war were made to build his tomb deep, which is cavernous inside into a rocky outcrop, is on a major energy line in Spain, so he can still exert his influence. However, many died in its construction. The conference held in the Tintagel Castle Hotel was also very memorable, perched high on the coastline cliffs with Merlin's Cave below and Tintagel Castle itself on an opposite cliff, which was all very atmospheric. Our lecture space looked out over the sea and cliffs, and in the evening, Tim Wheater played haunting music on his flute. Very early one morning I gave myself a fright as I went down to Merlin's cave on my own to do some photography. As I walked across the beach, I heard what I thought was an indistinct voice. Now I knew that the place was empty, and my stomach turned over, but I bravely continued to the cave, and was relieved when I found it to be a pigeon. (Just to put the story into context, some years earlier I had visited Tintagel with Barney Camfield, and meditated by the cliff waterfall, and had been told that this place was a communications point.)

Klaus Brudny

It seems mad now, but we went for a weekend conference in Mallorca. This was when we first came across Klaus Brudny from Austria, who worked with radiaesthesie. The most emotional moment was when he played the sounds that the planets make. When he played the Earth's sound I was moved to tears, as it sounded like a baby crying in the dark. On that same weekend, we were taken up into the Mountains, so that we could dowse and visit a nearby Cathedral. As we went up this impossible narrow road by coach, with a clear drop on one side, it was a harrowing journey, but we had to be content, as the driver's name was Gabriel, like the archangel.

There was also a Fountain holiday to Malta, and George de Trafford of the Maltese Fountain Group, showed us around some of the ancient sites of the island, like Hagar Qim, and shared esoteric knowledge.

Waiting in the airport lounge in Malta

Of course, Malta was a stronghold of the Knights Templar, and we visited their preceptory on the island, which was well worth the visit. Another place of interest was the Hypogeum, the site of an old underground temple. To get to it we had to go down a very long circular metal staircase, to the temple cut from stone. The atmosphere was very rarefied. I well remember the guide, (Rene Bugey,) who took us to all the sites in Malta, and by the end of the trip I believe that we had found another convert. Interestingly he came from a family of trapeze artists, but he couldn't follow in their footsteps because he was scared of heights.

As well as all these fabulous trips and events we did some local dowsing of an ancient sites in our area.

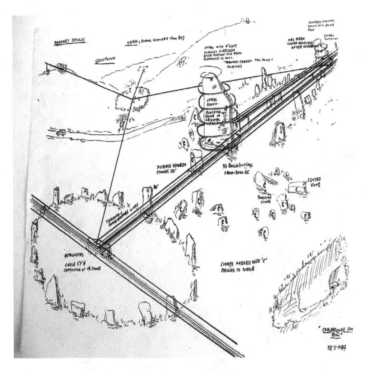

Challacombe, Dartmoor, England

In Torquay, there is a very old chapel on a hill, overlooking the bay, but surrounded and hidden by trees. As with most churches perched high on hills, it is dedicated to St Michael, although in previous times it was dedicated to the Virgin Mary. The place is a real mystery, and nobody knows it's true history, or why it is there. Some say there are tunnels to the nearby Torre Abbey – but they would have had to have tunnelled through a lot of rock. Some say that it was a hermit cell and others say that in its early history, before the trees came it was a signpost for seafarers.

When we first went to this site, it was rather run down, used by the homeless, drink and possibly drug takers, plus dog walkers. The small building itself is just walls and a roof. There was no floor to speak of, just uneven rocks. So, with rods in our hands we started to dowse the energy of the site immediately around the chapel, as it was. In a sense, we had to be fairly quick, as our energy interacted with the site, and would expand the lines and other energies. Below is a map of the energies we found outside of the chapel, on 22.2.1987, between 11.30am and 12.30pm.

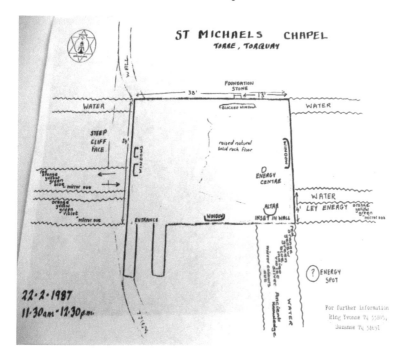

1st Diagram, dowsing St Michael's Chapel

We were able to find water at the site, the foundation stone, and of course, yes it was on an energy system. Having recently learnt of colour being found within energy lines, we tried out this theory, and the results are shown. We managed to get into the chapel later and found an energy centre within.

For the next few weeks we used the chapel as the focal point of our meditations, then went back and dowsed again on the 12.04.1987 between 11am and 1pm. We aimed for the same time of day, because energies can fluctuate over a 24hour period.

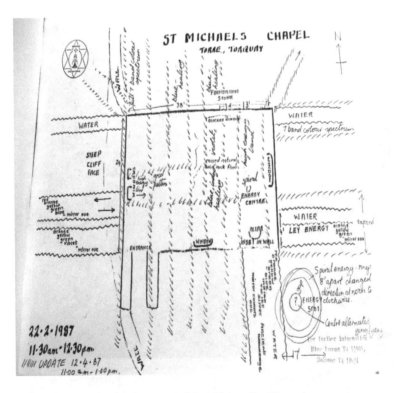

2nd Diagram of St Michael's Chapel

264

From this diagram, you can see that a lot of things have changed and expanded. Within and outside the chapel a chequer board effect could be dowsed, which for us meant harmony and balance. Both the energy spot inside and outside of the chapel had a spiral within it. We were surprised at how much of an effect we had made on the site.

As reported by Colin earlier in the book, of trying to stop a riot situation, the Torquay Fountain Group worked on a similar situation. Every so often something would happen in the town which would deserve the attention of the pure love energies. At that point in time our local newspaper came out daily. The following weekend Saturday 28th May 1988, two factions as well as the normal holiday makers would be visiting the town. The first was the home football game, between Torquay United and Swansea, tensions were mounting as Swansea supporters had a fearsome reputation for trouble, and there were fans travelling down without tickets. Now if that wasn't bad enough the National Front were coming down for a conference. The town was going into panic mode. On the Tuesday before the event, the Torquay Group decided to do a Fountain meditation on the Saturday morning, to try and ease the day. We sent out a calming, pure love energy to this groups, then waited to see what happened in the papers. The result. "All quiet at NF camp", the police said that the camp had not been brought to their attention at all. "Arrests – but police pleased", for the football match. A massive police operation to stop yobs marring the big match went off smoothly.

In September 1988, I was asked to take over the office reins by Peggy Bunt, I was thrilled, but it was a major task to take on, (and bear in mind I already had a full-time stressful job). I saw my role as the Co-ordinator for Fountain International, so I did everything office related, apart from Chris Miller whom I drafted in to be the treasurer, and Paul Keonig for one issue, then Morwenna Lloyd to edit and produce the Fountain International Magazine, when it was still hardcopy.

As I ran the Fountain International Office from my bedroom, quite often I felt the energetic "being" that was Fountain, and it was a heavy-duty energy.

The Conference Photo Opportunity Outside The Rozel Hotel

In those days it really was like having two full time jobs, with the mail, stock sales, posting out the magazine, dealing with phone calls, writing for the Magazine, solely organising a conference, which took over the whole of the Rozel Hotel, overlooking the sea at Weston Super Mare, (which is now expensive flats,) including accommodation, meals, speakers and taping etc, etc. During my tenure the conference always went to the Rozel, booking the same time each year.

But another strange fact. There is a smaller enclosed beach to the right of Weston's large beach, and the hotel overlooked it. Many years before as a small child I had nearly drowned on that beach, as I lost my footing down a hole, whilst walking in the sea. I can remember with clarity that time, and looking at the murky sand filled water, not knowing which way was up. It was only my mother's alertness and quick thinking that saved me!

Whilst I was running the office David Icke gave our address as a contact address in his book. Well the mail went wild, and it did get up to a hundred letters a day, much to the disgust of the postman.

At the 1992 conference, it was put forward that Fountain UK, needed a single focus for the United Kingdom, as the local focal point works on local problems, this new point would be linked into by all people working with the Fountain Concept, and the aim would be towards improvement in the spiritual energies of the UK as a whole, and to put energy towards solving problems particular to the UK. Also, the main point could be used as a reservoir of energy which groups could call on when they needed extra energy for certain projects. Silbury Hill in Wiltshire was the winner of the competition, as it was easy to visualise, due to its conical shape, with top removed.

During that period Fountain International was in a very healthy state, we had groups around the world, including 23 in Australia. But after four years, I was beginning to become stale, and knew that I should step aside for new energy, to take Fountain International on to its next step. I handed over to Rosemary Barry and indulged myself in my other interest complementary medicine.

But there was to be my second coming in 2011. More of this later.

Fountain International was based on research using dowsing. Colin in his infectious enthusiasm, retelling of his experiences, and demonstrations of dowsing inspired people to have a go for themselves. Some feel drawn to this show me method, in an attempt to verify something that cannot be seen by the naked eye, and not just for finding water. If this is you, two good places to start are, the American Dowsers Society and the British Society of Dowsers.

For Colin, dowsing was his main way of working. Even after the initial work and the forming of Fountain, he used this method to track interaction and changes in energy. Proving the effect of the "concept."

Having said all this, dowsing is not essential to the day to day Fountain International, the most important thing is working with the "concept" in your community, and as mentioned earlier dowsing is not the only way to verify results. Please don't feel that you have to be a dowser to do the "work", it is not essential.

There follows an article that Hamish Miller wrote for the Fountain Magazine. Hamish was a healer of note, who became a great dowser. In 1988, he described for Fountain members a meeting with Colin Bloy and how and why he started to dowse.

A Dowser's Dilemma
By Hamish Miller

"You can do it yourself", said Colin Bloy.

"Nonsense". I thought irreverently...then..."nice enough fellow, but a touch around the bend!"

I had listened open mouthed! For the second time I had tried to take in the import of what he was saying on the reality of dowsing energy changes that happen when healers go to work on people and communities using earth and etheric energies.

I had just asked him if he could find me someone in Cornwall who could dowse and check the field patterns and forms while we worked as healers in our various sanctuaries and while we spread the Fountain idea in the western tip of England.

"Yes, you can!" he said, reading my mind, smiling and metaphorically patting me on the head.

He was right of course.

A couple of weeks later, having beaten out the metal, and invoking Vulcan at every hammer blow...a decent pair of iron rods... designed to be unaffected by the howling winds on the top of the moors. I experienced a magic moment when the rods responded of their own volition and showed me were the weak, vestigial energy line between Trencrom and St Michael's Mount. An unforgettable moment which has led me to more and more fascinating people and places as time goes on.

The initial Dowser's dilemma was simply whether the findings were valid, whether the shapes and lines that were being picked up were believable...and, if they were whether they had any value or contribution to make to the scheme of things.

Some people said that the dowsing was unnecessary and that the healing was the important issue. Absolutely right! But if one compares two photographs of the same scene, one in black and white (which may be exquisitely beautiful!) and one in colour, at least there is an added dimension to the second which may trigger even greater depths of beauty.

A great deal of the future of Fountain is surely in the search for new realms of healing stimulated by the development of dowsing beyond the process of using tools, to "spiritual" dowsing by hands and mind on etheric bodies and concepts of human consciousness which has been lost for a very long time.

That dowsing works no longer has to be proved. British Telecom, the Electricity Board, British Gas, the various Water Boards, all use dowsers in problem areas and they never seem to pick up each other's pipes and wires and cables and things because they have trained themselves to be absolutely specific in defining what they are looking for.

My good friend Don Wilkinson was a legend in Cornwall. He not only found water with his very lively forked stick, but he predicted the depth and amount of flow available, and for the sceptical he has the ultimate answer. He comes in with his rig, drills where he puts the peg in, stuffs the pipe down, sticks on the valve on and says "There y'are guvnor" or words to that effect. Not only does he do this but says if he's wrong, he'll dig another hole for free! Now it wouldn't be a commercial proposition to do this if he was often wrong, and Don has very, very seldom had to drill twice! So his dowsing has proved to be accurate and sound many hundreds of times and there is no reason to question that practical, working dowsers who know how to interpret what the rods, pendulum, hands or whatever, are telling them about the earth energy fields should be any less accurate.

In the last few experiments in simultaneous dowsing of energy forms and changes, sometimes in areas hundreds of miles apart, have shown quite remarkable accuracy in interpretations of shape and size. In this case measured drawings have been exchanged in the post with no prior communication other than a telephone call to confirm the time of the experiment. In many cases dowsers have come up with similar drawings of entirely new shapes which had hitherto been unrecorded.

Here are some illustrations of typical simple forms which appear in the initial stages of Fountain community healing work.

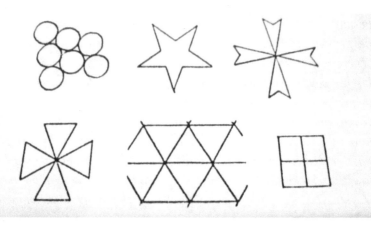

The second series is indicative of the much more complex shapes which exist after some years of progression into more profound interpretations of earth healing.

The forms are appearing in colour and sequences of colour, and in the case of multi=banded energy lines the colour sequence tends to be a mirror image of itself from the centre out. When one becomes aware of these sequences the inner lines occasionally cease to respond to a "simple colour" interpretation and change their reaction to a much more abstract concepts e.g knowledge, teaching, healing, communication.

The current dilemma is that we are trapped in semantics. "jargonese", historically defined meanings of words and concepts which are at the moment too "crude" to receive the accurate data from the thought forms with the energy lines.

Intuitive "dowsing" into New Age thinking by hundreds of groups and individuals around the world will gradually come up with positive answers. We are groping towards some of the knowledge that was part of the way of living of the old people. Their senses were fine tuned to the earth, planetary and cosmic energies, their "dowsing" was a natural function of being...and their quiet inner knowledge of the oneness of things around them allowed them to have a totally satisfying relationship with their Creator.

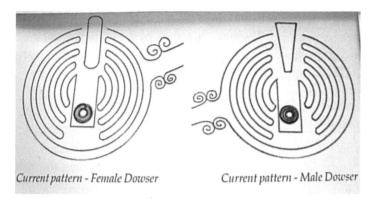

Current pattern - Female Dowser   Current pattern - Male Dowser

The most recent earth energy patterns in parts of the UK dowsed with painstaking accuracy, is produced above. It is a sophisticated, beautiful labyrinth and similar forms have been used by spiritually aware people for millennia. It has a deep significance in Greek, Egyptian and European history, and in Templar discipline. It is depicted on the floor of Chartes Cathedral and was carved around 2000BC on a granite wall in Tintagel, Cornwall...it has Atlantean connections.

Male and female dowsers agree on the labyrinth shape, but the earth connections come in from the opposite sides and the "entrance" is slightly a different shape.

Re-Declaration of the Church of Love

Andorra 29th March 1986

How did this come to be? In 1978 on a visit to Montsegur in the Cathar country of S W France, Colin Bloy had dowsed the meadow where 300 Perfecti were burned alive in 1244. The dowsing revealed a Latin text which referred to the rebuilding of the Church of Love in Andorra in 1986.

Colin Bloy had been delving into the history and legend of what happened to the last of the Cathar people who held out for so long at Montsegur against the crusade initiated by the Pope and the King of France in 1209.

For 35 years the Albigenses in the Languedoc area of south of France had been systematically hunted down and died in their thousands labelled heretics and enemies of the State.

By 1244 only a few were left, and the last of these, some 215 Cathar Pefecti were induced to surrender at Montsegur on the 16th of March. They were led out from the castle to a field below and burned in a communal funeral pyre.

Legend has it that four of the Perfecti escaped the previous evening with a "treasure" variously described as the Holy Grail, documents of great value, books, gold, and which some of us believe could have been the ability to transit the ultimate power of love, suing a combination of earth and etheric energies. These four people, and whatever they carried with them, have been the subject of countless stories and legends. Colin Bloy learned during his research that they had spent time in a cave somewhere in Andorra. This relates to an earlier section in the book where Colin tells of the finding of the "Grail Stone". Subsequent work with field patterns and research in the area led Colin back to Montsegur, and in the field where the

Perfecti died, a dowsable message in a mixture of Greek and Latin was discovered.

Translation of the text.

"In awe and wrath of God, and in that awe known by all evolved men. I build thee in the name of love. I nominate Pitirifio Itit Reog spokeman of all the Cathars. Rome hates Trionian Piddires, the oriflame bearing god of all trionian things, that difficult but faithful god. The powerful God of the Cathars fears nothing but was building his church at a bad time. He will build the church in 1986 in Andorra .... (an indecipherable name) will give the gospel. As a light bearing priest he excels. The far-off people of Londuri will approach. I will build the day the God of all Cathars lives again. The awe the temple of those divines will join eternity, and the God of all Cathars providing the ideology".

Notes

Pitirifio Itit Reog – presumably name of surviving Cathar Perfectus.

Trionis – Latin, the constellation of the Great and Little Bear. Presumed origin of triune, agnostic attribute of the Divine.

Piddires – a god name?

Oriflame – the oriflame was the forked pennant carried at the lance head by the Knights Templar.

Lonunorum – the people of London. Peter Dawkins has shown London to be the heart chakra of Europe and finds this reference entirely apt in any awakening process.

What we have here is the text which is a result of imperfect Latin and some Greek, and probably imperfect dowsing. It would be good if more dowsers could go to the Campels Cremats at the foot of Montsegur and check. One I know has, and is in general agreement that it exists as stated after a cursory examination. It takes a good hour to do it properly. A curious Frenchman was instructed in dowsing, read the first to words, turned pale and made a hasty retreat, which helped convince me of its objective reality.

The Cathar Prophesy of 1244AD

In March 1985 Colin was prompted to write the proclamation for the Church of Love, which took place on Good Friday 28th March 1986 in Andorra, he does not claim authorship. It was all written in ten minutes. He states, *"Although this was written to fulfil a 14th century prophecy that the Cathar Church would be restored in 1986. I believe it is a statement relevant to all Fountaineers and that we too are part of the Church of Love/Alphaega. It's a bit of a special church and I don't want you to get confused over the word "church", because it means "Communion or Fellowship", ecclesia in Greek, nothing more".*

Proclamation of the Church of Love

It has no fabric – only understanding.

It has no membership – save those who know they belong.

It has no rivals – because it is non-competitive.

It has no ambition because it seeks only to serve.

It knows no boundaries, for nationalisms are unloving.

It is not of itself because it seeks to enrich all groups and religions.

It acknowledges all great teachers of all ages who have shown the truth of love.

Those who participate, practice the truth of love in their daily being.

There is no walk of life or nationality that is a barrier.

Those who are, know

It seeks not to teach, but to be, and by being enrich.

It recognises the collectivity of all humanity and that we are all one with the one.

It recognises that the way we are may be the way of those around us because we are that way.

It recognises the whole planet as a being, of which we are part.

It recognises that the time has come for the supreme transmutation, the ultimate alchemical act, the conscious change of the ego into a voluntary return to the whole

It does not proclaim itself with a loud voice but in the subtle realms of loving.

It salutes all those in the past who have blazoned the path but paid the price.

It admits no hierarchy or structure, for no one is greater than another.

Its members shall know each other by their deeds, being, and their eyes and by no other outward sign, save a fraternal embrace.

Each one will dedicate their life to silent loving of their neighbour, and environment, and the planet, whilst carrying out their daily tasks, however exalted or humble.

It has no rewards to offer, either here or the hereafter, save that of the ineffable joy of being and loving.

Its members shall seek only to advance the cause of understanding within whichever church, group or family they happen to be.

They shall do good by stealth and teach only by example.

They shall heal their neighbour, their community and our planet.

They shall know no fear and feel no shame and their witness shall prevail over all odds.

It has no secrets, no Arcanum, no initiation save that of the true understanding of the power of love and that, if we want it to be so, the world will change, but only if we change ourselves first.

All those who belong, belong. THAT IS ALPHAEGA.

Many churches, groups and sects are impositions by the few on the many, preying on weakness. Alphaega is the reverse.

It liberates and promotes individual strength.

Such vestigial structure as it may eventually have, must come from those who know they are part of it.

Colin Describes the Church of Love

A pretty sanctimonious name, but it will do for the moment. Until we find something better.

Why Andorra? Well the prophecy of Montesegur, not far away, indicates it, and some strange formative things, at least for me, went on, some years ago, after finding the stone in Arsinal, a mile or two away from La Massana. Andorra is a strange and beautiful country. Isolated from airways, railways and motorways, you have to make a bit of an effort. It isn't for the effete, comfort seeking, jet age traveller, he or she would never make it. But once you are there, it's something else. It is the so-called oldest democracy in Europe, thus, one presumes the world, although women only got the vote recently. As a co-prinicipate, it was brought into being by Charlemagne, when the local inhabitants gave him such doughty assistance against the Moors, that he gave them independence, based on the twin suzerainity of the Bishop of Seo de Urgel, the nearest Spanish See, and the King of France and his successors. Thus, President Mitterand, (at the time of writing), is co-prince of Andorra. I was once grasped by the hand of Giscard d'Estaing in Massana, in error, I hasten to add, when he made a princely visit there, (perhaps alluding to Colin's distant relation to Spanish royalty.)

It was also outside the jurisdiction of the Inquisition, which is why the last Cathars made their way there, and tradition has is that religious attitudes of the various parishes are not necessarily in accord with Roman dogma, but a modus vivendi has been long establishes.

Andorra abounds with legends that occur in the rest of Europe. Why is the church of Saint Meritxell where it is, and the stones keep moving there? A statue, a black Madonna, was found in a bush indicating the site etc, etc. All the Romanesque 12th century churches, and various megalithic and petroglyphic signs indicate that here is a very special place in Europe.

Why there?

Apart from the whole Grail story of the Arsinal Valley, abutting on La Massana, and the fact than an associated plateau is called La Plana de Gral, those people who wish to be associated with the declaration of the Church of Love by being there, or by assisting at other meetings, at a similar time in their own countries, will be taking part in a gathering, which hopefully may be considered as the beginning of a very significant process in healing the planet.

Fountain Groups and other like-minded entities have specifically concerned themselves with their own communities, cleaning up and linking up with their neighbouring towns, cities and countries, but with the primary emphasis on one's own doorstep. Thus far, the evidence is positive, and the associated fields are developing in many countries. There is still a long way to go in that direction.

It is generally agreed that Fountain International is not didactic, that is to say it is not concerned with teaching. Enough groups exist for that purpose. Fountain Groups are about "doing" in one's own community, and those who consider themselves members are so because they already understand the general spiritual principles. They are non-competitive for Fountain work may be carried out by spiritual groups who are also concerned with other things.

However, whereas that is based on a perhaps novel approach to the subtle energies that go to make up the collective consciousness of the planet, and appears to be perfectly valid, many people have been concerned primarily with a "macro" approach to meet the most immediate problem – that is to say, preserving this particular seat of consciousness in the Universe.

Sending light and love to the planet has had, so far as dowsers are concerned, no discernible effect on the ley lines. Fountain work has. That does not make Fountain Groups necessarily better, but what does it mean, possibly, the traditional aphorism "Sort yourself out first, then your neighbours and community", in that order, has some validity.

If the process is, as it appears in its clumsy way, making progress, we are still left with the macro problem, and as Buckmister Fuller has said. *"The current situation is too dangerous to be resolved by anything less than Utopia."*

Whereas progress is being made in the re-invigoration of the pathways of consciousness that link the nations and communities, If the Church of Love has any significance, other than mere spiritual self- indulgence, it must be to unite all those people, whatever their formal national and religious associations, in the notion of pure love.

That's non-competitive and requires no re-alignment of allegiance, cultural, religious or national, as many re-groupings have tended to do. It is not involved in lengthy debates about how many angels you can get on the head of a pin, how many arms has Shiva which descendent of the prophet Muhammad is the most legitimate, whether Jesus was the true Messiah, or whether Buddha was a great messenger, it's about simple spiritual common-sense LOVE. The application of which, in whichever community or tradition you happen to be, is effective, if properly practised.

Carl Jung may be considered to be one of the great messengers, and his definition of the group consciousness seems pretty valid. He also defined the archetype that exist within group consciousness, and which superimpose themselves above rationale ethnic and cultural readings.

If you like, they are the bad gods. Whatever their names in the different mythologies and pantheons, they come down in practical terms to hatred, envy, greed, violence, egotism, and similar debasements of the human condition. They are there because they let it be there, not because they are imposed upon us.

It is my wish, if I may personalise the whole affair a little, that we take into account the following quotation from Barry McWaters book, "Conscious Evolution".

"Beyond the capacities of the individual, the group, properly supported by its members, and well blessed from above, may be the vehicle for transmitting high level energies necessary for the emergence of the New Age. If a small yet critical percentage of humanity is able to see the light, there will be intimations and ramifications for all the human family".

Thus those who came together in Andorra, and those who don't even know about us, can join together in the ultimate spiritual exercise, which may not be that day, but of which that day may be a processor, it may be possible to form the permanent hard use percentage for when no sacrifice is too great, for whom no reward is required, for whom pure love is all, that is easy to say people who are ready, having been through the agonies of total awareness, with all its horrors, to make that voluntary return to the group which can only be achieved through love, and form with themselves and all those who seek to unite with them, a composite group united in being, in the spirit – we're still all individuals in ordinary consciousness, which is prepared in a state of total meditation and self-forgetfulness, as one being, to go into collective consciousness of humanity and root out those negative archetypes, expecting them from that over-riding position of human evolution.

Consciousness is an objective field. Its archetypes are objective. Objective spiritual work, through meditation, dedication, and total visualisation is capable of performing the supreme alchemical act, if carried out in pure love, not easy. Human consciousness, in its higher states can make human evolution conscious.

The declaration of the Church of Love in Andorra on Good Friday, 29th March 1986, Grail Day, La Massana, at 11 am local time, may be a step in the right direction. That's what I hope the first group meditation will be about.

What will follow, I cannot know. But if its honest, it should be alright.

The strengthening of the feminine principle. Gaia which is part of the Jehovah Elohim, after the Archangel Michael has expunged those demons that torment humanity, should be the basic image. They are only names and emerge from a Judeo-Christian-Helleristic culture – they are real in whatever cultural forms they take, for all mankind when applied as archetypes.

Those who understand these forms in other religious – cultural contexts, please apply them in their own way, and fervently desire.

Colin Comments on Alphaega – The Next Step

The objective of the Alphaega Group is to unite all those of whatever race, religion culture or nationality who recognises that ultimate truth is Pure Love. (This name was happened upon before the Christian Church used it for religious education group. So we would not use it in the future.) Not just from the ivy clad armchair, as some academic conclusion, but as a persuasive. Consuming, and all imbuing, vibrant truth that changes one's life.

Whereas Fountain Groups are drawn from members of that community, which each one serves because they are an integral part of the collective consciousness of that group, so the Alphaega Group must unite all those components of mankind which make up the collective consciousness of the world.

Photographs of the Virgin Mary making an appearance at El Escorial in Spain are significant, in that, whereas it may be persuasively argued that a genuine manifestation of the feminine principle is taking place. I personally do not believe that the shade of the Mother of Jesus is there. What I do feel is that the feminine principle manifests within the vocabulary of the imagery that resides in the collective consciousness of those who focus their attention on that site, and it is a site which exists within the Roman Marian tradition. Whither Isis? What happens in similar sites in Japan?

Images of the Virgin Mary occur in Marian situations. In a very important sense, to the extent that it is cogently arguable that in the Aquarian Age, evolution is henceforth participatory, it could be very confusing and counterproductive, if a variety of the artefacts of human collective consciousness obscure the truth that unites all humanity.

Magic is a confusing word, rather live LOVE, but let us define it as something that does not, as some have decreed, go against the laws of nature, but something that begins where the laws of positivism end, because of the laws of nature are the laws of God, and God is infinite, the perception of rational man is limited to the five senses, and this perceives nature as finite.

Once one admits consciousness as an objective field, the new dimensions of reality become admissible. For instance, the world idea. As Sir James Jeans once said. "The more I look at the universe the less I see it as a great machine, and much more as a great idea".

Magic is about ideas, and about will. I doubt whether many would argue that there is a baser form of existence than the world in which we live. It is the densest known form of idea.

Consciousness is structured. It does not reside uniquely in the brain. It exists within and around the being, and perception varies according to the point on the ladder that the relevant state of consciousness is at any given time. At the Exeter Conference Peter Dawkins volunteered to have his 8th chakra examined, which is about four feet above the head. It is available to all to perceive this new chakra.

But the 8th chakra is the Christ Consciousness, the Buddhic, and for all I know there are African and Oriental terms for describing this, but it is where the perception through Pure Love exists.

Back to magic and will. Perhaps the term "Spiritual Science" for magic will make people feel more comfortable. But there is high grade and low grade magic. It all depends on the state of consciousness, and one would expect spiritual science, in a Steiner sense, to relate to the higher degree of consciousness.

It remains constant that the use of magic to further one's own material or emotional ends through the imposition of the will, through the etheric field to influence the behaviour and brain rhythms of another is wrong, and the eventual price one pays is self-destruction, but if in total humility, submission and love, and with total intent, one participates in the re-creation of the idea of perfection of this planet, the personal consequences to one's self are totally irrelevant. It is complete self -fulfilment as a vessel of consciousness. No more no less.

It is arguable, if the universe is a great idea, that something must have gone wrong, and there are all sorts of sophistries to cope with this – the concept of the original sin. God had to create evil if he created good, man is the basest form of idea, the earth is a training ground etc, etc. there is little profit in organising such concepts into an acceptable metaphysical model. The application of Pure Love to all situations soon resolves these problems.

What do we do now? – Colin Bloy

It would be logical that the consciousness is structured and an objective field, if Pure Love can only exist with the highest form of consciousness, and if the universe is an idea, then the equation Energy=Love=Consciousness is unavoidable, and if that is true, the notion of his being participative henceforth, with this 8th chakra in subsequent evolution, takes on a whole new meaning.

One of the problems, I feel, is that man's approach to the ideal is contingent, contingent upon his race, culture, nation, etc, which is why Mary turns up in the Marian cultures, and utterly confuses everybody. We tend to work from the ground up, whereas perhaps we should work from the top downwards and from the concept of Pure Love, develop new archetypes, common to all humanity, which represent no divisive influence.

It is really sad that Islam, Christianity and Judaism acknowledge the common patriarch Abraham, that the Dome of the Rock in Jerusalem is a sacred site common to all, yet they have massacred each over the millennia.

It must be axiomatic that there is only one truth, and it must be higher than any man-made or man modified religious system. If it is true that ultimate reality is Pure Love, Pure Consciousness and Pure Energy, then as the vessels of consciousness in this particular corner of the universe, our participation in our subsequent evolution takes on a new responsibility and a new reality.

If it is true that Marian manifestations in Marian cultures are artefacts, or archetypes, in the Jungian sense, from man's collective consciousness, it's equally arguable that they got there for cultural reasons – What's culture? It may perhaps, be defined as all that is relative, contingent, parochial, customary, traditional, shared, comfortable, recognisable, with any given group of human beings – but absolute it is not.

For instance, part of my personal cultural heritage is cricket. And I happen to feel that one of the best things that can happen to an Englishman is to beat the hide off the Australians in cricket, or anything else for that matter. At the same time, if they didn't beat us occasionally, they wouldn't be worth beating and I'm sure they feel the same way about us. I can get cosmic about it, but it's totally irrelevant to the basic drama of humanity, yet it can be temporarily absorbing. Similar cultural blindness was involved in the crusades, and El Salvador and Hondruras went to war over a football match. So, let us be clear away all dross, and go for the ultimate truth, for it the magical and spiritual efforts of mankind are available to build a new idea, that makes the world a better place. It would seem logical that we ought to have an agreed idea of what that idea of perfection should be – and I do believe that the Virgin Mary manifesting in all cultural systems is the answer.

Perhaps we should consider the archetype of man, rather than the archetype of the planet, for the cells go to make up the whole rather than vice a versa.

It goes without saying that the negative archetype of envy, greed, lust, egoism etc, are generally speaking universally accepted. The confusion arises, culturally in agreeing on the positive.

287

I believe, however, there is unity in those schemas of oriental provenance which show the chakra ladder of man. Leonardo's Man against the Macrocosm, Robert Fludd's version of the same thing.

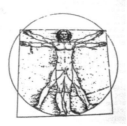

The more we bring this archetype of man into being through meditation, visualisation and the creation of the new idea, the better. At the same time, there is a cleaning up job to be done. Those negative archetypes lurk deep in the collection consciousness of humanity and will continue to lurk until such time as they are healed. They cannot be healed other than by the power of Pure Love, vindictiveness or trivialisation is only counter-productive, and furthermore only man himself can do it, because he is the vessel of consciousness on this planet.

Whereas Fountain Groups relate to individual communities, the call of Alphaega is to all humans, who with no consideration of self, without consideration of nation, race or creed, consider themselves ready to abdicate their personal identities from time to time, during an annual cycle of magical meditation, in favour of committing themselves to the creation of a group being on the astral plane, not the etheric, which has strength and tenacity of purpose, the unbending intent in Pure Love, in reality, to enter into the murky depths of the collective consciousness of humanity, and clean it out, as one would clean out a sewer.

Once again, there is no conceivable reward, furthermore, it is the most dangerous path on which any human being can set out. It can lead to insanity and death. This is not stated for melodramatic reasons, but simply as a signpost for the unwary. It is far removed from the "frisson" brushing shoulders with spiritual truth. It's not something you can let go of, once you are involved. If you're not 100% clear, stay away, 99% is not enough. It is not something which is in the slightest way self-indulgent. It's Pure Love or nothing. But that properly deployed is immutable. And fewer people than one might think are necessary. But if there is the slightest doubt don't.

Unbending intent will do all to heal the negative archetypes, build the idea again of perfect man. Man's future evolution becomes truly participative, and a great air of spiritual magic may be prepared in humility, submission and love.

It is not an act of "dementia religiosa", but a profound, total all absorbing commitment to changing the world from the depths of one's spirit. It does not imply living in a desert, eating locusts and honey, wearing sackcloth and ashes or any form of holier than thou spiritual narcissism or self-advertisement, just total quiescent, peaceful inner conviction and application. You can still go down to the pub for a drink, or whatever cultural equivalent exists.

(Sorry, old pre-digital photo)

On that appointed day of 28th March 1986, a small group of about 15 Fountaineers, stood on the appointed mound in the middle of Messana, Andorra. It was a fine day, and the place had an atmosphere of antiquity. Colin read the proclamation for the Church of Love, followed by his own Andorran Meditation. Designed start the ball rolling on the healing of negative archetypes, and the cleaning of the deepest levels of Gaia.

This meditation may last half an hour. Those who take part should be completely sure they are ready for it, and if they are, do it completely or not at all. PLEASE DO NOT TAKE IT LIGHTLY!

The Andorran Meditation - Colin Bloy

General Relaxation

1) Visualisation of the great column of light descending on the group. A hemisphere of golden light over the group. The

setting aside of the daily consciousness and the deliberate coming together in higher consciousness of all individuals to form in total love, one group being. The ego is of no significance.

2) The group being starts to identify with the whole planet. Starting at the very centre of the earth, in the mega heat and working slowly outwards in a great spiral, becoming one with the magma – then hardening rock – issuing slowly from the surface – becoming one with the mineral world in all its elements. Uniting with the dragon energy of the earth through all its mountains, valleys, fault lines, plains, rivers and seas, and out into space to the outer edges of the invisible fields that are part of the planet, as well.

3) The identification with the biological earth – the humus – organic life – primitive organisms – lichens – emergent plants – savannahs, grass, cereals, flowers, herbs, fruit trees, the great forests – and the whole process of life within the plant kingdom. Bring the dragon energy into it with love, gentleness and the authority of pure unselfish consciousness.

4) Now to the animal kingdom. The life-giving energies of the dragon now combined with the plant kingdom give rise to primitive life forms, which in turn evolve into the insect kingdom, and the whole of animal life – pulsing in harmony with the basic energies of the planet. The dragon lives in the animal world in harmony,

5) Back in time, to the various epochs, some millennia away, when emerging consciousness took human form. Through fits and starts, and external interventions, see human evolution as a being of higher consciousness, moments of harmony, moments of discord, confused at times, clear at

others, struggling with his environment – uncertain, at times lonely and desperate, at times illuminated and harmonious – ever struggling to make sense of his adventure on this planet.

6) See recorded history. The struggles for domination by one group over another. The emergence of the idea of love and its shattering as its fragility breaks each time it is put to the test.

7) See the emergence of tribes and nations, with all their pride, arrogance, glories and disasters. The many races, at time seeking to destroy each other, at times grouping towards understanding each other and reaching harmonious accommodation – then failing again.

8) See the occasional teacher who seeks to show the way in love and light – the occasional beacon that shines as one great messenger, speaks for a brief moment and fades. How his message is sometimes incorporated in state institution to have a longer but emptier lifetime and is perverted into a cause for bloodshed.

9) See how more recent great teachers represent the true understanding of love – whatever their cultural or ethnic circumstances – and see how some pervert the knowledge for personal gain, and how humans slowly and painfully grows in consciousness and awareness, but fail in lack of faith, to practice love in their daily lives, and develop instead the arrogance of reason and a people centred universe, which can be organised according to the will of the most powerful human groups. The rise of science and technology harnessed for state and political reasons to create domination for one group or other – and that the pursuit of reason alone has now

brought human adventures on this planet to the edge of total disaster.

10) See how human increasing penetration moves into the forces of life, the cosmos and is eventually showing that the materialist explanation is becoming increasingly unsatisfactory, and that the sciences of man are beginning to realise that what they are looking at is – HOW GOD WORKS – and that the missing part of all the equations is CONSCIOUSNESS – which is an objective field.

AND THAT THE HIGHEST FORM OF

CONSCIOUSNESS IS

THE PURE, UNSENTIMENTAL, UNCONDITIONAL

IDENTIFICATION WITH EVOLUTION OF

TOTAL CONSCIOUSNESS FOR THE WHOLE PLANET

-   LOVE

11) Go forward in time to a period when GAIA is finally manifest in a harmonious, complete, loving planet, in which all its members have evolved sufficiently to return to group consciousness in a totally voluntary and understanding act. When the whole human race acts as one with itself and all its component parts as a deliberate way of life, and in harmony with the rest of the cosmos.

12) Now take the archetype of human perfection – the androgyne – the sum total of male and female – of dragon and cosmos – yin and yang – complete and integrated – trembling on the brink of his cosmic destiny.

13) Holding that model, return to the present day and see people how they currently are. Now consider the labyrinth in history as myth, and in practice, as it appears in diagrams in many civilisations. The magnetic fields of the earth are like the labyrinth, which is the representation of the human brain, left and right hemispheres separated. See the new labyrinth developing in which the separate parts start to integrate, to become a totally integrated structure that may best be seen at Chartes Cathedral. See the coming together of human rational with intuition – see physical knowledge finally merged with spiritual knowledge.

Understand Golgotha, the place of the skull, and the crisis of consciousness that took place there and similar places in other human environments.

Understand the message of Osiris, and the bringing together again all the separate parts of man.

Understand the light of the East and the message of the Buddha.

Understand the real truth about Mohammed.

Understand the message of Quetzalcoatl and the unity amongst races.

14) Now see the planet energy, for ultimate energy is consciousness. Take the human archetype and the whole planet into your consciousness as one inseparable energy being. See the dragons of East and West, North and South cease their vortical movement and fuse into the straight lines of human consciousness. See the links between villages strengthen, between villages and towns, between towns and cities, between cities and whole nations, between nation and

nation, continent and continent. See the frontiers fall, and all divisions disappear. See the human body and the planet, as one whole vibrant being, in joy and harmony, with all its meridians and energy points functioning.

15) And now, go through that new and complete being, as you would through an individual when you were healing and clean it completely.

Take a clean blue light from above and use it as a broom which sweeps before it all human collective diseases – better known as the seven deadly sins.

Take them one by one

PRIDE, JEALOUSY, HATRED, GREED, SLOTH, LUST,

And the most dangerous of all, PRIDE OF SPIRIT

That somehow we are better than others because we are doing this.

This must be done in total humility.

Sweep out all these lurking demons and archetypes from the being Gaia and its inseparable human inhabitant, expelled once from all for all from our misery-ridden existence to the farthest and most distant corners of the universe, never again to trouble us.

16) See the great being, the archetypal consciousness of the whole universe in majesty, binding again all negative influences to his will, and bringing them back to whole again.

LEVIATHON BOUND

And know that it is through LOVE, that humans can henceforth participate consciously in his evolution on the Planet.

17) Holding the image of human perfection in harmony with the planet, healed of his diseases, come very slowly back, breath slowly, take a lot of time, don't talk. Relax very, very slowly, and when you really, really feel that you are back give thanks to God, embrace your neighbour and then you can jump for joy.

Some Post Andorran Thoughts on Alphaega

There was a photograph, taken at the time that showed a hemisphere of energy on the Andorran site during the declaration which is a remarkable testimony.

Healing is the Key.

First, we must heal ourselves – that is to say, become aware, become alive, become awake, and be sure of the sacred nature of being a vessel of potentially pure consciousness – Gurfjieff was significant here – pure consciousness is pure love, the stuff of healing – applied to ourselves first. Loving ourselves may seem like a superficially narcissistic self-indulgence, but of course it isn't. It means being totally aware of, and secure in the knowledge of ourselves, as vehicles of pure consciousness, and the consequent reverence and respect for ourselves, in the higher state, that that implies. It means getting rid of all dross we have acquired in what passes as education and formation in favour of ultimate truth, and the ability to observe ourselves for what we are, warts and all, and love the essence behind it.

Secondly, once that purgative discipline is accomplished, and only then, and in total humility and pure love, can one set about sharing with one's neighbour, through thought, word and deed – through sublimation, visualisation and projection – this is spiritual alchemy.

Spanish Radio & World Healing – Colin Bloy

In the radio studio

Colin Bloy was revered in Spain, and this is where he did the most of his one to one people healing, especially in his later years, and was very successful and well-known. His researches into healing are vast, and worthy of another book in its own right. For now, we will look at Colin's thoughts on world healing, albeit from 1989, but still relevant to today, followed up by his experiments of healing on Spanish Radio.

The evidence that the world is a living being is convincing. Metaphysically and physically, both philosophers and scientists are in general agreement.

Metaphysically, the totality of all things is implicit. In the positivist terms of physics, the concept of ecology and the mutual interdependence of the world's inhabitants, be they human, animal, botanical or mineral has now become a fact of systematic observation.

But the being is sick. GAIA, our mother is ill. What can we do? Clearly, we as individuals can stop polluting, visibly and invisibly.

One drop with another and another makes an ocean. Yet the problem is wider. Scientific observation has sounded the alarms at the physical level, and "green" politics is becoming the stuff of government. But that is perhaps a pragmatic way by which established politicians may remain in power rather than an authentic respect for the environment. What is important is that irreversible damage may take place.

The way to avoid that is to raise the level of consciousness so that everyday acts of every individual are sentient and caring. In short, that we all learn how to love. Not in silly, sentimental ways, but as a form of inner discipline in which personal egoism is transmuted into a general responsibility for the well-being of our neighbour and our environment, both ecologically and spiritually. That we stop thinking uniquely in terms of our own personal and short-term well-being and assume responsibility for others and the rest of the world, without any sense of reward, save that of realising ourselves as complete human beings.

Implicit is an abandonment of personal egotism. That in the Western world, the Age of Reason has produced the so-called triumph of individualism, which is only a stage for self-awareness in a materialist, non-spiritual society can be totally destructive. In the East, there is perhaps a greater historical predisposition for such a transformation. Yet the voluntary and conscious, deliberate and disciplined return to a self-awareness whose objective is to function uniquely in a loving relationship with one's neighbour, one's environment and the World, is the opening phase of the New Age.

New dimensions of understanding of the collective consciousness have emerged. The morpho-genetic field of the Cambridge biologist Rupert Sheldrake has shown that there are subtle energies that unite species, and thus the hundredth monkey syndrome is explicable. Sir George Trevelyan has spoken of Man's deliberate self-redemption.

Barry McWaters has proposed the model of conscious evolution and the fact that self-aware loving Man has the opportunity to participate in his future evolution, instead of being an unconscious puppet. Thus, Spiritual Science may be seen to be a reality.

Fountain International was formed in order to practise not only spiritual healing of individuals, but of communities. It worked, and there are many other groups like Fountain. The use of consciousness as a vehicle of new images of being within the psyche of the planet has changed the behaviour of many communities around the world. This is based on observations of how spiritual healing of individuals works, how ley lines, or pathways of consciousness unite communities and may be measured, and the geometrical forms that are created at focal points, analysed by dowsing.

The loving input of spiritual energy carrying new images of well-being of communities into focal points of those communities raises the level of awareness in a measurable way. And so more loving attitudes to one's neighbour, and one's environment develop naturally. The more people who participate the more effective it becomes.

Harmonic Convergence created a dramatic step forward in the potential of humanity. Man now has 16 chakras, on top of the normal 7 popularly known of. The ley system also functions on a 16 factor, all of which opens the door for humanity in ways we can only dream of. Yet for all of that Gaia is dying.

(In 1989 and 1990, Colin Bloy on the Spanish State radio network Radio Cadena Espanola, carried out two broadcasts, the first was a meditation on Spanish radio to eliminate the annual slaughter on the Spanish roads, and the second was a World Healing Day involving a group of healers and many thousands of listeners).

It occurred to me the other day, before going to Spain for the Annual Healing Course in a monastery to the north of Madrid, that it would be a good idea to suggest to Spanish National Radio that a repeated broadcast meditation in the period leading up to the summer exodus would be useful, revolving around the concept of personal responsibility on the roads. There was real carnage at that time.

I sent a message to Miguel Blanco, a good friend of Fountain, and presenter of a programme, on which we had earlier done healing programmes together. Individual healing where the audience participated in healing those around them who had difficulties. We had also done the first community healing programme together in Fountain mode. He thought that it might be a good idea, and within 3 hours of putting the idea to him, I was in the studio recording the meditation.

There was no rehearsal, the ink was scarcely dry on the paper. Miguel made a few corrections, and there it was, one take, done! I only stammered twice. Well, that's the Spanish way. "It's good let's go for it".

In the event, it turned out well. If there had been more time to worry over it, correct it, and pick over it, it might have lost its spontaneous flavour. There is no doubt that something like this could be extremely powerful if enough people participate. Rupert Sheldrake has identified the morpho-genetic field of species and confirmed the notion of critical mass. If enough people in Spain follow this meditation, and it is to be repeated frequently, it should work. Here is the text in English after the introductory relaxation:

"Let us get ready for a journey into space. We are going to the moon, from whence we will observe the world below us. From there we see clearly the ant hill that is humanity, or so it appears. But ants treat each other better than human beings do. They look after each

other, they communicate with each other, they share their food, and they don't kill each other with cars. But man does every day, and particularly at holiday time.

This is a time in which we are supposed to relax, a time of happiness, of re-creation, but humans kill each other with cars in the frantic and selfish desire to be first to get to their holiday places. Looking down from the moon, we can see that the causes of accidents are not road works or bad highways. The cause is personal egoism on the part of the drivers, our personal stress, our impatience, our lack of responsibility. The causes are in ourselves, and not in external factors. It is a collective human disease and is avoidable.

Let us come down, slowly, again to earth, realising that we are all members of this ant hill, and we all share the guilt. Who has not shown irritability whilst driving, in an act of irresponsibility? Who? Nobody. We shout, we give two fingers and increase our own irritation until we commit a stupid act ourselves.

We see more and more that it is a collective disease with a collective cause. Sitting in our chairs, let us consider what the individual can do to diminish and heal this collective disease. In the calm of our thoughts, we ask if we want to change the world, then where do we start? Is it with our neighbour, the man in the street or with ourselves? Yes, that must be it. With ourselves.

Thus, taking into account the phenomenon of the collective consciousness, and how it affects everybody's behaviour, let us begin to change our own attitudes towards driving. Whether we are drivers or not we can all participate in this exercise. Let us visualise ourselves and others always driving calmly, deciding that we are not competitive in traffic. It's not a race. If someone else does something silly, we do not react. We do not overtake except when we know it's 100% safe.

We are not going to be the cause of the death of a member of our family, or anybody else's. We will always leave room for the next man on the road, we will not impose ourselves on others through "machismo". We will not get irritable, we will not abuse other drivers, but in peace and serenity, we will arrive with the family intact where we are going to spend our holidays, doing no harm to other people's families – for my son is your son, your daughter is my daughter. That is love.

We will not die or kill protecting our right of way. Safety has right of way. Let the other pass, giving him a smile. Let us visualise other drivers doing the same thing, that the smile wins the day, not the word of abuse. When someone has problems with their car, we don't just hoot. We understand.

And having arrived at our holiday place, let's go home in the same way with peace, tranquillity and responsibility. Personal discipline is worth more than irritability. It is not a weakness. It's the toughest discipline there is.

And so, fixing this image permanently in our minds and consciousness, let us return to our daily lives..."

Colin's comments after the interview

Well, why not? My final message has a ring of naivety but a very profound truth behind it. Let us all participate in it for all the nations during the holiday period. Although we in England don't have the same mass exodus, this is nevertheless a human condition in which we can all help.

However, I am left with a sense of wonder that Spanish National Radio can just take a good idea and get on with it in three hours.

303

(The meditation on the radio, afterwards did seem to calm down the traffic mayhem that happened on the mass annual holiday exodus.)

Finally, it happened. I had thought September 29the 1990 was going to be the day but somehow the momentum lost its energy. Miguel Blanco phoned from Spain. "Look", he said, "let's do it on the Winter Solstice, Saturday 22 nd December. I was glad that he came through because a lot earlier effort now seems not in vain.

Felix Garcia, proprietor of the now famous Spanish esoteric magazine "Mas Alla de la Sciencia (Beyond Science) had the idea to do it, Miguel asked Fountain to arrange groups around the world, which he did. Link-Up, Fountain Magazine and Psychic News all ran the story.

Derek Austin and Michael Omejer put together in Broxmead studios a "Concerto for World Healing" as a contribution to the programme with their own magic music.

Now, the Spanish have their own inimitable way of arranging things and what appears to be total chaos suddenly crystallises into something that works.

I arrived in Madrid with Derek and Michael's tape and a list of phone numbers on the Friday. I phoned Miguel. "Don't worry", he said, "just turn up at the studio half an hour beforehand, and we'll put it all together". Knowing Miguel as I do, I trusted him completely and rightly. The new Association of Spanish Healers organised by Ramiro and Gloria Catalayud, who represent Fountain in Madrid, laid on a meeting of members in the new healing centre where a buffet meal was had with contributions from everybody. From there we went to the studio – including Christina, Alisa, Gloria, Ramiro and Jesus Morientes (an old friend of Fountain). At the studio doors, there were 60 people who wanted to enter to join us. The corridor outside the studio was full.

So, it began. In the small studio itself were Miguel Blanco, the presenter, Enrique de Vicente, his minder, Felix Gracia, Gloris, Jose-Antonio Campoy, director of Mas Alla and Carlos Mariano.

Suddenly it was all over in two hours. Miguel had previously publicised the event and did not have to explain much to the Spanish peak-time audience (12 midnight). We phoned Alexander Neklessa in Moscow – Roger Brown in Australia – Ginette Daubeton in Paris - Klaus Brudny in Austria – Chris Street in London – Sixto Paz in Peru – other friends in Mexico and Chile, Groups in Spain, the Centro Aquarius in Barcelona where seven nations are represented and the Fountain Group in Madrid where 57 people had stayed behind.

I felt for all those in England and many other countries who we could not phone but were standing by. Suzanne Thomas in Torquay. Elsie Starks in Bishops Waltham, Nina Betts with Derek and Sarah Austin, Sara Miles and George de Trafford, Rene Bugby in Malta. But we knew that they were there.

Things became so crowded and intense that Miguel cancelled the 1am News, not a thing that a presenter would normally do, but the programme controller accepted it.

Felix and Carlos did the meditation, which, with Derek and Michael's music revolved around the concept of the solstitial see with the collective consciousness and seeing it grow so that the application of pure love would govern our affairs in the future. We tried to phone Derek to thank him for his music but could not get through.

Then it was all over. The first radio broadcast for world healing that I know of. Spanish radio now has four firsts. Individual healing through audience participation, community healing in the same mode, healing through the studio, (Radio Catalunya) and now a world healing meditation.

It was certainly my fervent hope that now they have all actually happened, radio stations around the world will emulate Spanish Radio. They now know that it is accepted by the audience, and that radio and television broadcasts can carry spiritual energy.

May it be repeated everywhere. Radio is better than television for meditations because the usual image of the television is a distraction. Our own mental screen feeling the "word" is the greater magic.

We went back to the Madrid Healing Centre and danced flamenco. I walked home across the main artery of Madrid, the Castellana, and the energies were greater than ever by a factor of at least 100.

So there it is. Let's have more of it.

NOT FOR NOTHING HAS THIS OCCURRED IN THE BASE CHAKRA OF EUROPE.

The Birth of Homo Amans – Colin Bloy

When we had the symposium in Madrid in April 1995, entitled "The Waking up of Humanity – the Mutation from Homo Sapiens to Homo Amans," (from thinking man to loving man), we had as a logo, Neanderthal Man and Homo Sapiens, with Homo Amans as a winged man coming out of a box and flying free. That was a piece of inspiration by a Spanish commercial artist. Just before we had that symposium someone said, "Have you seen what's going to happen on the 22nd July?" For those who don't know, the horoscope of that day was a perfect Star of David. So far as I know from the astrologers I've talked to, that was without precedent and totally unexpected. No one knew at the beginning of the year, as far as I knew, that this was going to happen. What may it mean? The

astrologers of the Spanish Astrologers Association said that it looks as if this may be a genuine quantum shift for the benefit of humanity. I think that's the way most people took it. We certainly made a play of this at the symposium.

Then came the day, July 22nd. I had been dowsing the various fields in the various countries where I was and noticed that they started to fade, which is characteristic of a major shift coming up. Then we had a bank day with nothing. On the day itself there were quite a number of people involved in meditations and we made an appeal in Madrid – "Please let's free the world of wars and hatred and all other miseries. It really is time." But what happened the following day was something I certainly didn't anticipate. We had seen, in one or two cases, that very saintly people can transmute the energies of the heart chakra into spiritual love and that chakra actually starts to sprout wings. There's no doubt about it. It's palpable, photographable. There's the famous photograph of the lady visionary at St Damiano in Italy with big wings.

Just before July 22nd in Barcelona, Maria Angeles, whose known as the "Fastest Gun in the West" for her speed of healing, said to me, "I'm finding that one or two people now have got wings". So, I thought after that shift on July 22nd, I'd better look. I'd been checking people beforehand and I hadn't found any wings, even though she had. But on July 23rd, everybody had wings, greater or smaller. It became a bit of a frenzy, literally stopping people in the street outside the healing centre in Madrid to check them for wings. A beer delivery man bending over his crates had them too, and also the waiters. It really did happen. And down in Australia they've got them too (and the kangaroos have them!) It really has happened. Roger Brown and I looked round the various parts of Australia. Those of you who know the 16 chakras will remember that the archetype of the 12 chakra is wings. That is now the general energy *field. We've seen the Templar crosses. Every 2 or 3 years the field begins to grow and then we have a shift. In 1992 the 11th chakra of the egg or oval Universal Consciousness became the general field, at least in Spain, England, France, Malaysia and Australia. It's now wings, the 12th chakra of Angelic Consciousness, what Rudolf Steiner calls the angelic or archangelic formative forces, states of consciousness to which humanity can aspire, anybody if they wish. The great thing is to know that they were there.*

Healing over these years, in my experience and in the experience of others, has improved dramatically because we've been given access to these new sates of consciousness. We need to dissociate and move away from the emotional world where we do not heal. I'm sure you all know that, and into the world of spiritual love, which is universal and does not judge, so we never wish to heal one person more than another. Given these preconditions, it really is getting dramatic. All these tremendous things are happening. Maybe, the 22nd July was the birthday of Homo Amans.

During the last 12 months, we've discovered the work of Emma Kunz, the swiss German healer. Her healing, in public terms, was based on pulverised energised rock, herbs and so on, but she left behind this mass of so-called modern art, but it was not art, but drawings of etheric archetypes. She said, "This will be the medicine of the future." She died in 1962. There is a drawing of the etheric evolution of the foetus, from conception to birth, but not just as we are today, but as we will be in the 21st century which is Homo Amans. It confirms this interest we've seen in Templar work. This is pure Templar geometry. And the work of this remarkable life-long healer also shows that we're not alone in the perception that Homo Amans is here. I think he could go away again if we don't do things right, but I think that we probably will.

If Homo Amans really is with us, and there are wing inspectors around who'll check your wings for you if you are in any doubt! (or can you check them yourselves with your hands), the extent to which this fundamental shift in human consciousness has occurred shows that this exploration into consciousness which has been the adventure of Fountain and many, many other groups around the world is paying off. It is worth it. It is something that is relevant to the future of mankind. I must say I was very moved that day. It was extraordinary. We can take comfort from it and say, "Right, OK, now where are we going?"

For many millennia, the world as we know it has been a kind of reformatory for naughty souls. Karma actually comes out in healing, not so much as a punishment, but as the history of your soul, the history of your spiritual growth. Those who heard the Hassim tapes will remember that it was stated that those who don't complete karma in this lifetime won't be able to reincarnate on this planet. Which I think is very sad, because it's the best time coming up, if this analysis is right. Until this time, it's really been a sort of spiritual borstal.

You had to keep coming back until you learnt the consciousness of love. Spiritual love is not really difficult concept. It's just about living your life, so the planet survives. We don't have to be sanctimonious about it. It's much better to be involved in spiritual love because, when you are, the emotional love becomes so much easier, which is good news.

For various reasons, we have been able to see over the years that there is a plan for humanity. That's to say that the universe is not some extraordinary accident, nor is it some great machine. There is such a thing as personal responsibility because it is an evolving and imprecise universe within the plan. Free will could not exist if it were perfectly planned and organised and regulated. There are variables

310

in the universe. Healing couldn't exist if there weren't free will. Healers intervene. Accidents happen. Everything is not karmically determined. If there's no free will there's no moral responsibility. Happily the evidence is that there is. Sir George Trevelyan has been one of the great champions of the idea that the human race has a role to play in its own evolution and it's one of the great messages of all time. We're not asleep, we're not puppets, we're not mechanical toys. We can actually do something about our situation. We can love. Once we realise that, things start to change. My question is whether Homo Amans is a product of the change, a product of the waking up, albeit written generally in the plan. But that plan works better or worse, according to whether human beings consciously take part in it. It's the Elohimic Plan. We can read about aspects of it in the Bible and in the non-canonical texts and so on, but that old aphorism, "God helps those that help themselves", seems to be absolutely right.

When we take note of the fact that this school of karma has now come to an end in favour of a human race which is free of the karmic wheel, it has enormous implications. It may be that we are a seed planet of our galaxy. A human race that is riddled with the problems of karmic reform and merely being a place of teaching does not have the consciousness to go forward with a wider destiny. It may be that we are, in a physical sense, the only receptacles of consciousness in this part of the universe but that relieves us, liberates us, encumbers us with, asks us to partake in a hugely greater destiny than we have had before. But that destiny is meaningless unless we're karmically free as a race. Eight years ago, when we were looking archetypically as healers of karma, it was relatively rare to find someone who was karmically complete. With the 32 pathways all in place, now it's the contrary. It's not our work, it's happening. There are these external influences, which are helping and stimulating people to grown in consciousness and the understanding of love, and if we accept them, then we will grow faster. It really is happening.

So here we are with Homo Amans. Here we are with new fields in collective consciousness. Here we are with wings. Let's take advantage of a wholly new scene for humanity, the scene that sets us free. The inner peace that spiritual freedom gives is ineffable and is only within the grasp of poets to describe. It's certainly not capable of description in prose. But don't take the birthday of Homo Amans too sombrely. It's an occasion for happiness and a smile. The emotions are still around, we are still allowed to have emotions. But it's time for great reflection and great consideration of where we go from here, how we got here in the first place and what part Fountain can play, in its way, in the future of humanity and in the evolution of Homo Amans.

My Own Second Coming, And Fountain International Now.

No, I do not have delusions of grandeur, and don't see myself as the messiah. But when I stopped being Co-ordinator for Fountain International, to allow fresh blood to come in, and was released from the heavy workload, I went on my own path of discovery. I've always had an interest in complementary medicine, especially vibrational medicine, so off I trotted gaining certificates as I went. But during this period, I always held onto the Fountain concept and its importance, whilst any interaction with its members faded.

Whilst I was Co-ordinator, I mentioned that I had archivist tendencies, and always felt that I was guardian of the knowledge gained by Fountain. As the years passed, I held on to all my Fountain information. Which was no mean feat for anyone who delights in de-cluttering, like me.

I was saddened when I heard of Colin's death in 2004, as he was such a lighthouse for Fountain International, and had acquired such a wealth of knowledge. But, when any charismatic figure of a group, "leaves the building", there is a vacuum, and there is a tendency for people to fall away and move on to other things.

This was true in Fountain International's case, although all the old "Fountaineers" have such a fondness for Fountain International and the concept, it is always kept in the back of their minds.

After Colin's passing, I became aware that Fountain International was on a downward spiral to a point of non- existence apart from a static website, and committee. When I was attending a Megalithic Conference in Glastonbury, I bumped into Giles Bryant, who promoted Fountain at festivals, and wrote a Fountain Newsletter. After a chat, I realised that Fountain was important to me, and that such an easy, and all-encompassing concept to help heal the world should not be lost.

Another response to the state of affairs was TONGO an off shoot of Fountain International, instigated by Colin Kay and Joe Hoare which started around this time, based on the Fountain International concept. Their method is to radiate individual healing intentions for peacefulness and harmony into the general field and possibly to specific focal points. Individually and in groups this can be done as frequently as you like, and the more often the better. The link in happens on the 27th of the month, 7pm local time, wherever you are. It's a four-stage project:

Energizing the healing field
Measuring it
Recording it
Understanding it

If you would like to find out more about them, go to
www.tongo.org.uk

313

Not long after my meeting with Giles, the first whisperings started to come into my mind from Colin Bloy, urging me to organise a Fountain International Conference, to re unite old members, and perhaps attract new members. Now this wasn't met with great joy by me. I was fully employed, and felt that I had already done that, got the t-shirt. However, I found out that resistance was futile. Colin always knows, and gets what he wants, as others will also attest to after his death, he will nag and nag.

After some months of nagging, I succumbed and arranged a conference in my local town. It was difficult as I had no members list, but through word of mouth and advertising about twenty came. It was greatly enjoyed, and everyone felt that they had had their batteries recharged. Two more conferences followed, with Giles running alternate conferences on the opposite side of the country. (Giles has now started his own website www.worldhealingproject.com).

By this point I had gained a profit from my local conferences, and to cut a long story short. This money went on the building of a new website. www.fountaininternationalmagazine.com Those who know me, are aware that I am computer phobic, and this is one of the reasons why the website was built in a very simplistic way to accommodate this, as I would be the one updating it. When the website was being put up onto the internet, (September 2011), I was told that it could take a few days for it to be seen. I was very surprised when it turned out to only be a few hours, but it did splutter and die, to be reborn a second time, and again within hours. which makes me think that it was wanted by "higher management."

The previous incarnation of the "Fountain International Magazine", had been printed, and posted out, with the last issue in 2000, due to mounting costs. With computer technology, I am able to produce the

Magazine for a fraction of the cost, therefore I have never charged for the online Magazine, and it is purely run on a donation basis.

The Fountain International Magazine comes out four times a year, and it is around 40 pages per issue. It has been a joy for me to produce, and I am so grateful for all the high calibre contributors that keep it alive. In fact, I enjoyed doing it so much, I now also produce a free monthly newsletter, which can be signed up for on the website, and I will send it to you as an attachment.

Fountain International, during this time, has also gained a Facebook page, which is run by Steve Fuller, with Christopher Miller and myself team members, which people can interact with. www.facebook.com/FountainInternational

In days gone by Fountain International had used Silbury Hill as a focal point for sending energy to the UK.

With the turbulent changes that the world is going through today, I thought that it was a good idea to re-instigate the idea, but this time make it a Global focal point, especially as the readers of the Magazine come from all around the world. As the Earth's heart chakra/centre is in Glastonbury, it seemed a valid option, with Glastonbury Tor one of the easiest places to visualise. Hence the advert in our magazine for people to link up.

Linked Meditation, Glastonbury Tor, UK
Become Involved

Join with us for the daily sending out of Pure Love, Light and Balancing energies, at 7am GMT, daily, using the focal point of Glastonbury Tor, UK, to encompass the World and all within it.

This is a free activity that any human being can do, in aid of the world that we live in. All can participate and help, there are no barriers.

Not able to make the sending out time of the energies at 7am!

You can still join in and be of great value, by sending Pure Love energy to the Tor, putting on the intention that it is stored there until 7am the next day, when it will be sent out with the rest of the Pure Love energy into the world and to encompass all.

Everyone can make a difference, don't let anyone else including yourself, tell you different.

A thought is all it takes.

Fountain/Fountain International at the time of writing has been going for 36 years. But what happened after the meditation all those years ago regarding the problem of Mods and Rockers coming down on their motorbikes and mopeds from London to Brighton looking for trouble?

Motorbikes and cars still have events in Brighton, but the atmosphere is totally different. They include the Ace Café Reunion, Brightona, Pioneer Motorcycle Run, and Landrover Run. If we just look at the Ace Café Reunion for a moment, this is where various motorcycles descend of Brighton each year. The highest number so far of bikes turning up was 63,000, and it was recorded as a good-humoured event. A lot of these events are put on for the benefit of charities, especially those for children.

When I first started to write this book, my aim was purely seed scattering, for the future. But I feel that Fountain is starting to re-flutter, and when one thinks about it, now, is its time in these challenging days. So, why not give the concept a try in your locality.

I know that some things in this book are not going to be to everyone's taste, belief's or sensibilities, but take only that which resounds with you. After all I do not want you to be sheep, following blindly. This book is about empowerment. All of us have the power to aid the world in which we live, leaving it to others is no longer an option.

What happens next is up to you. In these scary times of change, it's a case of if you snooze you lose.

From such insignificant beginnings –

WHO'D HAVE THOUGHT IT.

Further Reading

The Sun and the Serpent – Hamish Miller and Paul Broadhurst.

In Search of the Southern Serpent – Hamish Miller and Barry Brailsford

Axis of Heaven – Paul Broadhurst and Gabriele Trso

The Spine of Albion – Gary Biltcliffe and Caroline Hoare

Sun, Moon and Stonehenge – Robin Heath

Earthstars – Chris Street

New View Over Atlantis – John Michell

Spiritual Dowsing – Sig Lonegren

Needles of Stone Revisited – Tom Graves

The Wessex Astrum – Peter Knight and Toni Perrott

Fairy Paths and Spirit Roads – Paul Devereaux

In Resonance with Nature – Hans Andeweg

Decoding the Sacred Network – Chris H Hardy

Ley Lines and Earth Energies – David Cowan and Chris Arnold

Recommended Website and Conference Organisers

www.megalithomania.co.uk